Education in America

SOCIOLOGY IN THE TWENTY-FIRST CENTURY

Edited by John Iceland, Pennsylvania State University

This series introduces students to a range of sociological issues of broad interest in the United States today and addresses topics such as race, immigration, gender, the family, education, and social inequality. Each work has a similar structure and approach as follows:

- introduction to the topic's importance in contemporary society
- overview of conceptual issues
- review of empirical research including demographic data
- cross-national comparisons
- discussion of policy debates

These course books highlight findings from current, rigorous research and include personal narratives to illustrate major themes in an accessible manner. The similarity in approach across the series allows instructors to assign them as a featured or supplementary book in various courses.

1. *A Portrait of America: The Demographic Perspective,* by John Iceland

2. *Race and Ethnicity in America,* by John Iceland

3. *Education in America,* by Kimberly A. Goyette

Education in America

Kimberly A. Goyette

UNIVERSITY OF CALIFORNIA PRESS

University of California Press, one of the most distinguished university presses in the United States, enriches lives around the world by advancing scholarship in the humanities, social sciences, and natural sciences. Its activities are supported by the UC Press Foundation and by philanthropic contributions from individuals and institutions. For more information, visit www.ucpress.edu.

University of California Press
Oakland, California

Library of Congress Cataloging-in-Publication Data

Names: Goyette, Kimberly A., author.
Title: Education in America / Kimberly A. Goyette.
Description: Oakland, California : University of California Press, [2017] | Includes bibliographical references and index.
Identifiers: LCCN 2016045251 (print) | LCCN 2016046783 (ebook) | ISBN 9780520285101 (cloth : alk. paper) | ISBN 9780520285118 (pbk. : alk. paper) | ISBN 9780520960718 (ebook)
Subjects: LCSH: Educational equalization--United States. | Education—Social aspects—United States. | Equality—Social aspects—United States.
Classification: LCC LC213.2 .G69 2017 (print) | LCC LC213.2 (ebook) | DDC 379.2/6—dc23
LC record available at https://lccn.loc.gov/2016045251

Manufactured in the United States of America

26 25 24 23 22 21 20 19 18 17
10 9 8 7 6 5 4 3 2 1

To Michael, Jasper, and Meara

Contents

Figures

Tables

Acknowledgments

I would like to thank those who provided encouragement and feedback on this book. Thank you to Naomi Schneider, Executive Editor at the University of California Press, and her assistant, Renee Donovan, for seeing this through. I would like to thank John Iceland for recommending that I write this book and providing advice throughout the process. Also, I appreciate the careful and detailed comments of the anonymous reviewers of this manuscript. The work is better because of their thoughtful feedback.

I would like to thank all of the students who have taken my sociology of education undergraduate and graduate classes, and to the talented graduate students with whom I have had a chance to work. My thoughts were formed in conversation with you, and I am lucky to have the opportunity to have these conversations about educational inequality regularly. Thank you to Joshua Freely, Danielle Farrie, Melody Boyd, Helen Marie Miamidian, Shannon Feliciano, and Jessica Brathwaite (who is a coauthor on a chapter in the volume).

I am thankful to have mentors and colleagues to help shape my work on education and stratification. Yu Xie, Annette Lareau, Josh Klugman, and Maia Cucchiara are some of the many people who have encouraged and influenced me. I would like to thank my colleagues at Temple for their support.

Finally, thank you to my family, Michael, Jasper, and Meara, and to my parents, Frank and Maureen Goyette.

1 The Promise(s) of Education

We have all had experience with the education system in some way or another. Most of us (those who were not home-schooled) have been in some type of primary and secondary schools. You may be a student now in a college or university. You may be a parent of a student. We all know education "from the inside." We have seen its effects firsthand.

Some of you may be in college classrooms right now. You are likely high school graduates who have "made it" to or perhaps even through college. You might think if you have made it this far education has worked for you. You did the work you needed to do to get to where you are now. The education system correctly recognized that work and sorted you into the right place. You earned your place as a high school graduate or as a college student or graduate. You probably haven't thought too much about how your race, socioeconomic background, or gender shaped your education because you "made it." Whether you are black, white, Hispanic, or Asian, rich or poor, male or female, you made it through high school and into college. There are plenty of examples of people who went through the education system and "made it" like you—even those who were very poor, like former president Bill Clinton, who achieved the most prestigious occupation in the United States thanks, in part, to the success of the US public education system.

Table 1-1   Educational Attainment of Adults Aged 25–44 by Parents' Education

Parents' Education	High School Degree or Less	Some College	Bachelor's Degree or More
Both parents with high school degree or less	53%	27%	20%
One or more parents with some college	22%	46%	31%
One parent with bachelor's degree	15%	27%	58%
Both parents with bachelor's degree	3%	13%	84%

SOURCE: Jeff Larimore, "Does It Matter Who Your Parents Are? Findings on Economic Mobility from the Survey of Household Economics and Decisionmaking," July 2015, www.federalreserve .gov/econresdata/notes/feds-notes/2015/findings-on-economic-mobility-from-the-survey-of-household-economics-and-decisionmaking-20150720.html.

Who gets to "make it," though? Who are the people that don't make it? Are there any patterns that we can see in who gets higher levels of education and who does not? Is this related to their socioeconomic background, race, gender, or other characteristics? Social scientists and the public at large generally consider educational attainment, what kinds of degrees people are able to achieve, a measure of success. How much education one eventually gets, whether a high school degree, associate's degree, bachelor's degree, or more, is thought to be one indicator of status and social mobility in the United States, and one that correlates highly with other indicators of "success" like higher income, professional employment, even marriage. We know, though, that there is much inequality in eventual educational attainment across social groups: inequality by socioeconomic background, inequality by race and ethnicity, and, to a much smaller degree, inequality by gender. For example, in a survey conducted by the Federal Reserve in 2014, the Survey of Household Economics and Decision-Making, researchers found that parents' education was strongly related to their children's adult education attainment in their sample of about 1700 respondents aged 25 to 44. Table 1-1 shows that a majority of those whose parents had a high school degree or less had also attained a high school degree or less as adults, while more than 80% of those who had two parents with bachelor's degrees also attained a bachelor's degree or more as an adult.

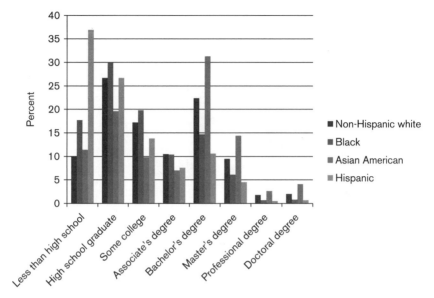

Figure 1-1. Educational Attainment by Race and Ethnicity for Those 25 and Older, 2014.

SOURCE: US Census Bureau, Educational Attainment in the United States: 2014—Detailed Tables, 2014, table 3, www.census.gov/hhes/socdemo/education/data/cps/2014/tables.html.

Figure 1-1 shows that the eventual educational attainment of the adult population also varies substantially by race and ethnicity. Looking at adults 25 and older, we see that Asian Americans have the highest rate of attaining bachelor's, master's, professional, and doctoral degrees, followed by non-Hispanic whites. Hispanics have the highest rates of not completing high school, while blacks have the highest rates of attaining a high school degree and attending college but not receiving a degree.

There is less inequality in educational attainment by gender than there is by socioeconomic background and by race or ethnicity. Looking at the degree attainment of men and women in the United States 25 years and older, we see an interesting pattern. Men tend to be slightly overrepresented among the least *and* most educated. For example, figure 1-2 shows that men tend to have less than a high school degree or only a high school degree more than women. Women are slightly overrepresented among those who have some college, associate's degrees, and master's degrees.

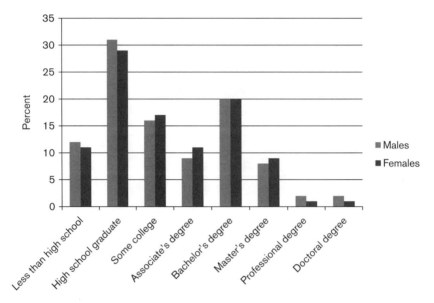

Figure 1-2. Educational Attainment by Gender for Those 25 and Older, 2014.

SOURCE: US Census Bureau, Educational Attainment in the United States: 2014—Detailed Tables, 2014, table 2, www.census.gov/hhes/socdemo/education/data/cps/2014/tables.html.

Men and women appear to be equally likely to have bachelor's degrees, but men are more likely than women to hold professional or doctoral degrees. This figure represents men and women of all ages above 24, so if women continue to enter and graduate from college at higher rates than men, as is the current pattern, we may see this pattern change among younger ages first—with more women attaining bachelor's degrees particularly. As more women attain bachelor's degrees and some of them continue on to further education, it is possible that differences in professional and doctoral degrees will diminish.

From the above table and figures, it appears that there are differences in whether people "make it" to college and beyond particularly by socioeconomic background and race. These differences in eventual educational attainment are consequential. Systematic differences in educational attainment by socioeconomic background, race and ethnicity, and gender lead to differences in occupational attainment, marriage and family formation, voting behavior and civic engagement, and health outcomes. This book explores public schooling in the United States that leads up to this eventual attainment. Do schools themselves shape these patterns?

Horace Mann, and many others following him like John Dewey, famously called education the "Great Equalizer." He declared, "Education, then, beyond all other devices of human origin, is *the great equalizer* of the conditions of man,—the balance-wheel of the social machinery."[1] It is hard to agree on what Mann meant by this, though. Did he mean that different groups—defined by race or ethnicity, socioeconomic background, gender, disability status, or other characteristics—should have similar outcomes such as grades, test scores, college attendance, or eventual attainment? Should these groups have equal opportunities? What does "opportunity" mean?

Before diving into these questions, though, we should understand the role of education as an institution and an organization. In most societies, in the past 100 to 200 years, education has not simply occurred organically through social interaction; it has also been established as an institution.[2] Being institutionalized means that "education" occurs in particular places during specific times, and people have clearly delineated roles in that institution. So, for example, much education in the United States occurs in places called schools from 8 AM to 3 PM and is led by people called teachers. It is no longer perceived as something that occurs organically when a child talks with an adult or observes an insect and makes a conclusion about its behavior; rather, it is what occurs during the school day in a school taught by a teacher.

Another feature of institutionalized education is that it is bureaucratic. That means that rules determine what is acceptable and unacceptable in that institution. According to Max Weber, as time goes on, those rules become more and more complex.[3] Rules determine who can be called a "teacher." In the United States, it is typically someone who has at least a four-year college degree and has been certified to be a teacher. Rules determine when and how teachers are hired and can lose their jobs. Rules determine students' behavior in the institution—line up, no chewing gum, hands to yourselves are some of those rules. There are often consequences to breaking rules. Schools can put students in detention, suspend them, or expel them.

Institutionalized education strives to be, and in many places is, universal. Institutionalized education, to be successful, should reach all members of a society at some point in their lives. In most societies, this occurs during childhood, often from ages six to 12, though much education may occur before and after these ages, depending on the society. Institutionalized education tends to expand in scope over time. It encompasses more and more children of a particular age and then expands to include children and young adults from different ages—younger (preschool) to older (college and graduate school). Institutionalized education strives to include children from all parts of its society—rich and poor, of all races and ethnicities, boys and girls, of all abilities.[4]

Often when we consider the institution of education, we think about the ways we shape it. We consider the ways we use education to further our goals for society, whatever they may be. But we could also consider the ways that education shapes us as a society. Education as an institution validates certain types of knowledge over others. It provides legitimacy to certain fields and not others. It provides credentials that signal which fields and careers have status and prestige. The institution of education is not just something that reflects a society's views, but also something that shapes and changes a society.[5]

The main purpose of the institution of education is to prepare young members of a society for their adult roles in that society. Two ways that youths are prepared for these adult roles is through socialization and through sorting or stratification. Émile Durkheim, a nineteenth-century sociologist, refers to socialization as the ways that members of a society learn that society's norms and values.[6] Stratification occurs when young members of a society are trained for particular roles in the economy, polity, family, or other institutions. When education stratifies or sorts students, it differentially allocates resources and knowledge to different members of society according to different attributes, that is, education gives people different knowledge or resources based on their future roles in society.

According to Durkheim, education teaches us how to behave. It teaches us norms, values, and beliefs that are important to our culture, our society. It teaches us what knowledge is valued by our culture and society. Education is referred to by Durkheim as an agent of cultural transmission. According to Durkheim, the institution of education should be the main institution through which the individual learns the ways of a given group or society. It should be the place an individual acquires the physical, intellectual, and moral tools needed to function in a society.

How exactly, though, does this socialization occur? How do we learn to negotiate our places in society, appropriate social rules or norms, social values, about what is acceptable and valued in schools? Sociologists have identified two different types of "curricula," that is agendas or plans by which skills, knowledge, rules, and values get transmitted or communicated to students. The first is the formal curriculum and the second is called the hidden curriculum.[7] The formal curriculum is what is explicitly taught in schools. This is the knowledge or set of skills we are most likely to identify when asked what we learned in school. We know we are required to learn algebra, to study American history. The curriculum also points to the areas of these subjects that are important to learn. For example, we know that the Revolutionary War was an important part of American history because we spend a lot of time learning about it, there are a lot of materials, textbook pages, and the like devoted to it, and we may even get tested on it. We know that *Catcher in the Rye* and *The Scarlet Letter* are important books to read. We learn about subjects and predicates, prepositions and dangling participles in order to learn the "correct" way to speak and write. We also learn the school rules—they are posted and explicit, and the consequences for breaking them are clear. We may also learn values from the formal curriculum. In many schools, there are curricula designed to teach children not to bully. The formal curriculum is explicit; it is stated. We recognize what we are learning.

The hidden curriculum is subtler than the formal curriculum. We may not always be aware of the lessons we learn from this hidden curriculum. From the hidden curriculum, we may learn what is expected of us based on our anticipated roles in society, the unspoken rules we should follow in order to be rewarded. Rules that have to do with how we are expected to behave may be based on our race, our gender, or our socioeconomic background. We may begin to negotiate our positions in society and form expectations of ourselves and the rules by which we think ourselves and others should live based on the messages sent from this hidden curriculum.

Let me give you an example of what I mean by the hidden curriculum. Researchers observing in school classrooms have found that teachers call on boys more than girls.[8] There may be many reasons why this occurs (boys are louder, teachers want to encourage more participation from boys), but, regardless of why this occurs, this practice may communicate to girls, without them explicitly realizing it, that what they have to say is less valuable than what boys have to say. Girls are subtly taught that their thoughts or answers are not as important.

Durkheim also talks briefly about another activity that education carries out. Not only must education provide common societal principles and values for people, but it must also ensure that people fill the diverse roles that are important for society. Some people need to farm, some people need to heal others, some need to build shelters. Educational institutions sort youths so that particular people fill each role. Education in this sense stratifies people.

These adult roles carry different amounts of responsibility and varying rewards. These rewards often, though not always, reflect how much a student has to invest to be trained in a particular field, how difficult that job is, and how much we as a society value that role. For example, doctors may be paid more than accountants because they need to invest more in their training. Professional athletes are highly paid because the society values their abilities. We rely on the institution of education primarily to sort students into these adult roles of doctor, accountant, athlete, and so on.

Table 1–2 shows you some occupations taken from the Bureau of Labor Statistics in 2014. Here you see occupations like waiter/waitress, real estate agent, teacher, doctor, and lawyer. The middle column shows the entry level of education generally needed for that occupation. Waiters and waitresses need no formal degree, for example. Occupations like postal workers and plumbers typically require a high school degree or the equivalent. Dental assistants and court reporters need vocational training, while registered nurses and preschool teachers have associate's degrees, typically. Bachelor's degrees are required for occupations like airline pilots and investment bankers, while postgraduate degrees are needed to become doctors, lawyers, and veterinarians. How much education you get determines what kind of occupations you can have, what kind of roles in society you can fill.

The third column of the table shows the average annual earnings of those occupations. The table clearly shows a pattern: those occupations with higher levels of required education also get higher rewards. Janitors,

Table 1–2   Selected Occupations by Entry-Level Education and Average Annual Earnings, 2014

Job Title	Entry-Level Educational Level Required	Average Annual Earnings
Waiter/Waitress	Less than high school diploma	$18,540
Retail Sales Worker	Less than high school diploma	$21,410
Janitor	Less than high school diploma	$22,320
Garbage Collector	Less than high school diploma	$22,970
Secretary	High School Diploma (or Equivalent)	$35,330
Real Estate Agent	High School Diploma (or Equivalent)	$41,990
Plumber	High School Diploma (or Equivalent)	$49,140
Postal Service Worker	High School Diploma (or Equivalent)	$53,100
Cosmetologist	Vocational Training	$22,770
Dental Assistant	Vocational Training	$34,500
Firefighter	Vocational Training	$45,250
Court Reporter	Vocational Training	$48,160
Preschool Teacher	Associate's Degree	$27,130
Laboratory Technician	Associate's Degree	$47,820
Web Developer	Associate's Degree	$62,500
Registered Nurse	Associate's Degree	$65,470
High School Teacher	Bachelor's Degree	$55,050
Investment Banker	Bachelor's Degree	$71,720
Chemist	Bachelor's Degree	$73,060
Airline Pilot	Bachelor's Degree	$98,410
Mental Health Counselor	Master's Degree	$41,500
Librarian	Master's Degree	$55,370
Sociologist	Master's Degree	$74,960
Economist	Master's Degree	$91,860
Psychologist	Doctoral Degree	$69,280
Veterinarian	Doctoral Degree	$84,460
Lawyer	Doctoral Degree	$113,530
Physician or Surgeon	Doctoral Degree	$187,200

SOURCE: Bureau of Labor Statistics, US Department of Labor, *2014–2015 Occupational Outlook Handbook*.

who need no degree, make about $22,000 a year, while postal workers who need high school degrees earn $53,000 a year. High school teachers who have bachelor's degrees earn about $55,000 a year, while psychologists who need advanced degrees make $69,000. There are some exceptions to the pattern. Airline pilots make almost $100,000 a year on average with bachelor's degrees and mental health counselors with master's degrees make less than $42,000 a year, but generally as the required education increases so do the income rewards. This is the basic picture of stratification: you need particular levels of education to get certain jobs and these jobs have different amounts of resources or rewards associated with them. The education you attain may not completely determine the job you will get, but it increases the probability that you will get certain jobs.

Many have made the argument that this sorting occurs most efficiently when it is only based on students' talents, abilities, and hard work.[9] The society works best when those students who are most talented and are willing to work the hardest are the doctors we depend on to save lives. We want students who have a breadth of knowledge and who are willing to think deeply about complex issues to govern our nation. We want students who are good at math and able to put in the time to understand complex tax codes to be our accountants. Should we ever have legal problems, we want those who are good at argumentation to defend us. And, when we watch sports, we want to be amazed by what athletes are able to accomplish.

There are two theories about how students get sorted through educational institutions into their adult roles. The first theory is that students wind up there based solely on their achieved characteristics. Sociologists like Talcott Parsons believe that students' achievement is mostly determined by their abilities, talents, and hard work. Schools are perceived as institutions that level the playing field, that sort people into different places based solely on their talent or ability, not on their ascribed characteristics—that is, characteristics that people are born with and cannot get rid of. Characteristics like race, gender, and socioeconomic background should have no role in how students are sorted according to this theory. These characteristics should not affect the choices students make about their own academic careers, nor should they affect people's assessment of their performance, or the ways that they are taught.

On the other end of the spectrum are people who believe that a student's educational chances are determined by ascribed characteristics. Some social theorists believe that school does not sort people on the basis of talent, but rather that school is an institution through which groups maintain power and privilege. Students of the upper classes may be sent to better schools where almost all students are guaranteed a college education. Ascribed characteristics affect the way students are taught. Students who have upper-class parents may be perceived differently from those who have working-class parents based on the ways they behave in classes, the ways that they speak, and the knowledge they have when they start school.[10]

Sorting, or stratification, occurs imperfectly when there are large race or ethnic, socioeconomic background, or gender differences in the composition of different professions. Discrimination operates such that students are not sorted purely based on talent or ability. Once discrimination falls away, in theory, at least, sorting should become more efficient. This may be simplistic, however. Positions in society are rewarded differently with money, status, and prestige. Individuals may want to maximize the rewards they or their children gain as adults. Education becomes a place where individuals compete for the rewards of adult life—money, power, prestige, status—and groups with resources and power may work to maintain them.

Education then carries out two crucial activities in society. Simply, what we learn and how we learn provide a common set of beliefs, assumptions, ideas about the world and ourselves—these things can hold a society together. We learn the importance of democratic principles and individualism in our classes, through school rules, through interactions with teachers and peers. We learn how to behave in a society. In a very simplified sense, we learn how to be the same, what it means to be American, living in a Western country. We also learn to be different. Through our educational "achievements," we are slotted into different social roles. We learn the appropriate skills, norms, and behaviors for those roles. Socialization refers to how we learn norms, behaviors, values, and beliefs. Stratification refers to the process by which we are sorted into different roles in society. The two concepts are not distinct. How we are stratified alerts people to how we should be socialized, and how we are socialized more easily enables us to be stratified. Whether we come from poor households or wealthy households may lead us to be placed in different schools. Students in more-advantaged schools may be taught and social-ized differently than those in poor schools. How we are socialized in schools may reinforce our social positions or it may enable us to break out of them. Socialization and stratification occur together: they reinforce each other, but also challenge each other.

We, as members of society, occupy several roles in relation to the insti-tution of education. Most of us were or are students. In that role, we may have advocated for the most resources possible, to put ourselves in the best position to occupy an adult role with status, prestige, power, and high income. We may be parents with children in schools. In this role, we may be concerned that our children are able to have the same lifestyle we enjoy or a better one. We may rely on (and even push schools) to maximize the resources our children receive in order to ensure that they have advan-tages and are able to compete with other children. We may be teachers or considering becoming teachers. In this role, we may want to ensure that all the children we are teaching have opportunities to learn and thrive. And, we are all members of society. In this role, we may want to be sure that all children have access to the education that will best sort them into adult roles (we want the most talented scientists, engineers, doctors, law-yers, and so on) in a way that is not based on their ascribed characteristics. We want all children to have equal or, at least, fair opportunities to learn and to achieve without regard to their gender, race, ethnicity, religion, socioeconomic background or class position, or other characteristics.

These tensions in our roles in relation to education are well captured by the scholar David Labaree.[11] He argues that schools are both a public and private good. The public functions of education are to educate citizens to participate in a democracy and to train students to fill necessary roles in a changing economy. The private function of education is to prepare stu-dents to compete with one another for valued social positions, increasing social mobility for some. The tensions between the public and private functions of education lead schools to be less effective at either one of them, though Labaree suggests that schools are increasingly used as vehi-cles for social mobility (or to maintain status and prestige) at the expense of those public functions that would provide more equitable educational opportunities in the name of democracy and labor market efficiency.

It is easy to see how this conflict might play out for individuals and families. If I want the most resources I can garner for myself so that I can attend a prestigious college, I may not be in favor of equalizing resources across a neighboring district so that a poorer school can have better technology. My interest in education as a sorting mechanism may conflict with my ideals that everyone should have an equal opportunity. These types of conflicts are found throughout the educational system.

Throughout this book, I will provide some descriptions of how students' ascribed characteristics affect where they go to school, what those schools look like, and what they achieve within those schools. I will question why students achieve differently by their ascribed characteristics. Do schools contribute to differences in outcomes across students? Do they maintain, exacerbate, or ameliorate differences that may result from experiences outside of schools in families, in neighborhoods, and with peers? Can schools alone erase gaps across students by socioeconomic background, race and ethnicity, gender, and other ascribed characteristics? The answers to these questions are complex, but generally, some of the best research to date shows that schools actually reduce inequality by social background when students are in schools. Much of the persistence in educational inequality by socioeconomic background comes from students' experiences outside of schools. This is not true for racial and ethnic differences, though. These differences appear to grow the more time students spend in schools, suggesting that something about the schooling experience exacerbates rather than reduces gaps by race and ethnicity. And, between boys and girls, differences in educational achievement tend to be small. These small differences tend to be to the advantage of girls, with the exception that girls are less likely to take advanced math and science courses and perhaps consequently less likely to enter Science, Technology, Engineering, and Mathematics (STEM) fields once they graduate from high school.

It is important to keep in mind that students' experiences and outcomes vary not only by each of their ascribed characteristics—whether one is black or Asian, rich or poor, boy or girl—but also by how those various identities are combined to create different experiences. For example, a poor Asian student may face different stresses, pressures, and discrimination than a poor black or white student. A black boy may experience perceptions of criminality and aggression that are different from the perceptions faced by black girls, who may be seen as independent and hardworking. School experiences and outcomes may result not simply from the "addition" of one's identities, that is, from being Hispanic + being a girl + having educated parents, but those experiences may be dependent on one another. The roles and expectations that affect educational outcomes may be different for girls in Hispanic families, those in Asian families, those in white families, and those in black families. Expectations for education for girls may be different based on whether they are in poor or wealthy families. This idea is called "intersectionality." Identities cannot be neatly separated into distinct categories, but overlap in ways that have implications for society's perceptions of individuals and the allocation of power and privilege.[12]

In this book, I will revisit the conflicts and questions that make the goal of reducing inequality of both experiences and outcomes in schools complicated and elusive. I focus exclusively on public education. Some may argue that families should be able to pay for specialized or higher-quality education that they may perceive exists in private schools, but what should be done about those schools that are meant for all students, public schools? In addition, since higher education and, to some extent, preschool education have been considered optional, I focus on those grades where school attendance is generally mandatory, grades one through 12, or more generally, elementary and secondary schools.

The remainder of the book will cover the following topics. Chapter 2 describes the beginnings of public education in the United States. I discuss the expansion of education and its eventual universalization. I spend a portion of this chapter discussing the various theories for why public education expanded and the rationales that were popular during its expansion. In chapter 3, I describe two of the main ways of perceiving education as an institution. Functional theories suggest that education, at its best, can be meritocratic. When this works well, children are sorted based on talent and hard work. When the institution is inefficient, race, socioeconomic background, and gender may influence the sorting process. On the other hand, conflict theories argue that the institution of education reflects and reproduces differences of race, socioeconomic background, and gender. Those groups with more advantages are able to control educational resources in such a way as to further reproduce their advantage. This chapter aims to make these theories explicit by giving examples of how they have been used to explain social inequality. These theories are revisited in future chapters to show how they can be applied to inequality by socioeconomic background and race. In addition to these two perspectives on education, other theories of inequality like symbolic interactionism are briefly reviewed.

Chapter 4 explores how socioeconomic background affects the characteristics of the schools that students attend. Then I look at patterns of inequality in outcomes by socioeconomic background in education. Finally, I discuss theories about why there are socioeconomic differences in these educational outcomes.

In the next chapter, chapter 5, I briefly describe the history of segregation and attempts at desegregation in the United States. As in the previous chapter, I provide some description of the average schools attended by Asian, black, Hispanic, and white children in the United States in terms of their socioeconomic and racial compositions, teacher profiles, and class sizes. I also look at school outcomes like the persistent "black-white test score gap," as it is popularly called, as well as descriptive statistics on racial differences in grades, retention, graduation rates, and enrollment in college. I include some discussion of differences in schools that may influence these outcomes like AP and advanced math course-taking, special education enrollment, and disciplinary practices. Where it is possible, I show how these indicators have changed over time. I also discuss some of the research on immigrant children and, in particular, English Language Learners (ELLs) and explore the degree to which there are differences in experiences and outcomes within this population. I touch briefly on the small amount of research devoted to the experiences and outcomes of multiracial children.

And, in chapter 6, I look at differences by gender. For the last several decades, women have graduated from high school and enrolled in college in greater proportions than men. This is true, not only in the United States, but in many nations across the globe. Girls, generally, tend to get higher grades in high school, are held back less, and are suspended or expelled less than boys. However, boys and men tend to study math and science at higher rates than women. In this chapter, as in the previous two,

I focus particularly on differences within schools like AP and advanced math course-taking, in disciplinary practices, and in outcomes like test scores, graduation rates, and college enrollment. I discuss some of the explanations for why women achieve more than men in school overall, but still study math and science at lower rates.

In chapter 7, I provide some comparisons to other countries—some with relatively high rates of educational inequality (Argentina and China), and some that have lower rates (Finland and South Korea). I describe inequality in learning outcomes by parents' income, gender, and urban/rural residence. I discuss how the organization and purpose of education in various nations may be related to inequality in outcomes. For example, centralized funding, universal preschool, and generous welfare states tend to show lower inequality, while governments with residential registration systems and high rates of privatization show higher inequality. This chapter relies on data showing inequality in outcomes on the international PISA tests.

Chapter 8 focuses on recent federal reforms, particularly starting in the 1980s with the report *A Nation at Risk*, continuing through the No Child Left Behind Act of 2001, and ending with Race to the Top and the current movement toward a Common Core. My coauthor, Jessica Brathwaite, and I describe reform movements focused on choice and privatization that have been attempted in various states: magnet schools, voucher programs, charter schools, and other types of school choice programs. In this chapter, we review the literature that reports on whether these reforms have reduced inequality across schools and improved outcomes for students in low-performing schools. Finally, in chapter 9, I again engage the questions posed in this introduction. Is US education a meritocracy? Can it be? What sorts of policies could be tried? What are the trade-offs to these policies? Why is reducing educational inequality so difficult?

2 Competing Visions of Public Education

WHO AND WHAT SHOULD IT BE FOR?

Education's purpose—what it should do and for whom—has been discussed and contested from the founding of the United States. Should education primarily be a private good for the wealthy to use to secure positions in the government or ministry? Is education a public good to provide common socialization in democratic and "American" values? Should education be used by a society to prepare its members for a changing economy? Is education the main tool for social mobility? Competing visions of what education should do and whom the institution of education should serve have undergirded arguments for its expansion in the United States. Underlying most of these arguments and visions is the idea that everyone should have access to education, though there is less agreement about how "equal" educational opportunities should be across social groups.

Back in the seventeenth century, only a small proportion of people in the world had experience with formal education. Most learning was done in families on farms or with employers when youth were apprenticed to tradespeople. The same was true in the United States. Few people who immigrated and settled had experience with formal education, and even fewer of those who were native-born (American Indians) had any experience with schooling. Formal schools were built in the colonies early in the founding of the United States, though, and, throughout the nineteenth century, this schooling expanded to encompass more and more students— not only the male, wealthy, privileged, native-born, or white, but also females, poor students, immigrants, and minorities (though often these students were taught in separate, segregated schools). Schooling also grew to encompass more and more of a youth's life. Schooling first became common for those in grammar or primary school, and then expanded to fill the middle school years. High schools expanded after middle schools began enrolling a majority of preteen and teenaged children. We might see parallels in this type of expansion today in both directions—schools reach younger populations through the extension of preschool and prekindergarten programs and through higher enrollments in two- and four-year postsecondary programs and institutions, as well as master's and professional programs.

Those who promoted the expansion of education had many, sometimes conflicting reasons for it. Some argued that education was necessary for learning new skills required in an industrial economy. Parents, who by and large farmed before the Industrial Revolution, could not be relied upon to teach children these new skills. Others suggested that citizens of a new democracy had to be educated to be informed voters. Children needed to learn civic values, as well as have the basic skills (reading, writing, and arithmetic) that would allow them to make good voting decisions. Still others worried about immigrants in a relatively young country. Children of immigrants had to be taught how to be "Americans." These proponents argued that immigrant and native-born alike had to learn a common history and the values and norms of those who had settled the country.

In this chapter, I describe the history of how education expanded to include nearly all youths aged six to 16 and children of all gender, race, immigrant, and socioeconomic background groups. I focus on the arguments for why this expansion occurred. The tensions between these arguments provide some context for how inequality in education—both experiences and outcomes—has been and is still viewed today.[1]

A BRIEF HISTORY OF EDUCATION IN THE UNITED STATES

European Settlement

Much of the first formal, institutionalized education in the United States occurred in missionary schools. Many French settled in the United States, from Canada to Louisiana. Jesuit priests often traveled with settlers and educated the Native Americans and children of the settlers. Spanish Franciscan priests taught Native Americans in a few missions in California. However, the establishment of the English colonies led to more institutionalized educational systems there.

Although there was variation in its scope and form, generally this education shared some characteristics. Education was religious, primarily. There were also social class differences in who got formal education, at different levels. Education past the first several years was reserved for those boys who were advantaged. The children of those who were not among the elite received minimal education in primary or town schools, where they learned the 4 Rs (reading, 'riting, 'rithmetic, and religion). Male, upper-class students went to middle and high schools or trained with tutors. Elite male students learned the classical languages, Latin and Greek, in Latin grammar schools. The first was established in Boston in 1635. Some from these schools would attend Harvard, the first of the colonial colleges, established in 1636. Except for Dame Schools (like kindergarten, where children were taught a little reading and writing, and girls were taught to sew and cook), education was, at first, only for boys. While formal schooling was established in the colonies early on, most children got their education through their families and farms or through apprenticeships.

As the settlements grew, though, education became more institutionalized. For example, in 1642, the Massachusetts General Court required parents and those who were masters to apprentices to be sure children could read and would be able to understand religious and colonial laws. In 1647, the General Court required every township of 50 households to find and pay for an elementary teacher with the Old Deluder Satan Law. Every township of 100 households or more was to also find and pay for a Latin or secondary teacher as well. These laws established a precedent that taxation was to be used to support the schools. These laws marked a transition from thinking of schools as private or religious entities to thinking that schools are responsible to and paid for by the public. Schools existed to serve the needs of the colonies for both religious and civic education.

Schooling in the eighteenth century in the United States varied greatly by region. While in the northern colonies, some types of public schooling were commonplace (though most schooling was reserved for elite boys), the situation was different in the southern colonies of Maryland, Virginia, Georgia, and the Carolinas. In these colonies, it was common for plantation owners to hire tutors to teach their sons and daughters. Some poor children were able to attend schools run by charitable or religious institutions like the Society for the Propagation of the Gospel (SPG). Many youth without resources became apprentices. Generally, though, education in these colonies was a private matter for families or for individual churches.

The situation was different still in the Middle Atlantic colonies of New York, New Jersey, Pennsylvania, and Delaware. There was a much greater diversity of settlers in these colonies. There was no one language, religion, or cultural heritage that united all of the settlers. In this region, parochial schools of many religious denominations were established. Apprenticeship was also common, and there were a few private schools that prepared students for trades. Throughout the eighteenth and early nineteenth centuries, school systems varied by region. There was no one schooling system that was the same throughout the country. Schooling was far from universal in all regions; though some colonies had established public schools, others relied more on religious and trade schools.

Education in the Early National Period

Starting with the founding of the nation in 1776 and continuing through the early years of the nineteenth century, education very slowly expanded. As in the northern colonies, education more and more became a state, though not a federal, responsibility. Education was not mentioned as a right of the citizen or as the responsibility of the federal government in the US Constitution, ratified in 1788. Control over education was left to states to determine, which has shaped the US perception of education as a local institution. The federal government was not completely uninvolved, though, and it set national precedent for using taxation to fund schools with the Northwest Ordinances of 1785 and 1787. The Ordinance of 1785 stipulated that each territory that was settled set aside the income from the sixteenth section of each township to pay for education in that township (a township was six square miles, subdivided into 36 sections). While not in the US Constitution, the Ordinance of 1787 affirmed the federal government's support of institutionalized, public education, saying that it was "necessary to good government and the happiness of mankind."

Slowly in the United States, education was thought to be more important for citizenship and less for religious purposes. Benjamin Franklin, Noah Webster, and, especially, Thomas Jefferson realized that for the new nation to be able to govern itself, citizens had to know enough to cast responsible votes. Nationalism and democracy needed to be taught in schools. Thomas Jefferson (1743–1826) wrote the "Bill for the More General Diffusion of Knowledge" in 1779, which argued that schools should produce literate citizens, the state should be responsible for providing schools, schools should be secular, not religious, and schools should sort students according to academic talent. The bill promoted a three-stage plan that included three years of publicly supported elementary school with further schooling for those who paid tuition, then the establishment of 20 grammar (secondary) schools for the academically talented, with scholarships for poor students, and finally the founding of the College of William and Mary for the top graduates from the grammar schools. Like the elementary and grammar schools proposed by Jefferson, William and Mary was a public school, supported by funds from the State of Virginia. Jefferson saw two purposes to education: one was to educate all citizens so they could be responsible voters, while the other was to select and nurture those who were perceived to be most talented, regardless of their ability to pay tuition.

Benjamin Franklin (1706–1790) best represented advocacy for teaching science in schools during the period. He promoted a utilitarian and scientific education, which was the basis of the English grammar school he founded in 1749. This school, the Philadelphia Academy, was significant because it presented an alternative to the more common Latin grammar schools in the northern colonies. The emphasis in the Latin grammar schools was on classics and elite culture, not on practical or scientific knowledge. Franklin's Academy was the precursor to other academies and ultimately the public high school.

Noah Webster (1758–1843) best represented the argument for teaching nationalism in schools. Webster wrote the *American Spelling Book,* published in 1783. This book standardized the language to simplify it, and he changed spellings of words so as to create "American English" as opposed to "British English" (for example, changing "honour" to "honor"). Webster is best known for writing the *American Dictionary,* which we know as *Webster's Dictionary,* though he also wrote a number of textbooks for schools.

While these famous figures influenced school change in the eighteenth century, the nineteenth century ushered in the most dramatic changes in the US educational system. Changes in how family and work were organized from before to after the Industrial Revolution influenced many educational reforms. With several important inventions in the eighteenth and nineteenth centuries (like the steam engine, cotton gin, telegraph, and sewing machine), production using machines became more efficient and transportation became faster. This spurred the growth of factories, where goods could be produced and more easily transported across the country. As more and more family members were drawn to work in factories, American society changed from a rural, mostly agricultural society to an industrial society concentrated around urban centers. This change required workers with at least basic literacy skills. Further, as more family members went to work in factories, fewer adults were left at home or on farms to supervise and teach children. Families were not around as much to socialize children, nor were they able to teach the new skills that were valued in factory production.

Schools responded to these new needs in several ways. Industrial schools were established based on the ideas of William Maclure (1763–1840), who taught how science could be used in industry and agriculture. He believed that schools should promote social change, and, with Robert Owen (1771–1858), founded the New Harmony school in Indiana, based on his beliefs that all children deserved a practical education that cultivated their individual interests and curiosities. Maclure believed that children needed a practical education that provided them with useful skills, and also that education could be a vehicle for equalizing outcomes across working-class children and more advantaged children.

Monitorial or Lancasterian schools were founded based on the ideas of Joseph Lancaster (1778–1838), who focused on the efficiency of the educational system. A master teacher would train "monitors," who would then teach other students. These schools aimed to teach as many students as possible the basic skills that were necessary in the new industrial economy. In addition to these two types of schools, "Sunday schools" were established for those children who worked six-day weeks in factories. It was only on Sundays, when the children were not working, that they had free time enough to be taught the basics of reading, writing, and religion. Some Infant schools were also established during this time. These schools were the forerunners of the modern day-care center. They were thought up by the Scottish industrialist Robert Owen to care for and educate the children of the young mothers who worked in his factories.

The precursors to the types of schools that exist today, though, were the Common Schools, which largely developed in the middle of the nineteenth century. The Common School was most like New England's publicly funded and locally controlled schools. One enthusiastic supporter was Horace Mann (1796–1859), whose quotation is found in chapter 1. Henry Barnard (1811–1900) was also a supporter, and he became the first US commissioner of education, from 1867 to 1870. The creation of this post suggested greater federal interest in public schools. Mann, Barnard, and others like them generally believed like Jefferson that all students in the nation needed an education. In addition, he saw public education as a way for the children of all social classes to compete socially and economically with those who had more resources. Not everyone supported the growth of Common Schools, however. Opponents of the Common School included owners of factories, mines, and plantations who did not want to lose cheap child labor. Also, individual ethnic and religious groups who wanted their children taught in their own languages, religions, and traditions did not want to see their children educated with religiously or culturally different children. And, similar to arguments that often surface in debates about education today, some of the public did not want to pay taxes (or more taxes) to support a public education, and there were politicians who responded to this.

The Common Schools encompassed both urban public schools and small country schools. These schools were run by locally elected school boards, with few rules or regulations from the state or federal government.

As Common Schools increased in number, they typically encompassed grades one to eight, and in the bigger, urban schools, each grade was in its own classroom, with its own teacher. As the numbers of students in these schools increased, age, rather than ability, determined which grades children were placed in. These schools were free of tuition because they were supported by local taxes. Eventually, schooling in these or other schools became mandatory, and, in part because of this, schooling in the United States was soon considered "universal," meaning it encompassed close to all children from the ages of six to 13. The South was the last region to have compulsory, public schooling, established after the Civil War.

The growth of high schools was also occurring during this period, but they rapidly expanded after 1874. In 1874, the Supreme Court of Michigan ruled that school districts could support high schools with taxes in a case called the Kalamazoo case. After this, the numbers of high schools and those enrolled in them grew. The mission of high school also changed. It was no longer only for elites headed to universities; it was also meant to provide vocational skills that students of all groups would be able to use in the labor force.

Twentieth-Century Trends in Education

As schools were increasing their enrollments and beginning to serve a much more diverse student body, girls and boys, wealthy and poor, and students of different races and ethnicities, reformers thought more deeply about the purpose and effectiveness of education. Progressive education, part of the larger progressive movement in the United States, which lasted from about 1900 to 1920, countered the idea born from the Industrial Revolution that schools should be like factories. In traditional schools, as in factories, efficiency was a main goal. To serve large numbers of students, students sat in rows, quietly in classrooms, focusing on the same curriculum. Emphasis was on basic skills and science. Education that could serve large numbers of students in classrooms most efficiently was the model of the nineteenth century. Progressive education, on the other hand, was based on writing from philosophers like Rousseau and educators like Maria Montessori (1870–1952). The philosophy of pragmatism with its emphasis on problem-solving and exploration, espoused most famously by John Dewey (1859–

1952), motivated Progressive education. Progressive educators moved away from memorization of facts to focus on problem-solving and hands-on learning. Curricula were not uniform and standardized, but guided by each child's interests. Different methods were used, including small-group learning, independent research, farming, field trips, and others. While few public schools became Progressive schools, ideas from the movement began to make it into public school curricula and practice. Teachers began to recognize individual learning styles, and they adopted hands-on projects and small-group learning to accommodate them. Progressive education focused on the needs of the individual child, rather than the need to educate large numbers of children most efficiently.[2]

During most of the history of the United States, blacks and whites—and in some instances, Hispanics and whites, and Asians and whites—were educated in separate schools. The same was also true of many Native Americans who were educated in tribal schools, though there was an explicit attempt to integrate many Native Americans into public schools. This separation of students by race was justified by the Supreme Court's 1857 *Dred Scott v. Sanford* decision, which upheld the notion that people of different races could be separated as long as the facilities and resources provided to them were "equal." The notion that the schools serving black (or Hispanic or Asian) children and white children were indeed "equal" was challenged throughout this time, but court cases asserting this were brought to the Supreme Court in the 1950s, beginning a period of school desegregation.

The end of legal school segregation and attempts at school desegregation were major turning points in American education, beginning in 1954. Federal attempts at desegregation began after the *Brown v. Board of Education of Topeka* decision in 1954, in which the Supreme Court unanimously struck down the "separate but equal" doctrine in American education. However, despite this decision, the federal government had little means to enforce it. While the government could send National Guard troops to protect black students attending white schools, it had little other means of promoting school integration. It was not until the Civil Rights Act of 1964 and Title I of the Elementary and Secondary Education Act of 1965 that the federal government had a way to promote integration by threatening schools with a loss of federal funding meant to subsidize schools serving higher proportions of children in poverty.

Many school reform efforts have followed the movement for desegregation, and these will be reviewed in chapter 8. By the 1950s, arguments for universal schooling (and what "universal" meant) had been laid out, for the most part, and nearly all children between ages six and 15 were spending time in schools, whether the schools were of similar quality or not. So, let's review some of the arguments for expanding education in the eighteenth, nineteenth, and twentieth centuries. Remember that mass education experienced the greatest growth as the country was also rapidly growing in terms of population and economic strength, as it was industrializing. First, there is the argument that schools needed to provide skills necessary for jobs that were growing as a result of industrialization. Workers needed skills that families could not give them. Because of industrialization, many families, working outside of the home, no longer had time to educate children. According to this argument for expanding education, some type of care and socialization should be provided for these children. Not only should students be taught new skills; they also have to learn new norms and values in order to be a compliant workforce. Others argued that schools were the necessary and appropriate place to sort people into different roles. Those who argued that education should be meritocratic suggested that family background should not determine children's place in the new economy, and that children should be sorted into adult roles and occupations according to the skills they acquire and display in schools. In order to do this most efficiently, schools had to provide students equality of opportunity to learn and display these skills. Still others argued that schools needed to reach all American children to keep social order and build nationalism. Schools were needed to teach all Americans loyalty and responsible citizenship, but American values and norms must particularly be taught to immigrants and the poor.

The purpose of the institution of education and one's stake in it could be viewed differently depending on one's social role. Factory owners may have wanted their workers to learn those skills that are necessary to be efficient workers in schools, but no more. These owners may also have wanted to limit the time children spend in school in order to maximize the time they were available as cheap workers. Politicians may have wanted to expand education so that everyone had the tools to vote, while at the same time maintaining an elite educational tier to train future politicians. Poor parents

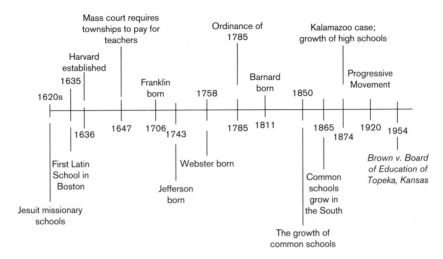

Figure 2-1. A Timeline of US Education.

may have desired expanded education in order to give their children an opportunity to compete with wealthier children for the same types of jobs, while wealthier parents may have promoted the sorting function of education by advocating for special types of education (an elite tier or a tracking system) to preserve the occupational position and status of their own children. Some immigrants and minorities may have promoted more inclusive education for their children, while others argued that separate schools were necessary for learning about their ancestry and cultural traditions.

To put this history in some context, figure 2-1 shows some of the major events and proponents of expanding education. From this (incomplete) timeline, you can see that over the course of the almost 400 years since the colonies were established, and the 240 years since the country was founded, truly public schooling—schools for all children from all social classes and immigrant and ethnic backgrounds—has been a reality for a bit less than 150 years. And, for blacks in the United States, schools that weren't explicitly separated by race have only existed for 60 years. Though the United States was one of the first and fastest countries to expand its education system to include nearly all students in the United States,[3] compared to political and other types of institutions in the United States, public schooling is relatively new.

On the surface, the varied goals of American education may seem not to be incompatible. The institution of education could potentially teach American values and basic skills for new workers. It could provide opportunities for all students and then sort those who displayed particular talents and abilities into valuable social roles and well-paid occupations. Education here serves as a public good—good for all members of society equally. However, some goals could also be in tension: If education is the means through which children get sorted and socialized, wouldn't those with privileges want to maintain those privileges through the institution? Would families look for ways to ensure their children had advantages that others did not? Families' interests in securing good occupations and futures for their children may work against the interests of those who want to ensure that all children have equal educational opportunities to succeed. And, here, education has a private function: it is used to secure social mobility for children or to maintain social position for advantaged families.

This tension is also manifested in the ways that sociologists have tried to understand how education shapes and is shaped by society. Two ways of looking at education, loosely grouped together under "functionalist" and "conflict" perspectives, view education's operation as an institution in opposing ways. Functionalists tend to see education operating in the interests of society—as a public good that, when ideal, harmoniously socializes and efficiently sorts youths into their appropriate adult roles (without regard for ascribed characteristics like gender, race and ethnicity, socioeconomic background, and others). Those who subscribe to the conflict position see education as being used primarily to fulfill the function of maintaining social status positions in society. Education is used as a private good by families to either increase their social mobility or maintain their advantaged status. Those with power and privilege based on ascribed statuses like boys, whites, and the socioeconomically advantaged have more resources to use to maintain their social positions. These two perspectives, and the assumptions that underlie them, are explored more fully in the next chapter.

3 What Does Education Do?

PARADIGMS AND THEORIES ABOUT
HOW EDUCATION WORKS

Sociologists who study education spend a lot of their time thinking about two questions. First, how does education, as a social institution, work? Second, they wonder who it works for, that is, are their some groups that benefit more than others? In this chapter, I present some perspectives that address these two questions. While there are two general "camps" into which many education researchers fall, called "functionalism" and "conflict," I will also explore how symbolic interactionists and other theorists view some of the practices of education.

Many of the theories about how education works can be categorized by two different paradigms of how sociologists view education. Paradigms are different from theories in that paradigms are a connected set of assumptions about how a system works. These assumptions themselves are not often directly tested, but theories can be derived from them, using specific measurements of the concepts implied by paradigms. These theories can be tested. Both of these paradigms present a consistent set of assumptions about the role of education in socializing and stratifying younger members of society. Sociologists, like Talcott Parsons, for example, consider education to be functional. This is an optimistic look at education that believes that education is generally progressive: that it imparts useful knowledge, rationally and efficiently sorts people into the positions that they are best suited for, and reduces initial inequalities between members of society. In the 1970s, another view of education emerged—a more pessimistic view. This view, called the conflict paradigm, is expressed by sociologists like Randall Collins and Samuel Bowles and Herbert Gintis. Essentially, they argue that the ways that education socializes people and sorts them into different roles (or stratifies) reproduce existing inequalities.

FUNCTIONALISM

The functional paradigm encompasses many people's ideas and opinions about what schools do. According to the functional paradigm, schools equip children with the skills and knowledge they need to fill their roles in society. They provide what is called "human capital" by economists. Schools may also, apart from teaching these skills, teach students how to learn; so they teach students not only specific skills, but also ways to go about finding answers to their own questions. Schools equip students with basic skills (math and reading skills) so that students can build upon these, exchanging their "human capital" for jobs and other adult roles.

Students are equipped with these basic skills so they can be sorted rationally and efficiently into the positions for which they are best suited. Schools, according to this view of education, are supposed to level the playing field. Students learn the same things, so that the classes or tracks into which they are placed (Advanced Placement, honors, college prep, general, vocational, or whatever) are based on their "natural" ability, talent, or propensity to work hard. According to functionalists, if students have the same basic skills, then performance must be based on achieved characteristics, like talent or hard work. Ascribed characteristics, like those that an individual may have at birth, such as socioeconomic background, race and ethnicity, gender, and so on, should not have any influence on how a student gets sorted into academic positions and, later, into careers or other adult roles.

Talcott Parsons is an example of a functionalist. Talcott Parsons was a famous sociologist, writing primarily in the 1950s and 1960s. He talked about how institutions in a society work together to benefit one another—and how the relationships in some institutions reinforced those in other institutions. Parsons saw the school as an institution that sorted children into their later social roles. He said this sorting occurs on two axes: people are sorted according to ascribed factors and according to their achievement. He saw achievement as the more important axis.[1]

Parsons recognized two types of achievement. He said that people could achieve cognitively, that is, they could learn to master certain skills. He also said there was "moral" achievement—moral achievement occurs when people mature, learning to be adults and responsible citizens. They learn good work habits and take leadership positions in a society. Moral achievement occurs when students' behavior exemplifies the values that the society holds.

Parsons saw the school as a "transition" institution between family and home and work and the larger society. Parsons argued that schools should and do resemble families at the earlier stages of children's education (his example being that teachers are mother figures) and that later on education becomes more and more like a job with more formal relationships between teachers and students.

Functionalism assumes that members of societies share some of the same values. The first is the value of a meritocracy. Societies must believe that it is better for ability (achieved characteristics) to matter more than background (ascribed characteristics). Meritocratic societies can be more desirable or "better" in a couple of ways. First, they can be better morally. We may believe that people who work hard and are talented should be rewarded for that—it is a moral value we have. We may also believe that meritocratic societies are more efficient—if people who are talented at medicine become doctors, it is better for the patients than if a person who has no aptitude for medicine inherited being a doctor from his or her father or mother.

Functionalism also assumes that societies value democracy and diversity. Functionalists assume that students educated in schools will learn democratic principles in order to become better citizens and members of society. Functionalists argue that education increases tolerance for others and, because of this, education is a great vehicle for increasing social harmony.

No one suggests that education is perfect—schools aren't completely able to reduce inequality. But the consensus among functionalists is that schools do help—they work, at least some of the time, and the better the schooling, the more likely it is that initial inequalities will be reduced. It is a goal toward which functionalists continue to strive using the existing educational system.

Functionalists, in general, do not wish to see overall inequality in society erased. The sociologist Kingsley Davis[2] argued that inequality motivates people to take the most difficult jobs in that society. Doctors are paid more than sales workers because they need to go to school longer and spend time studying intensively for exams. According to functionalists, in order to ensure that there are people to fill the more difficult and demanding roles in a society, we need to give higher rewards to those roles. Functionalists, then, generally do not protest all inequalities, only inequality in opportunity. Students should all have the same chance to become a doctor, but once a doctor they are entitled to earn more money than sales workers.

An "ideal type" is abstract. At its most basic level, an ideal type is a concept that captures the essential features of some phenomenon. It is an ideal—it is not meant to be attained but is simplified to characterize something. Ralph Turner[3] contrasts two "ideal types" of education, which he calls "sponsored mobility" and "contest mobility." Sponsored mobility is often found in European societies, and Turner uses Great Britain as an example of where sponsored mobility systems occur. In those education systems characterized by sponsored mobility, education is typically stratified by elite status. Elites in society go to particular secondary schools called grammar schools, while nonelite students attend other types of schools called modern or technical schools. The schools of elites lead to adult roles with high responsibility and privilege, while schools for nonelites prepare them for clerical, manual, or other types of work. Students with talent or ability can be chosen for grammar schools, despite their social status, through exams. These exams are typically given after primary and middle school years, and once students are placed into a grammar or modern school, there are very few changes between these types of schools.

Contest mobility, on the other hand, is best represented by the US system of education. In this system, students compete at nearly all levels for their adult occupational and social roles. Selection into the elite is not controlled by the elites themselves or determined by examinations; rather, it is a prize that is competed for at all levels of education—up through and even beyond admittance to college. Students compete to achieve better grades, better test scores, more advanced classes, and more extracurricular activities or leadership positions in order to be admitted to colleges or colleges with high prestige. Competition may further occur in these institutions for graduate schools or for first careers. In contrast, students in sponsored mobility systems begin preparing for their adult roles as early as secondary school.

The view of education as a contest that eventually selects the most talented individuals supports a functionalist view of education. In its ideal-typical form, US education allows every student to compete, without regard for their social status or other ascribed characteristics. This view of education has been criticized for being too idealistic, though. When education is perceived as a contest, there is much at stake for both the winners and the losers. Students with advantages may use their resources to preserve those advantages so they can be sure to be "winners" in the contest. With so much at stake at all levels of education, the motivation to use one's resources in the competition may be great. The contest may not be fair in a sense—there may be no "level playing field" on which people compete, so those with advantages may find it easier to win privileged adult occupations and roles.

Just to summarize, two main assumptions of functionalism are (1) as schools improve, schools (and society in general) become more meritocratic, and (2) schools teach students basic skills they need to compete in the labor market, so there is a clear link between the skills needed by employers and what students learn in schools. You might ask yourself whether or not you agree with these assumptions. Are students sorted less by their ascribed characteristics over time? Some may answer "yes" to this question. While girls and women were historically excluded from schools in the United States (and still are in some countries and regions of the world), the enrollment of women in colleges and universities now exceeds that of men.[4] Others of you may say "no." While racial segregation of schools declined from 1960 to 1990, segregation has once again risen (although there is some evidence for a decline or at least leveling off in recent years).[5] There is also evidence that although primary and secondary school enrollment is nearly universal in the United States, and college enrollment has been rising dramatically since the 1950s, the influence of parents' socioeconomic background on children's occupational attainment has not changed over the past several decades.[6] How much ascribed characteristics matter for students' schooling experiences and outcomes will be more fully explored throughout the chapters of this book.

You may also ask yourself to what extent schools teach students what they need to know to compete in the labor market. Are schools teaching skills that can be used for jobs right away? Are schools providing students with skills that will enable them to more easily learn what they need to know for specific jobs? It seems that a popular complaint is that employers cannot find workers with the "right" skills for their positions. If students are not being prepared for their roles in the labor market, what might they be learning in school?

CONFLICT PARADIGM

Randall Collins[7] questions the link between the skills we learn in schools and the skills needed by employers. He reasons that those who do well in school should have higher earnings than those who do not, if rewards accrue to those who show mastery of skills. Grades should be related to income: the higher your grades, the higher your income. Researchers find no such relationship. Collins argues that, rather than imparting specific cognitive skills, education imparts credentials. These credentials allow access into a more elite community and employers look for these credentials.

Collins fits into the conflict paradigm of education. Essentially, those who follow the conflict perspective believe that, rather than leveling the playing field, education reproduces initial social inequalities. It reproduces relations of dominance between classes, between social elites and nonelites, between those with and without privilege. In this view, education is designed to maintain the status quo relations of power in a society.

The conflict paradigm was largely formulated in the 1960s and 1970s in response to changing ideas about society. In the United States, the public was increasingly suspicious of authority. Activists became worried that businesses and industries were destroying the environment. Interest groups, and later more of the general public, saw more and more evidence that politicians were corrupt and hungry for power—less concerned with ideals and visions and more concerned with their own personal prestige. People began to identify racism and sexism, following the lead of the civil rights movement and the women's movement of the 1950s through 1970s. One view of the world that began to take shape during this time was that societies were manipulated by those in positions of power, for example, politicians, corporate leaders, those who had lots of money, employers. Society, as a whole, was not moving toward a more just and tolerant world; rather, people in positions of power were manipulating relationships and resources in their interests and the interests of their children. Many in the United States began to think that change was not possible within such a system, and that change could only be accomplished by a wholesale redistribution of power among societies' members.

The assumptions of the conflict paradigm matched the changing mood of the general public during the 1950s through the 1970s. First, those who subscribe to this paradigm believe that society is conflict-ridden and divisive. Groups compete to gain control over the educational system. There is always struggle over whose values and ideals will be taught in schools. Second, they believe this struggle is unequal. One side always has more resources or power than the other. Because of this, equality of opportunity is not realistic. This "reality" is hidden because those in power control the means of communication and produce a rhetoric of equality of opportunity in schools. Finally, those who ascribe to the conflict paradigm perceive that the skills we learn in schools are not connected to the skills demanded by employers. Employers care more about our attitudes and values than they do about specific skills. Particularly, employers want workers who will be docile, loyal, and compliant. This is what really gets taught in schools through the hidden curriculum. Also, employers want to build, or at least maintain, the status of their occupations. Because of this, employers seek to hire those with credentials like certificates or degrees. These certificates and degrees confer status, so the higher the level that is required to enter an occupation, generally the higher the perceived status of that occupation.

There are disagreements among those within the conflict paradigm, so not all conflict theories look the same. Generally, conflict theories can be divided into neo-Marxist and non-Marxist. Neo-Marxist conflict theories are generally derived from the ideas of Karl Marx, while those of non-Marxists are based more on the ideas of Max Weber.

The neo-Marxist view may be best expressed by Samuel Bowles and Herbert Gintis. In their book *Schooling in Capitalist America*, published in 1977, Bowles and Gintis argue that schools serve the interests of capitalism. Schools reproduce the values and personality characteristics that are necessary for capitalism to work. These values and personality traits depend on the class position for which students are being trained. Those who occupy positions of authority, who may own or manage work places, value creativity, flexibility, and innovation. Those traits allow businesses to compete and survive. These traits are not valued among workers, however. Manual workers and others who answer to bosses are valued for being punctual, respecting authority, and being loyal.

According to Bowles and Gintis, school tracks that prepare students to be workers teach students the importance of rule following and obedience. In higher-level classes, like honors or college-track classes, initiative may be more important. How does this look in practice? Observers of high school classes have noted several differences between honors and vocational-track classes that may be predicted by those within the conflict paradigm. For example, students in honors classes are often given more flexibility with their time and movement. During study halls, honors students may be allowed to leave the school campus or take study time in special student lounges. Students in vocational tracks may be more likely to need hall passes to move around during class hours. As another example, students in honors classes are more often graded based on the content of their ideas and less on grammar and spelling. Students in lower tracks may be graded on the neatness of their handwriting and their ability to follow directions. As a final example, students in higher-level classes may be given "projects" without specific directions. Students may produce art or video or write poems or plays to express ideas. Students in upper-level classes may work in groups. Students in lower-level classes are more likely to work on projects with very specific directions, alone. These different values and norms are taught to socialize people into different positions in the society—in this case, in the economy.

You might ask: Why do people not notice these differences? Can't students and their parents see the differences between how students in upper-level classes or tracks and students in lower-level ones are treated? To some extent, they can, and they seem normal. Students in upper-level classes are perceived to "earn" their privileges. Further, parents of students in upper-level tracks are often employers, professionals—somewhere in the upper-middle or upper classes. They desire that their children learn creativity and encourage initiative. Lower-middle and working-class parents value obedience in their children because it is something that they were taught. Because of this, they think it is natural and normal that students have to obey certain rules and do not have a lot of freedom of movement.

Bowles and Gintis reject the notion that schools are meritocratic: they only make people think they are meritocratic. If this is the case, though, why do people believe that schools are meritocratic? Schools seem to foster competition that sorts the "winners" into valued roles. One way that schools judge who is the most talented is through the use of presumably "objective" tests—IQ scores, SAT tests, or other "proficiency" tests designed to measure innate ability. Some suggest that these tests aren't good measures of innate ability because children come to school with different levels and types of knowledge and these levels and types of knowledge depend on their parents' background.[8] A child who has a parent who works two jobs or whose parents both work long hours may not be as prepared as a child who has a stay-at-home mother or father, or may not be as prepared as a child who is put in a challenging day care. Some say IQ measures occur too late—that they measure what has been learned in the home and other social environments (and this is related to socioeconomic background). IQ and other ability tests do not measure a child's capacity to learn. Others suggest that ability tests have biases built into them—that they ask questions that members of the middle and upper classes are more likely to know the answers to. For example, the word "regatta" has been used on ability tests like the SATs. Certainly people who participate in regattas are more likely to know what they are. People who participate are likely to be wealthy; not too many poor families take part in annual regattas. So there are arguments that these tests can't gauge innate ability and are only used to justify existing inequalities by making them seem achieved.[9]

Grades are another criterion people use to justify students being sorted into different groups, but researchers question whether or not grading is a truly objective practice.[10] Grades have been found to be related to students' behaviors and other mannerisms, especially at younger ages. It is common on elementary school report cards for children to be assessed based on how polite they are, how well they listen, and how well they interact with other children. Grades may be highly subjective—subject to teachers' views of who we are and what we say or do. Grades may not reflect talent or hard work, but rather how talented a teacher thinks a student is and how much work a teacher believes a student did.

So what do Bowles and Gintis think is the answer? How can education be reformed? Their answer is to overthrow capitalism—a pessimistic view of the chances for educational reform indeed. As long as people have more resources and power, they will act in ways so as to protect and enhance their resources and power, and inequality will be sustained.

Randall Collins, whom I mentioned before, subscribes to a non-Marxist conflict view, meaning that his ideas are based more on the writings of Max Weber. Weber contrasted the "cultivated man" with the "specialist man."[11] He argued that over time education was being used to confer credentials to those who passed particular examinations. With these credentials, even those who were not among the elite originally could claim the elite status of particular occupations. Credentials, conferred by educational institutions, were a way and now may be the main avenue to achieve status in a society that was ever bureaucratizing and becoming more meritocratic.

Randall Collins built upon these ideas in his book called *The Credential Society*, published in 1979. Collins argued that education does not equip students with skills for the work force, but rather with credentials to enter into different social positions. Credentials are signs or signals that tell others we belong to that group; they are like admissions tickets. Without credentials, we cannot get into certain occupations. Even if we possess the knowledge and skills, we still can't get in.

Collins, in contrast to the functionalists, sees education as an increasingly irrational and inefficient institution. He argues that more and more people are spending time in educational institutions that aren't preparing them for their careers. Perhaps at some point you or one of your friends has asked: Why do I have to go to college? And maybe your parents, friends, or family replied, "To get a job." You may have pushed further, asking, "But, what will I learn in college that prepares me to be a travel agent? a boutique owner? a chef?" Collins argues that more and more occupations require credentials, that is, college degrees, because there is a perception that as society becomes more complex, so do occupations. Further, the status of occupations is often determined by the amount of education associated with them. The more butchers who are required to have college degrees, the more status butchers will have, and the more people will perceive that butchers need special skills and training. The more special skills and training thought to be required by a position, often the higher the income associated with that position.

Collins calls the idea that jobs are becoming more specialized and requiring more skills the "myth of the technocracy." Collins attempts to prove that it is a myth that occupations in societies are becoming more complex and skilled in several ways. First, he notes that education has increased more rapidly than have highly skilled occupations. While there are a little more than three times as many college graduates now as 50 years ago, there are about two and a half times as many professional and technical occupations now as in 1960.[12] Collins finds that jobs generally require the same types of skills as they did 50 years ago—with some moderate changes in things like the use of technology. Collins argues that skills (like the use of technology) are not acquired in schools mostly, but are acquired on the job through training or accumulated experience. Finally, Collins says that education (and presumably the skills acquired through education) does not increase productivity. Educated workers are no more efficient than those who learned their skills on the job.

So, if schools are not teaching skills necessary for particular occupations, what do they do? School, according to Collins, teaches status cultures. Schools teach the values, beliefs, and norms of a particular group or groups in a society. Collins argues that these are often the values, norms, and beliefs of the elites of a society. The elites are people who have relatively more power and resources in a society than others: they may have more power (the ability to exert one's will on others) because they have more money, are in political positions, are in control of media and other types of communications, or for other reasons—race, religion, gender, sexual orientation. The values of these people become the values that are taught in school.

Collins suggests that elites in the United States have Anglo-Saxon, Protestant values. What gets taught in schools, then, is the value of hard work and the value of a broad, liberal arts education. But, Collins says, these values are not taught homogeneously. Schools in the United States tend to be more decentralized than in other nations—states and local communities have a greater degree of control over what gets taught in schools than the federal government. Because of this, different communities' values can be taught in schools. We have seen that recently in Colorado—in Jefferson County, the school board proposed to change the history curriculum to reflect patriotism and downplay civil unrest. This proposal met with opposition from both teachers and students, but neither the state nor federal government intervened. In another example, a Kansas school board proposed not only to teach evolution in schools, but to include creationism as a viable theory alongside evolution, despite protests from the scientific community. These examples show how local communities have a lot of control over what values get taught in schools.

Collins argues that diversity in the United States and local control over schools lead to a great deal of variation in what is taught in schools, in curricula, and in the skills that are taught. Because of this Collins suggests that what you learn in school is not as important in an employer's eyes as how much school you get, that is, how many years you have spent in school. He calls school "cultural currency"—like a dollar. The condition of the dollar, whether it is ripped and dirty or shiny and new, is not as important as the number of dollars you have. Schooling can then be exchanged (like money) for desirable occupations. The more levels of schooling or degrees a student has, the better or more desirable the occupation she or he can get. Collins also argues that there is "inflation" of educational credentials—the more money in an economy, the less it is worth, or the more goods cost. Similarly, the more education people have, the more certain occupations require—regardless of the skills imparted by the education or the skills needed in that occupation.

So, according to Collins, schools don't serve the needs of society efficiently at all. Students have to get more and more education to get the jobs they want whether skills are being taught in educational institutions or not. Employers want more of their employees to have higher levels of education because that generally brings higher status and pay to occupations. Educators want to see people go to school for more and more years so more and more professors like me have jobs.

Figure 3–1 shows this growth in enrollment in both two-year and four-year institutions. In the 1970s, only about 25% of adults aged 18 to 24 were enrolled in any postsecondary institution. About 17% were enrolled in four-year schools and a little over 6% were in two-year colleges. In 2012, those percentages have grown dramatically. Over 40% of young adults are now enrolled in any college or university, with a little under 30% being enrolled in four-year schools and 10% being enrolled in two-year colleges. This number captures the percentage of the young adult population that is currently enrolled in these institutions, not the proportions that have ever enrolled in these institutions, which is indeed higher. In addition, this figure does not capture growing numbers of nontraditional students (here defined as those who return to school past the age of 24, though there are many other definitions, as well), which in 2011–2012 was about 38% of all college students.[13]

Here I have presented two general ways of thinking about education and how it operates. Both functional and conflict paradigms present views of how education and society fit together. They attempt to answer questions about why and how education socializes and stratifies.

Both conflict and functional paradigms are concerned with how students get sorted into their adult roles and how this relates to their ascribed and achieved characteristics. Some researchers and social theorists have attempted to delineate the mechanisms through which this sorting happens. Two main approaches to how students get sorted into adult roles have emerged. The first follows the classic Blau and Duncan Model of Status Attainment, and then the Wisconsin Model of Status Attainment, linking socioeconomic background to eventual occupational attainment first through educational attainment, which is influenced by a student's academic performance, significant others, and educational aspirations.[14] The second tradition of research, social reproduction theory, highlights the roles of cultural capital and habitus in shaping educational outcomes.[15] Both may be relevant for understanding how students get sorted into adult roles.

Figure 3-1. Percentage of 18- to 24-Year-Old Adults Enrolled in Any Postsecondary Institution and by Institution Type, 1973–2012.

SOURCE: US Department of Education, Institute for Education Science, National Center for Education Statistics, *Digest of Education Statistics*, 2013, table 302.60.

RESEARCH IN THE TRADITION OF THE BLAU AND DUNCAN AND WISCONSIN MODELS OF STATUS ATTAINMENT

The Blau and Duncan Status Attainment Path Model specifies some of the mechanisms through which parents' (specifically fathers') social status is transmitted to their children. Education is a main factor through which this transmission occurs. Fathers' education and occupation influence the years of schooling, or educational attainment, of their sons, and the educational attainment of sons influences their first and subsequent occupations. Other factors related to fathers' education and occupation influence their sons' eventual occupational attainment, but education is the main intervening factor in this transmission.[16]

The Wisconsin Model of Status Attainment added to the Blau and Duncan Model by further exploring how parents' education and occupation

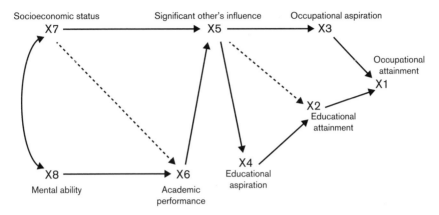

Figure 3-2. Wisconsin Model of Status Attainment.

influence their children's educational attainment (see figure 3–2). This model firmly established social-psychological factors, like educational aspirations, as important mechanisms in explaining the effects of family background on one's achievement.[17] According to the original Wisconsin Model, there is no direct effect of family background on a child's later socioeconomic status beyond the indirect effects of motivational factors. However, later elaborations of this model show that the effects of parents' status on educational attainment cannot be completely explained by students' motivations. For example, Wilson and Portes contend that parental resources and evaluations of students' ability by others may also play prominent roles in status transmission.[18]

The original Wisconsin Model shows that parents' socioeconomic status indirectly influences students' educational aspirations through a weak influence on academic performance and a strong effect on what significant others like parents, teachers, or coaches aspire for students. Students with less-advantaged parents perform less well on standardized tests and get worse grades than those whose parents have more advantages. This influences the perceptions of the parents of these students, their teachers, and their friends, and these perceptions then influence students. The encouragement of significant others and the information and examples they provide for a student enable them to attain various levels of educational credentials.[19] Significant others have also been found to influence a student's self-concept. Students whose parents aspire for them to achieve high levels of education have more confidence in their academic ability than those whose parents do not. Confident students set higher aspirations for themselves than those who feel less certain of their abilities.[20] The Wisconsin Model suggests that academic ability and the influence of significant others are the primary mechanisms through which socioeconomic background influences educational aspirations.

The influence of these mechanisms may not be the same across groups, however. Cheng and Starks find that in general parents' expectations influence the expectations of white students more than they do those of black, Asian American, and Hispanic students.[21] However, close relatives have a stronger impact on the expectations of blacks and Hispanics. Other research also identifies differences in the influence of educational aspirations and expectations on educational outcomes by race.[22]

The Wisconsin Model of Status Attainment highlights the important roles of academic performance and significant others in shaping educational aspirations and expectations and ultimately educational attainment. These factors have been measured and quantified in models describing how parents' social resources influence their children's adult occupational roles, but other researchers argue that there are unmeasured influences that operate on children, linking them to their adult roles, through means other than their performance and their stated motivations.

SOCIAL REPRODUCTION AND EDUCATIONAL OUTCOMES

A second research tradition that focuses on the effects of ascribed characteristics on educational attainment is the social reproduction theory promoted by Bourdieu and Passeron and others.[23] Bourdieu and Passeron highlight the roles of noneconomic capital in social reproduction. Individuals possess social and cultural resources in the form of attitudes, values, preferences, and behaviors that can be invested and converted into educational, occupational, and economic gain.[24] Bourdieu's term "cultural capital" refers to the cultural symbols that indicate the social position of an individual. These may include types of speech, knowledge of high culture, travel, and one's educational credentials. Individuals may be judged according to the cultural capital they have. For example, DiMaggio finds that students who know about or participate in high-cultural activities like art or music lessons are graded more positively by teachers even after accounting for their test scores.[25]

Another concept important to social reproduction theory is habitus. Habitus refers to an individual's set of dispositions, goals, and strategies for attaining the social resources and position he or she desires. Habitus is an interconnected set of perceptions of opportunities and appropriate ways to pursue those opportunities. According to social reproduction theory, habitus differs according to social position, and this serves to reproduce socioeconomic background differences, and perhaps other differences by ascribed characteristics like race.

The examination of different goals, different values, and the acceptable means to pursue them among social groups is not novel. For example, Melvin Kohn identified variation in values for children held by middle-class parents and working-class parents. He found that middle-class parents emphasized inner-directedness—creativity and curiosity—while working-class parents valued outward-directedness, values like obedience and politeness. He connected these values to later life opportunities. Children from working-class families exhibit values that better prepare them for lower-prestige jobs in which obedience is valued, while middle-class students are encouraged to exhibit the creativity and curiosity that will prepare them for professional, higher-status employment.[26]

More recently, researchers have explored the connection between social class and the meaning and experience of education. Lareau, for example, identifies different perceptions of education among working-class and middle-class parents, which affect their interactions with schools.[27] In later work, she describes how children in middle- and upper-class families are raised according to a philosophy called "concerted cultivation." Parents foster their children's talents and abilities through extracurricular activities and other opportunities, while also encouraging children to speak up for themselves and be comfortable and confident around adults, particularly those in authority. Children in working-class families are raised according to a philosophy of the "accomplishment of natural growth."

These children play among relatives after school is done, structure their own leisure time, and are not taught to challenge adults in authority positions, like teachers and doctors.[28]

The social reproduction approach suggests that students have different habits, ideas, beliefs, norms, and perceptions of their place in the world. Their goals may differ, and they may hold different strategies for how to achieve the goals they have. Bourdieu and many others after him suggest that the habits, values, and norms that are privileged in schools are the ones that are consistent with those in power—those who control the institution or field (education) in which students find themselves.[29] Oftentimes (though not always) the habits, norms, and values of those who are in power within an institutional field are consistent with those of people in power in the society more generally. Those in power, whom the society privileges, may be elite, middle- or upper-class, highly educated, or white, for example. This different evaluation of students based on their cultural capital or cultural resources is difficult to measure in empirical models and, social reproduction theorists may argue, is absent from models of status attainment.

OTHER APPROACHES

There are other sociological approaches that are important for understanding education, too. Symbolic interactionism is a perspective that shows how interactions that occur in and are shaped by schools teach students how to interact outside of schools and into their adult lives. Symbolic interactionists, the most famous of which is Erving Goffman, talk about how people perceive their roles and act them out.[30] People learn to act like doctors or patients, for example.[31] It is in schools that students begin to learn these roles through interactions with teachers, students, and other school personnel. Students learn this through the "hidden curriculum," which may teach them the appropriate behaviors for girls versus boys, privileged versus nonprivileged students, smart versus not smart kids, or white, black, Asian, or Hispanic students. Barrie Thorne, for example, shows how girls and boys learn their gender roles through repeated interactions with each other and through school structures, which give them different roles and different spaces to occupy.[32] Other studies look at how students are racialized into different roles. Asian students, for example, may be perceived to be the most hard-working or talented students, the "model minorities," while black students may be perceived as troublemakers.[33]

Symbolic interactionists study the mechanisms through which students learn roles and behaviors. These roles and behaviors are learned through repeated, patterned interactions with teachers and other students. While these interactions may be perceived as "natural" by observers (boys play more active, competitive games, while girls' games are more cooperative and take up less space), many symbolic interactionists interrogate the ways that the organization of schools facilitates these interactions. Playgrounds may be set up with large athletic fields and smaller spaces for cooperative games, which lead to boys and girls occupying different spaces. Schools may "track" students in ways that separate students by race, such that students notice that Asian and white students comprise Advanced Placement and honors courses, while black students disproportionately occupy vocational courses.[34] From these observations, students learn where they belong based on their race.

Symbolic interactionists generally fall into neither the functionalist nor the conflict paradigms squarely because they are concerned with how students learn their roles, but not with whether these roles are the ones they are best suited for based on talent or ability. Many symbolic interactionists, though, investigate theories derived from the conflict paradigm because they look at how interactions learned in schools reproduce differences across students that lead to stratification based on race, gender, or socioeconomic background that is unrelated to the talent or ability of students.

Philosophers of education have also devoted much time to thinking how education does and should work. Beginning with John Dewey in the early twentieth century and followed by Paolo Freire in the 1970s, these thinkers believe that education should be transformative and used for social change.[35] Like those within the conflict paradigm, they believe that education in its current form often reproduces social inequalities, but at its best, education can be used to liberate students from their social positions. According to Freire, educational institutions have to adopt a "critical pedagogy" for this liberation to occur. Students must be taught how to critique those social structures and ideologies that keep those who are oppressed in their positions. Students look for how power operates through their curricula and in school organizations and structures.[36]

Although the conflict and functionalist paradigms are often presented as opposing views of education, they do not necessarily have to be so. Does education sort some people in such a way as to minimize the effects of socioeconomic background, race and ethnicity, gender, and other individual characteristics on their adult roles? Does education (sometimes at least) sort those who have the most ability and show the most effort into our most important social positions? Many of our presidents, most recently Bill Clinton and Barack Obama, came from humble origins through the highest-prestige schools in the nation on their road to the presidency. But there are also many examples of students in underperforming schools, with high teacher turnover, high rates of school violence, and school buildings that are in disrepair.[37] These schools are not distributed randomly; they are located in neighborhoods, rural or urban, that are disproportionately poorer. Can students in these schools get an education that is equal to that of those students with the most-qualified teachers, new textbooks and technology, and sparkling swimming pools? Much of the research suggests that education either works efficiently to sort students (or, if improved, can do so) or reproduces the advantages of students who already have social advantages—parents with high incomes, higher education, and good jobs, white students, native-born students, and so on. It may be, though, that these two positions do not have to be exclusive. Can education both sort (some) students into positions that best match their talents and abilities while at the same time reproducing social advantages for those who have them? Is a better question to ask the extent to which education does each, while acknowledging that it can do both?

After reading this chapter, I want you to take out a piece of paper and draw a line on it. The line represents a continuum. On one end, write "functional paradigm," and on the other write "conflict paradigm." Where do you think education as an institution falls on this line? Is it closer to how functionalists view education or is it nearer to the conflict perspective? Representing paradigms about education this way suggests that the purposes and workings of education may in some instances be best classified under one paradigm and at other times the other. These tensions may exist, and we may ask ourselves, what kind of balance do we see in education at this moment? Where would we like to see our ideal version of education on this continuum?

In the next several chapters, I will present some empirical data concerning social inequalities in educational experiences and outcomes. I will review some of the reasons that people propose for differences in outcomes, and these explanations usually fall into a functionalist or a conflict perspective. Some explanations focus on families, peers, or neighbors, suggesting that schools may even ameliorate these differences (as perhaps functionalists might suggest), or that schools passively reproduce but do not exacerbate differences. Other explanations implicate schools more directly in reproducing differences or contend that schools are powerless to (or can only weakly) combat the larger social inequalities that have occurred over generations of rich and poor, black and white, and girls and boys. The next chapter, chapter 4, will describe variation in patterns of educational achievements and experiences across socioeconomic background. In this chapter, I look at whether and how parents' education and income may matter for students' school profiles, grades, test scores, and college enrollment. Chapter 5 will explore variation in experiences and outcomes by race and ethnicity, while chapter 6 will take up these same topics by gender.

functional
paradigm

conflict
paradigm

4 Inequality by Socioeconomic Background and Class

This book began with several questions: Should reducing inequality be one of education's main goals? Is it in tension with other goals? If, indeed, we agree as a society that reducing inequality *should* be a goal, what do we mean by inequality? Should children have equal educational experiences regardless of social background characteristics? Should students of all races, rich and poor, girls and boys have equal educational outcomes? In chapter 2, I show that one of the concerns of educational reformers throughout US history has been to ensure equal opportunities for students of all socioeconomic backgrounds. Later, this concern was extended to women and to racial minorities. However, as the previous chapters have discussed, the institution of education has many goals and oftentimes these goals can be in tension. For example, if education is used to sort students into adult roles—some of which are better rewarded and have higher status than others—then those with resources may use them to ensure their children are best prepared to occupy those roles. The goal of equal educational opportunity becomes more difficult to achieve when a more-advantaged group uses its resources to maintain its advantage. This is what the conflict paradigm of chapter 3 suggests. On the other hand, there have been educational reforms that have attempted to equalize the educational environments and outcomes for all students. Attempts to sort students into adult roles without regard for ascriptive characteristics are consistent with the perspective of functionalists.

As the questions above suggest, equality is hard to define. What do we mean when we say "educational equality"? For many, it means that educational outcomes are the same by socioeconomic background, race, and gender. Especially in an era of increased testing and accountability, educational equality occurs when blacks and whites, rich and poor, and girls and boys have nearly identical average test scores, or when they graduate from high school or complete college at the same rates. Given other differences between these groups in society, one wonders whether schools alone can erase these gaps, though. How do schools affect gaps in educational outcomes? Do they make them better, make them worse, or have little effect? What are other explanations for these gaps that schools may have little control over, and how might they contribute to the persistence of inequality in educational outcomes?

Apart from assessing educational inequality by outcomes like grades and graduation rates, scholars and journalists have noted that there is inequality in school resources and environments by school poverty or racial composition.[1] These differences are similar to the concept "opportunities to learn," which refers to differences in curricula, differences in teacher effort and ability, and perhaps other organizational differences between schools (though opportunities to learn can also differ within schools).[2] Student learning is influenced by both opportunities to learn and the ability to take advantage of those opportunities. These scholars and journalists have noted that children attend schools that look and feel different, and many children are aware of these differences. While some question how these differences affect outcomes, others argue that these differences, this type of inequality, should be remedied, whether or not it improves student outcomes necessarily. There is much debate about how school resources and environment influence inequality in educational outcomes, but some argue that even if they don't affect outcomes, inequality in resources and in school environments should be minimized because schools are public goods.

In this chapter, I want to provide a picture of both types of educational inequality. I will start by showing how educational resources and experiences in elementary, middle, and high schools differ across students by socioeconomic background. Next, I will present tables that describe how outcomes vary by student socioeconomic background. This ordering is not meant to suggest, though, that differences in school resources and environments cause differences in educational outcomes. I will discuss debates about whether and how differences between and within schools influence educational outcomes. However, I will also present other explanations for differences in outcomes by socioeconomic background that may be hard for schools to remedy, even if all agree that schools should reduce socioeconomic inequality in educational outcomes.

Before showing some of these tables and figures, first I want to distinguish between social class and socioeconomic background. Those who reference social class often refer in some way back to the social theorist Karl Marx. When Marx talked about social class, he was explicitly connecting individuals to their economic roles or their relationships to the means of production of a good or service. If an individual controls the means of production (for example, by owning a factory or business), then he or she is part of the bourgeoisie. If he or she works for the owner of the factory or business, he or she is part of the proletariat. Marx believed that one's relationship to the means of production conditions the ways that she or he views the world. Bowles and Gintis see social class similarly to Marx in that they believe that whether one is in a working-class or middle-class family conditions how one accepts the hidden curriculum in schools.[3] Those whose parents are workers are conditioned by school rules to occupy this role in the economy through attention to punctuality, obedience, and conformity, while those whose parents are in the middle or professional classes become used to group work and expressing themselves creatively, and they are encouraged to think critically. Class is most strictly measured according to one's position in the labor force, that is, how much autonomy a person has in his or her job. On the one hand, those in professional occupations control much of their time. They do not typically report to bosses, so although they may work many hours, those hours can be in the evenings or on weekends. Professionals typically have more flexibility. On the other hand, those in manual occupations do not control their time or have much flexibility. To take time off, they must often ask for permission from a supervisor or boss.

This concept is useful because how a student or how a student's parent views authority and work time can influence educational experiences and outcomes. According to Bowles and Gintis, students who are taught to respect and not question authority, and who are taught conformity and obedience to rules, will not be surprised when that is what is required of them in the labor force. Time is also important for students' families. Working-class families may find it difficult to attend school functions (like meetings with teachers) during working hours.[4] In addition, parents who work fixed hours may perceive their work time and their leisure time as separate, and expect that children's school time and playtime are as well. When children are done with school, they may be expected to have free time to play and hang around with friends and family.[5] On the other hand, for professional parents, who are used to overlapping work and home lives, children may be expected to do school work at home, as well as cultivate themselves through extracurricular activities.

Socioeconomic background is a more expansive concept than social class. This concept finds it roots in the work of Max Weber, primarily. Weber talks about "status," which groups people according to their honor, prestige, or religion. Status can be expressed by "shared lifestyles," such that those with the same status share similar tastes, values, behaviors, and beliefs. Status is multidimensional in that it is not defined by how much money a person makes or how much wealth he or she has, nor is it defined by whether a person has a boss or flexibility at work. It is often dependent on how much education a person has or the collective educational experiences of that person's family. The literature on educational homogamy (how people who are similar tend to marry each other) shows that those with similar educational profiles tend to share similar values, beliefs, and tastes. So, oftentimes one of the best proxies we have for measuring the status of a student's family is the educational attainment of his or her parents. This is crude, of course, as there can be a lot of variation across students whose parents have the same educational levels, but it is one of the best ways to capture this multidimensional concept since education very closely correlates with parents' occupations and incomes. To the extent possible, in the following tables and figures, I will show student experiences and outcomes by parents' education or income; however, both concepts are important and have different implications for understanding inequality in education.

Unfortunately, we sometimes do not have access to the educational profiles of students' parents. Sometimes, the only information we have about
students is whether or not they receive free or reduced price lunches, which
are determined by "poverty thresholds" and "guidelines" issued by the US
government. Poverty thresholds, or the "poverty line," are used by the US
government to estimate the proportion of people in poverty. Generally, they
are based on a calculation that determines how much food that would sustain families of different sizes costs, and assumes that this cost is about a
third of the income a family of that size needs. The poverty line for a family
of four nationally in 2014 was $23,850. Poverty "guidelines" use percentages
of this threshold to determine who should be eligible for which programs.
Students in families with four members who made less than $31,005 per
year (130% of the poverty line) in 2014 were eligible to receive free meals and
those who made $44,123 (185% of the poverty line) were eligible for reduced
price meals. However, in order to get it, students' families must apply for it.
Many families do not apply, either because they do not want to rely on government subsidies or because they are ashamed to do so. Some may not be
aware that they are eligible. Receiving free or reduced price lunch then is
likely an underestimate of the population of people who are actually eligible
for it. However, when no other measures are available, receipt of free or
reduced price lunch approximates a student's poverty status.

STUDENT EDUCATIONAL EXPERIENCES

Some schools are well kept. They have campuses. They may even look like
Ivy League colleges. There are art galleries, spaces for studying, athletic
fields, swimming pools. These schools are set apart from their surround-
ings—maybe they are set off the road or on a hill. Other schools look much
different. Jonathan Kozol goes to schools in inner cities in East St. Louis,
the Bronx, and Chicago. These schools are often run-down. They don't
have enough resources. Some schools do not have athletic fields. Schools
are not set apart from the areas in which they are found—they are on a city
block, just another building. They look like factories. One school that
Kozol visits is an old skating rink. Some schools have bars on their win-
dows and look remarkably like jails. Others have security cameras, guards,

and metal detectors. Students notice these differences, particularly, students who are in schools with less advantages. Students in inner-city schools, for example, wonder why they do not have the same types of schools as students in suburbs.[6] How this influences students' motivation or behavior is a question that remains to be answered, but one could speculate that students in inferior schools may feel like society cares less for them because as a whole we are unwilling to redistribute resources to improve conditions. This is very hard to measure and it is unclear how this relates to academic outcomes, if at all.

Socioeconomic Segregation

One way in which students' school experiences may differ is the extent to which poor students are concentrated in schools with other poor students, and the extent to which wealthy students are surrounded by other wealthy students. This socioeconomic segregation of schools appears to be increasing, at least over the past two decades, in part as the wealthy become more concentrated in neighborhoods and schools.[7] The segregation of one group from another is often measured with a dissimilarity index. For example, in 1999–2000, nationally, the segregation of those children not eligible for free or reduced price lunch (nonpoor) from those who were eligible (poor) children was .52 on the dissimilarity index. A dissimilarity index of .52 means that 52% of either poor or nonpoor children would have to switch schools for the proportions of poor and nonpoor students in each school to be the same as the overall proportion of poor and nonpoor students in the metropolitan area. In 1999–2000, the average poor student in public elementary schools attended a school that was 63% poor. The average nonpoor student's school was only 27.5% poor.[8]

Table 4–1 lists some school districts in major metropolitan areas in the United States. Those with the most segregation, like Bergen-Passaic, NJ, and Newark, NJ, have dissimilarity indices that show that more than 70% of poor or nonpoor students would have to change schools for their representations in schools to be the same as in the metropolitan area. On the other hand, those with the least segregation, like Greenville-Spartanburg-Anderson, SC, and Raleigh-Durham, NC, show that anywhere from 29% to 35% of poor or nonpoor students would have to move to have distributions

Table 4-1 Segregation Indices for Those Eligible for Free and Reduced Price Lunch and Those Who Are Not across Selected Metropolitan Regions

School District	Class Segregation
Bergen-Passaic, NJ	.705
Newark, NJ	.703
Milwaukee-Waukesha, WI	.650
Detroit, MI	.639
Cleveland-Lorain-Elyria, OH	.630
Philadelphia, PA	.627
Boston, MA	.617
Orange County, CA	.605
New York, NY	.576
Los Angeles-Long Beach, CA	.566
Buffalo-Niagara Falls, NY	.565
Richmond-Petersburg, VA	.564
San Francisco, CA	.563
Hartford, CT	.561
Baltimore, MD	.560
Denver, CO	.558
Cincinnati, OH	.550
Rochester, NY	.549
Houston, TX	.541
Nassau-Suffolk, NY	.539
Dallas, TX	.532
Oakland, CA	.530
Albuquerque, NM	.529
Columbus, OH	.527
Atlanta, GA	.521
San Diego, CA	.508
Minneapolis-St. Paul, MN	.508
New Orleans, LA	.503
Fort Worth-Arlington, TX	.492
Pittsburgh, PA	.484
West Palm Beach-Boca Raton, FL	.484
Fort Lauderdale, FL	.477
Indianapolis, IN	.469
Washington, DC	.465
Shreveport-Bossier City, LA	.463

Jackson, MS	.462
Charleston-North Charleston, SC	.459
Miami, FL	.454
Norfolk-Virginia Beach-Newport News, VA	.452
Riverside-San Bernadino, CA	.452
Augusta-Aiken, GA	.444
Las Vegas, NV	.437
Columbia, SC	.432
Birmingham, AL	.430
Baton Rouge, LA	.415
Jacksonville, FL	.412
Mobile, AL	.417
Memphis, TN	.402
Louisville, KY	.394
Portland-Vancouver, OR	.389
Greensboro-Winston Salem-High Point, NC	.388
Tampa-St. Petersburg-Clearwater, FL	.382
Orlando, FL	.370
Charlotte-Gastonia-Rock Hill, NC	.347
Raleigh-Durham-Chapel Hill, NC	.343
Greenville-Spartanburg-Anderson, SC	.294

SOURCE: John R. Logan, *Whose Schools Are Failing?*, US2010 Project, tables 3 and 4.

of students in schools resemble the distribution of poor and nonpoor students in the metropolitan area. Generally, dissimilarity scores for these metropolitan regions range between 40% and 60%. Dissimilarity scores over 60% are considered quite high. Percentage scores of 40 to 60 suggest moderate segregation of the poor from the nonpoor.

Per Capita Spending

There is much debate over whether and how much school resources matter for students' educational outcomes, but it is one way that students' school environments differ.[9] Schools that have more funds at their disposal may have newer textbooks, better technology, more sports equipment, or better-kept grounds, whether or not these differences ultimately affect student educational outcomes directly. Those who argue that funding does not matter suggest that the differences in achievement outcomes observed across schools with different levels of per pupil funding are due to the socioeconomic backgrounds of the students or to overly bureacratized, inefficient schools.

Funding for schools comes from several sources, but the source of most of this funding is local property taxes. This money is often then supplemented by states to provide students with what they judge to be an "adequate" level of education, though the definition of "adequate" can vary from state to state, and "adequate" is not intended to mean "equal."[10] Often states use what is called a "funding formula" to figure out how much supplementary money districts need. Additionally, for those schools whose free and reduced price lunch population exceeds 5 percent, the Title I program of the federal government provides extra funds to be used at the school's discretion, weighted according to the population of students in need. Because the funding a student has access to is based on both the state and the district in which students reside, I present below the per capita funding by state (adjusted for regional differences in cost of living) and then by select cities (to approximate differences between schools within the same state).

Table 4–2 shows the differences in per capita funding in 2012 across all states in the United States and Washington, DC. Roughly, southern and mountain states tend to spend the least per pupil on education. For example, Texas spends a little over $8,000 per pupil and Utah spends over $6,000. Arizona and California also have low per pupil spending at a bit above $8,000 per student. On the other hand, states in the midwest, northeast, and mid-Atlantic regions tend to spend more. Vermont spends over $18,000 per pupil (adjusted) and New York spends over $17,000. Connecticut spends over $15,000 and the other midwestern, northeastern, and mid-Atlantic states range from $12,000 to $14,000 per pupil. There are some notable exceptions to this pattern: Alaska spends over $18,000 per pupil and Wyoming over $17,000.

These differences are quite big. A student in Texas has half as much spent on him or her compared to a student in New York. Clearly, the state in which a student lives influences how much money is spent on his or her education, but what about within states? Are there big differences across the schools within states?

Let's take Texas as our first example. Table 4–3 shows that from 2007 to 2009, those schools with the lowest proportions of poor students were

Table 4-2 Per-Pupil Educational Expenditures in 2012, Adjusted for Regional Cost Differences

State	Expenditures	State	Expenditures
Alabama	$9,563	Missouri	$10,798
Alaska	$18,113	Montana	$13,224
Arizona	$8,101	Nebraska	$13,457
Arkansas	$11,224	Nevada	$8,141
California	$8,308	New Hampshire	$14,561
Colorado	$9,020	New Jersey	$15,421
Connecticut	$15,172	New Mexico	$9,736
Delaware	$13,902	New York	$17,326
District of Columbia	$13,917	North Carolina	$8,670
Florida	$9,120	North Dakota	$13,443
Georgia	$9,394	Ohio	$12,010
Hawaii	$12,727	Oklahoma	$8,624
Idaho	$8,123	Oregon	$10,415
Illinois	$11,730	Pennsylvania	$13,653
Indiana	$11,230	Rhode Island	$13,814
Iowa	$11,929	South Carolina	$10,141
Kansas	$11,399	South Dakota	$10,742
Kentucky	$10,713	Tennessee	$9,113
Louisiana	$12,375	Texas	$8,113
Maine	$14,613	Utah	$6,688
Maryland	$12,435	Vermont	$18,882
Massachusetts	$13,157	Virginia	$9,784
Michigan	$12,038	Washington	$9,346
Minnesota	$11,547	West Virginia	$13,227
Mississippi	$9,587	Wisconsin	$11,968
		Wyoming	$17,758

SOURCE: Annie E. Casey Foundation, Kids Count Data Center, National Kids Count, Per-Pupil Educational Expenditures Adjusted for Regional Cost Differences Using the National Center for Education Statistics (NCES) Geographic Cost of Education Index, www.datacenter.kidscount.org /data/tables/5199-per-pupil-educational-expenditures-adjusted-for-regional-cost-di#detailed/1 /any/false/868,867,133,38,35/any/11678.

Table 4–3   Cost-Adjusted Local and State Revenues per Pupil in the Ten Least
Equitable States by School Poverty Composition

State	0% Poverty	10% Poverty	20% Poverty	30% Poverty
Alabama	$9,698	$9,240	$8,804	$8,388
Illinois	$11,082	$10,348	$9,662	$9,021
Maine	$12,880	$12,373	$11,886	$11,418
Nevada	$11,646	$10,214	$8,958	$7,856
New Hampshire	$14,801	$12,746	$10,977	$9,454
New York	$18,629	$17,907	$17,213	$16,546
North Carolina	$11,422	$10,302	$9,291	$8,379
North Dakota	$10,637	$9,917	$9,245	$8,618
Pennsylvania	$13,675	$13,226	$12,792	$12,373
Texas	$9,526	$9,134	$8,758	$8,397

SOURCE: Baker and Corcoran (2012): table 1.

spending a little under $10,000 per pupil. In those schools with the highest poverty, a little over $8,000 was spent per pupil. In Pennsylvania, over $13,000 was spent on students in the lowest-poverty schools, while high-poverty schools received about $12,000 per pupil. In Illinois, $11,000 was spent on students in low-poverty schools compared to $9,000 in the highest-poverty schools. There are states, though, that direct resources to their poorest schools to equalize per capita spending. New Jersey and Ohio spend more on their poorest students than they do on their least poor. Researchers find a general correlation between states that rely most on local property taxes to fund their schools and inequality in funding between the most and least poor schools.[11]

TEACHER QUALIFICATIONS

Schools with higher concentrations of students in poverty, and perhaps fewer funding resources, may differ from schools with lower concentrations of students in poverty. Using data from the National Center for Education Statistics, figure 4–1 shows that students in high-poverty

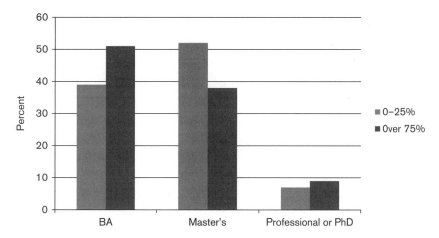

Figure 4-1. Teacher Degree by School Poverty Composition, 2007–2008.

SOURCE: US Department of Education, National Center for Education Statistics, Schools, and Staffing Survey (SASS), "Public School Teacher and Private School Teacher Data Files," 2007–2008, *The Condition of Education,* 2010, figure CL-7.

schools (above 75% receiving free or reduced price lunch) are less likely to be taught by teachers who have master's degrees. Over 50% of teachers in low-poverty schools have master's degrees compared to less than 40% in high-poverty schools. Teacher qualification has been found to be correlated with student achievement, though not consistently.[12] In addition to qualifications, teacher experience and retention may differ across schools with different compositions of students in poverty. Teachers who teach in low-poverty schools are generally more likely to be retained than those in high poverty schools.[13] As an example, in my city of Philadelphia, 67% of teachers in elementary schools with fewer than 80% in poverty remained at those schools three years later compared to 53% of those in schools with poverty rates of over 90%.[14]

Class Sizes

Another measure of school quality that some have argued is consequential for student outcomes is class size.[15] Some argue that the more students in a class, the harder it is for teachers to maintain order and for students to get individualized attention. Table 4–4 shows that class sizes vary little in

Table 4-4   Teacher/Pupil Ratio in 2009 and Teacher Retention in 2012–2013

Free or Reduced Price Lunch Eligibility	Average Number of Students per Teacher in 2009	Percentage of Teachers Who Stayed in the Same School, 2012–2013
0–25%	16.5	87.2%
26–50%	16.1	85.5%
51–75%	15.8	84.3%
76–100%	15.6	78.0%

SOURCE: US Department of Education, National Center for Education Statistics, *Digest of Education Statistics,* 2011, table 68; US Department of Education, National Center for Education Statistics, Teacher Follow-Up Survey (TFS), "Current and Former Teacher Data Files," 2012–2013, Schools and Staffing Survey, table 2.

both by school poverty status. Those schools with the least concentrations of poverty (25 percent or less) averaged about 16.5 students per class in 2009 compared with 15.6 in the highest poverty schools (over 75 percent).

The previous tables and figures provide some differences between schools with many students in poverty and those with few. Poor students tend to be segregated from wealthier students, with less overall funding available in most states, and may have teachers with lower qualifications, but, across the nation, are in classes of similar sizes. Whether these different educational environments may be related to the varied educational outcomes between students by poverty status, income, and parents' education is a question that researchers have grappled with, and one that I will address after I present some differences in educational outcomes by students' socioeconomic background.

EDUCATIONAL OUTCOMES

There are a variety of educational outcomes that can be used to assess educational inequality by socioeconomic background. These outcomes are related and affect students cumulatively. For example, if a student is held back in first grade, then that student may perceive that she or he is not "good at school" and may have low expectations for future education that affect future grades, course-taking, high school graduation, and college enrollment. While these measures are all related and influence one another, they measure different aspects of student experience as well. Whether one is held back a grade may be a result of noncognitive (behavioral) traits, such as delayed social skills or an inability to focus. One's grades may reflect ability and persistence, while test scores may tip more toward ability or proficiency. High school graduation reflects persistence in school (maybe more so than ability), while college enrollment may measure tested ability and perceptions that one can afford to attend and do well in college.

Educational Expectations

Though educational expectations are not strictly outcomes, they are often used as a way to assess students' perceptions of educational possibilities. They may reflect some combination of baseline expectations shaped by families and significant others, but they may also change as students get more information about their academic performance (like grades or test scores). Figures 4–2 and 4–3 show how much education students expect to achieve by their parents' highest educational attainment and by their family income. Both figures tell the same story: the fewer social resources, the lower a student's educational expectations. For example, about 9% of those whose parents have a high school degree or less plan the same for themselves compared to about 1.5% of those whose parents have graduate or professional degrees. About 58% of those whose parents have graduate or professional degrees plan to achieve the same compared to only 22% of those whose parents have a high school degree or less. Similarly, almost 8% of those whose families make $35,000 or less per year expect to attain a high school degree or less compared to less than 2% of those whose families make more than $75,000. Nearly half (48%) of those whose families make $75,000 or more a year expect to attain a graduate or advanced degree compared to about 26% of those whose families make $35,000 or less per year.

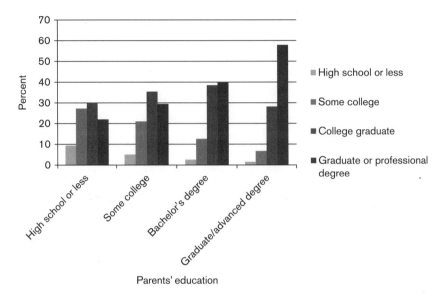

Parents' education

Figure 4-2. Educational Expectations of Students by Their Parents' Highest Educational Attainment, 2004.

SOURCE: National Center for Education Statistics, Institute of Education Science, US Department of Education, Xianglei Chen, Joanna Wu, and Shayna Tasoff, *Issue Tables*, "Post-Secondary Expectations and Plans for the High School Senior Class of 1003–4," NCES2010–170rev, http://nces.ed.gov/pubs2010/2010170rev.pdf.

Grade Point Average and Grade Retention

Researchers find differences in grades across students whose parents have different levels of education, which may both influence and be influenced by different expectations about education. Here I show differences in high school grades because it is in high school where grades become most easily quantified and compared as GPAs. At the elementary levels, grades may reflect some combination of cognitive and noncognitive skills (like being able to sit still and listen carefully), while in high schools, GPAs are thought to more reflect cognitive skills. The High School Transcript Study of 2005 shows that those whose parents have the least education, less than a high school degree, have GPAs about 0.3 lower than those whose parents have a college degree. This is shown in table 4–5.

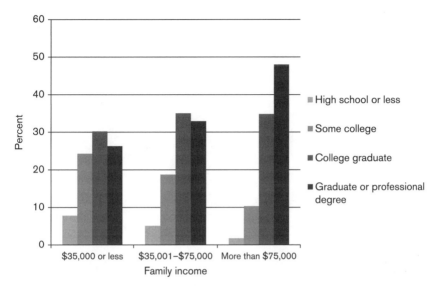

Figure 4-3. Educational Expectations of Students by Family Income, 2004.

SOURCE: National Center for Education Statistics, Institute of Education Science, US Department of Education, Xianglei Chen, Joanna Wu, and ShaynaTasoff, *Issue Tables,* "Post-Secondary Expectations and Plans for the High School Senior Class of 1003–4," NCES2010–170rev, http:// nces.ed.gov/pubs2010/2010170rev.pdf.

Table 4-5   Mean GPA of High School Graduates by Either
Parent's Highest Level of Education, 2005

Parent's Highest Education	*Mean Grade Point Average*
Less than high school	2.79
High school graduate	2.85
Some postsecondary	2.95
College graduate	3.12

SOURCE: The Nation's Report Card, *America's High School Graduates: Results from the 2005 High School Transcript Study,* www.nationsreport card.gov/hsts_2005/hs_stu_5d_3.aspx.

Table 4-6   Retention Rates by Grade and Parents' Education, 1994–1995 through 2009–2010

Grade	High School Dropout	High School Degree	Some College	College Graduate
1st	9.0%	7.4%	5.6%	4.3%
2nd	3.3%	2.4%	1.8%	1.5%
3rd	3.4%	2.3%	1.6%	1.0%
4th	2.6%	1.9%	1.4%	0.7%
5th	2.3%	1.5%	1.3%	0.8%
6th	3.0%	1.9%	1.5%	1.1%
7th	3.1%	2.7%	1.8%	1.2%
8th	2.5%	2.1%	1.9%	1.3%
9th	5.0%	3.8%	2.5%	1.1%
Total	3.8%	1.9%	2.2%	1.5%

SOURCE: Warren, Hoffman, and Andrew (2014).

And, in table 4–6, we can see differences in the rates that children are retained in their grades by parents' highest level of education. Retention rates can be based on cognitive performance, but also can reflect noncognitive skills, especially at younger ages. Retention rates are highest in first grade and then again in ninth grade, generally. From table 4–6, we see that 9% of children whose parents dropped out of high schools are retained in first grade compared to only 4.3% of the children of college graduates. In ninth grade, about 5% of those whose parents dropped out of high school are retained compared to only 1.1% of those whose parents have college degrees. The overall retention rates for those whose parents dropped out of high school is 3.8% across all grades compared to 1.5% for those whose parents have a college degree.

Test Scores

While grades often reflect noncognitive abilities that include behaviors, persistence, study habits, and others, some tests are designed to measure "proficiency" or "ability." The National Assessment of Education Progress

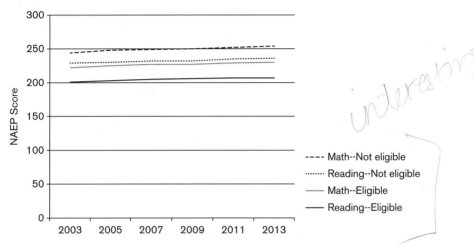

Figure 4-4. Average Fourth Grade Reading and Math NAEP Scores by Poverty Status, 2003–2013.

SOURCE: US Department of Education, Institute of Education Sciences, National Center for Education Statistics, National Assessment of Educational Progress (NAEP), 2003, 2005, 2007, 2009, 2011, and 2013 Mathematics and Reading Assessments.

(NAEP) tests were constructed to compare students' achievement nationally, as a way to assess how much variation there is in student content learning and how it varies across social groups. NAEP tests measure proficiency in subjects like reading, writing, math, and science in grades four, eight, and 12. Figure 4–4 shows changes in average fourth-grade NAEP test scores for individual students and compares those students who are eligible for free and reduced price lunch (labeled "eligible" in figure 4–4) with those who are not. Although scores have steadily improved in both reading and math from 2003 to 2014, the gap between poor and nonpoor students has stayed the same. Poor students score about 20 points in math and almost 30 points in reading lower than nonpoor students, pretty consistently over the years.

Different from proficiency tests, tests like the Student Aptitude Test (SAT) and, to a lesser extent, the ACT, which claims to measure material learned in high school to prepare for college, are designed to measure aptitude and the likelihood of doing well in college. These tests have been

Table 4-7   Mean SAT Scores by Family Income and Parents' Education

	Reading	Math	Writing
FAMILY INCOME			
$0–$20,000	436	459	429
$20,000–$40,000	467	481	455
$40,000–$60,000	489	500	474
$60,000–$80,000	504	512	487
$80,000–$100,000	516	526	501
$100,000–$120,000	527	539	513
$120,000–$140,000	531	542	518
$140,000–$160,000	539	552	527
$160,000–$200,000	544	558	534
More than $200,000	569	588	565
HIGHEST LEVEL OF PARENTAL EDUCATION			
No High School Diploma	421	447	418
High School Diploma	462	473	450
Associate's Degree	480	485	463
Bachelor's Degree	523	539	512
Graduate Degree	560	575	551

SOURCE: The College Board, *2014 College-Bound Seniors: Total Group Profile Report* (New York: College Board National Office).

used as measures of "ability," particularly the ability to perform well in college classes. There is much controversy about the extent to which they do, and the extent to which they were designed to maintain advantages for those who are already socioeconomically advantaged, however.[16] Table 4-7 above shows SAT scores by family income and the highest level of education of either parent in the household. It shows that the higher the family income, the higher the average SAT score. There is a more than 100-point difference in reading, math, and writing scores between those whose parents make less than $20,000 and those whose parents make more than $200,000. Students whose parents have graduate degrees score about 100 points higher on all three SAT tests than those whose parents have only high school diplomas.

Course-Taking

Differences in test scores likely affect students' beliefs about their academic ability (their academic "self-concept") and this influences the types of courses they and others believe they should take, particularly in high school. Klugman has argued that Advanced Placement (AP) courses are perceived as "marks of distinction" for students who are bound for college.[17] College admissions officers perceive that students who take these courses are ready for more challenging college-level material and so may be more inclined to be favorable to them during admission. The same may be said of dual-credit courses, which count for both high school and college credit, and for International Baccaluareate (IB) courses, which are based on European college-preparatory courses (0- and A-level streams).

Table 4–8 shows differences in the likelihood that students will take advanced courses by school poverty composition. The table shows that the greater the percentage of students who are eligible for free or reduced price lunch in a student's school, the less likely he or she is to take any dual-credit, AP, or IB courses. This is particularly stark for AP courses. The percentage drops from almost 45% of students who attend low-poverty schools earning some credits in AP courses to less than 30% who attend high-poverty schools. Not only is the likelihood of taking any of these courses greater in low-poverty schools, but the number of these courses taken by those who take at least one is also greater for those in low-poverty schools. The mean number of credits achieved in these courses among those who take them is higher for those in low-poverty than high-poverty schools. Students in low-poverty schools achieve almost two credits on average, while for those at high poverty schools it is closer to one. Students enroll in AP courses when they are motivated and advised to take them by knowledgable parents or guidance counselors, but these courses also have to be available for students to take. In his research in California, Joshua Klugman found a greater number and variety of AP courses in low-poverty schools, largely because parents demanded such courses be offered.[18]

Table 4–8   Percentage of High School Graduates Attaining Any Credit and Mean
Credits Attained in Dual-Credit, Advanced Placement (AP), or
International Baccalaureate (IB) Courses by Those Who Take These
Courses by School Poverty Composition, 2009

Percent Eligible for Free or Reduced Price Lunch	Dual-Credit	AP Courses	IB Courses	Mean Total Credits in Dual-Credit, AP, or IB Courses
0–25%	9.3%	44.9%	1.5%	1.75
26–50%	9.2%	31.3%	2.1%	1.17
Over 50%	9.1%	28.6%	2.8%	1.05

SOURCE: National Center for Education Statistics, *Digest of Education Statistics*, 2011, table 163.

Dropout Rates

Students with low grades and test scores, who are not taking challenging courses may be less committed to staying in school and may consequently drop out. Students may also face competing demands on their time—from taking care of families to working in jobs—that may influence the likelihood of dropping out. Problems in homes and neighborhoods that make going to school difficult and the inability to see how more education can lead to better opportunities may also lead students to skip more and more classes and days of school, which may eventually lead to them being considered a "dropout." Figure 4–5 shows status dropout rates by family income. Status dropouts refer to those aged 16 to 24 years old in the population who are not enrolled in school and have not attained their high school degree. These youths may not necessarily have made conscious decisions to discontinue schooling (and may have intentions to return), but for perhaps complicated reasons wind up not having high school degrees or being enrolled in school after age 16. Here family income is divided into quartiles that represent the lowest 25 percent of family incomes, the middle 25–49% and 50–74%, and those who earn more than 75% of families. The pattern shows that from the 1970s to 2012, dropout rates have declined for all groups, and they have declined most precipitously for low-income students. However, there is still a sizeable gap between those with the

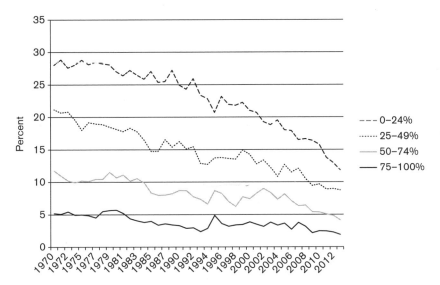

Figure 4–5. Percentage of 16–24 Year Olds Not Enrolled in Schools with No Degree by Income Quartile, 1970–2012.

SOURCE: US Department of Education, Institute for Education Statistics, National Center for Education Statistics, *Digest of Education Statistics*, 2013, table 219.76.

highest-earning parents and those with the lowest. In 2012, more than 10% of those in the lowest-income families had dropped out of high school compared to less than 2% of those in the highest-income families.

College Enrollment Rates

Those who drop out of school, who do not earn a high school diploma or a Graduate Equivalency Degree (GED), are typically not eligible to enroll in college. Figure 4–6 shows the college enrollment rates of those who completed high school or a GED within the past 12 months who had enrolled in a two-year or four-year college by October of the following year from 1975 to 2012. There are some encouraging findings. For everyone, including those in the bottom 20% of family income, college enrollment has increased. For those with the lowest income, it has increased from about 30% in 1975 to over 50% in 2012. It has also increased for those in the

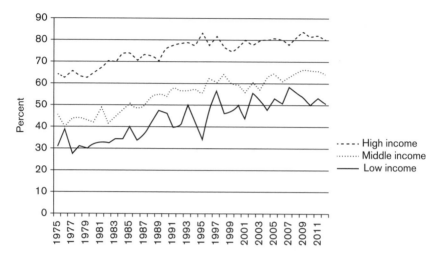

Figure 4-6. Percentage of Recent High School Completers Enrolled in 2-Year and 4-Year Colleges by Income Level, 1975 through 2012.

SOURCE: National Center for Education Statistics, *Digest of Education Statistics,* 2013, table 302.20.

highest income group. In 1975, about 65% of recent high school graduate enrolled in college, while 37 years later that increased to over 80%. Gaps between income groups remain persistent, though, such that there has been a difference of about 30 to 35 percentage points between those in the lowest and highest income groups over time. It is important to look at patterns of enrollment among recent high school graduates because the more time elapses after high school graduation, the less likely an individual is to eventually enroll in college.

CAN SCHOOLS CLOSE THESE GAPS? EXPLANATIONS FOR DIFFERENT ACHIEVEMENT BY SOCIOECONOMIC BACKGROUND

The above figures show some progress in the educational outcomes of rich and poor, and those whose parents have more or less education. NAEP scores have increased slightly for everyone, as have college enrollment rates. Dropout rates have declined over time. This means that on average, a low-income student whose parents may have high school degrees or less scores a bit higher on the NAEP, is less likely to drop out of high school, and is more likely to enroll in college than a similarly situated student 20 or even 10 years ago. The gaps between rich and poor and between those with the least- and most-educated parents remain quite persistent, however. While gaps by income quartile declined quite dramatically in high school dropout rates, these gaps persist in about the same magnitudes between the poor and nonpoor for NAEP test scores, and gaps by income group persist for college enrollment. What are some explanations for why children from lower socioeconomic strata get lower grades, do worse on achievement tests, drop out of school more, and enroll in college less? Do schools influence these differences, and if so, how? If the sources of differences are in multiple sites (family, peers, neighborhoods) and are influenced by other social structures like health care, the labor market, and the criminal justice system, can schools alone eliminate gaps?

Unequal achievement could have several different sources. The first is the individual. Some researchers contend that one large source of unequal achievement is the student's own innate abilities and talents. They see intelligence, often measured by the Stanford-Binet IQ test, as the source of achievement differences. Largely, intelligence is perceived to be a function of a student's genes. Students are smart because their parents are smart. This argument gets much more controversial when we talk about the average achievement of groups—it can lead to dangerous assumptions about the intellectual capabilities of particular groups of people. There may also be individual-level differences in children's health and nutrition that are related to their achievement, and these have been linked more convincingly to their socioeconomic backgrounds.

Another explanation for unequal achievement among individual students and among groups of students is that students come from home environments with different resources, values, and cultural traditions. Those students who come from homes in which parents read a lot, are involved with their schooling, are invested in children's education, and model achievement-oriented behavior are likely to have higher levels of achievement according to researchers. This is easy to see at the individual level, but harder to relate to groups. Do families with different socioeconomic backgrounds or class positions have different cultures and different values that promote or obstruct their success? Many researchers contend that they do—although this is difficult to measure and test.

Neighborhoods and peer environments are other contexts in which students find themselves. Neighborhoods can provide role models, community health services, access to grocery stores and nutritional food, and amenities that help children learn and keep them safe and occupied. Neighborhoods can provide social capital in the forms of supervision, information, and support. Peers can shape expectations of future education and careers, and can reinforce the importance of getting good grades, studying hard, and going to college, as well as provide information about courses, colleges, and other aspects of students' educational careers. While researchers note there are differences by individual families in their choices of neighborhoods, they also clearly link these choices to their socioeconomic backgrounds. For peer groups, students may make different friend choices that shape them, but how convincingly are these choices linked to socioeconomic background? How different are peer groups comprising working-class students compared to middle-class or rich ones?

And, finally, there are schools themselves. Do schools influence the gaps in academic outcomes between students, and if so, how? For decades now, researches from James Coleman in his famous *Coleman Report* to contemporary researchers like Sean Reardon have found that schools appear to do little to exacerbate inequality by socioeconomic background.[19] Students begin school with wide gaps in academic outcomes, and those outcomes either stay the same or become somewhat smaller throughout the school year or over the years of schooling.[20] Schools appear to have little influence on differences in academic outcomes and researchers puzzle over why this may be the case. In the next sections, I will spend a little more time discussing these sources of unequal achievement, particularly looking at why it is that schools may not solely be able to close the achievement gap.

Individual-Level Explanations: Intelligence or Ability, Health, and Nutrition

There are two issues to address when talking about differences in "intelligence" or "ability." The first is: To what extent are intelligence or ability differences inherited? Answering this question is important for people who want to discover ways to minimize inequalities in achievement. If intelligence differences are inherited and not shaped much by one's environment, then inequalities are very difficult to minimize. Short of requiring that a mother's and father's average IQ equals 100, there is little we can do to equalize the gene pool. So, this is one important question. The second question is: Can we and how do we really measure intelligence? Are Stanford-Binet IQ, or any other standardized tests, the best way to do this? Are there other ways?

Let's look at the first question. Is intelligence inherited? Many researchers say it is. I would say most of us probably realize some genetic influence on our natural abilities. The question is to what extent our genetic makeup influences our intelligence and achievement. There is some evidence that argues that environment matters very little in determining a person's intelligence.[21] Researchers have reached this conclusion through studies of identical twins placed in different environments. Identical twins who share the same sets of genes will score very similarly on IQ tests no matter what environment they are placed in. The IQs of children who are adopted are much more likely to resemble their biological parents' IQs than they are to resemble the scores of their adoptive parents.[22]

Many of these studies have been criticized for not being methodologically rigorous enough. Regarding twin studies, it is hard to really measure differences in environment—presumably some level of wealth and comfort is required for children to be adopted and adoption agencies make sure that children are raised in healthy environments, so the differences in the home environments of identical twin adoptees may not be so dramatic. Generally, there is little disagreement that there are innate differences between the capabilities of people, but there is disagreement over the extent to which these capabilities are also shaped by other forces—particularly home environments and schools.[23]

The presence of genetic differences in talent or capability seems plausible when we look at differences between individuals. Can this same argument be used to generalize to groups of people, however? Do people in different social classes have inherent genetic differences that can explain their differences in average achievement?

In order to have genetic differences explain differences in tested IQ among different social classes, we have to assume several things. First, we assume the United States is meritocratic such that those with the highest tested scores rise to upper social classes. Then we have to assume that spouses choose each other based on their tested scores. There are reasons to suspect that each of these may not be true—tested IQ differences may be due to a lot of other traits associated with being in an upper class, for example, the ability to afford different educational resources, the ability to provide an educationally stimulating home environment for children, and the ability to get children into specific schools of high quality.

Second, let's consider immigrants. White immigrants to the United States during World War I—Italians, Greeks, Spanish, Portuguese—scored as low on Stanford-Binet IQ tests as did blacks at that time. However, over time the average scores of these groups increased much more than those of native-born blacks. Over time, scores of these groups became indistinguishable from those who had lived in the United States for many generations. This suggests that social environment matters for IQ scores.[24]

The second issue to consider is whether or not we can really measure the concept of intelligence well and whether standardized testing is the best way to do so.[25] What is intelligence? How well do conventional IQ tests get at this concept? Many researchers have argued that the early home environment of a child is what is measured by IQ tests and not the child's innate intelligence. IQ tests are not administered at birth, but at ages five, seven, and so on. Children are affected by their environments by this time—and, these researchers argue, there is no way to accurately assess how much of a child's measured IQ is due to what the child has learned by age seven and how much is due to a child's capacity to learn.

One criticism of IQ tests is that they are culturally biased.[26] IQ tests may use words that children from poor or working-class families are unfamiliar with. Another criticism is that intelligence means different things in different contexts. What is intelligent in school is not necessarily what is intelligent on a farm. Intelligence may be culture- or context-specific. Intelligence differences that appear on standardized tests may not necessarily or only be reflections of innate differences but may indeed show what we already know about the United States: that it is highly stratified by socioeconomic background. Showing this on a test does little to show its root causes.

Other differences between children that are at the individual level that may be related to academic outcomes and socioeconomic backgrounds are differences in health and nutrition. Children in poverty are more likely to have vision problems than children who are not in poverty and this has been shown to affect their academic achievement.[27] Children from less-advantaged socioeconomic backgrounds may also have poorer hearing, which directly affects their ability to learn. Less socioeconomically advantaged children are also disproportionately more likely to suffer from conditions that lead them to be distracted in school or absent from school altogether, like dental problems, asthma, and other conditions. Poor children may be more likely to be exposed to lead and to have been exposed to smoking, alcohol, and the poor nutrition of mothers while in utero, all of which have been linked to worse health and higher rates of disability. Children from less-advantaged socioeconomic backgrounds may also suffer from nutrition problems: iron deficiency, undernutrition, or obesity, which may affect their concentration in schools and overall feelings of well-being. Although poor children have access to supplemental federal and state health insurance, poor children are still underinsured compared to those who are not in poverty.[28]

Family-Level Resources: Financial Capital

Families can influence children's educational outcomes in numerous ways, and there is even some evidence to suggest that this influence extends beyond one generation. The conditions that parents themselves experience as adolescents have been shown to affect their own children's educational attainment, even after accounting for their current income, particularly for parents who grew up in low-income families.[29] One common explanation for why less-advantaged students do not attain as much education as more privileged students is that they have fewer financial resources available to them. This has many effects at all ages. At the youngest ages it means that children may not get exposed to as much information—children who have computers are comfortable using them, children can get information from books if they own them. Researchers say that resources are important apart from the information they provide to students. Educational resources in a child's home also communicate the importance of education to a child. If children have a place designated for them to study—perhaps their own desk—they learn that it is important for them to do so. Wealthy parents can provide children with exposure to a variety of life experiences such as trips abroad or summer learning camps. They can take children to museums and cultural events. Well-to-do parents can buy expensive, "high-quality" day care. Children with financial resources may attend special after-school clubs or classes to improve their academic performance.[30]

With regard to dropping out of school, resources could affect a student's decision to leave. Students may feel the need to make money immediately to help out one's family or gain independence. And the same could apply for college. Colleges cost a lot of money. Not having money may affect a student's assessment that he or she is able to go to college.[31] Poor students may lower their expectation to go to college or may not be able to afford the tuition and time out of work. The opportunity cost, the cost of not earning money in the labor force, may be higher for lower- and working-class students in that they and their families immediately need the money from their earnings.

Family-Level Resources: Cultural Capital, Expectations, Values, and Parenting Styles

Resources also allow parents to transmit "cultural capital" to their children. Children are taught about certain forms of music, literature, and art, and, based on their knowledge of these cultural forms, they are differentially treated in school. For example, teachers may perceive a child who expresses interest in Mozart as intelligent. That child may then be tracked into higher-level classes in elementary school. According to Bourdieu, cultural symbols form a coded language that alerts hearers to the social class and, therefore, the presumed intellectual capability of the speaker.[32] Parents with more-advantaged socioeconomic backgrounds are likely to have knowledge about and access to these elite cultural forms. These parents may be able to afford to send children to after-school music lessons and buy children instruments so they may participate in orchestras. They may take children to art or other museums on weekends.

Another theory about the connection between parents' socioeconomic background and children's performance focuses on parents' expectations. Those parents who have themselves attended college expect that their children will also attend college. Children, influenced by their parents, set such expectations for themselves. Further, researchers contend that parents' expectations of children affect their educational outcomes independently of children's own expectations. Parents' expectations may influence their willingness to help children financially through school, as well as their desire to become actively involved in helping children plan their educational futures.

Researchers starting with Melvin Kohn have identified parenting styles that stress limit-setting, democratic decision-making within families, and parental involvement in children's academic lives. This "authoritative" parenting enables children's academic success and is associated with middle- and upper-class families. "Authoritarian" parenting, a parenting style of families in which decisions are made without children's participation and parents tend to be less involved in students' school careers, inhibits children's academic success. Authoritarian parents are more often those with lower socioeconomic status.[33]

Other researchers have found that parents with less-advantaged socioeconomic backgrounds tend to talk to and read to small children less than those with more advantages. Children then arrive in kindergarten or first grade with much different vocabularies.[34] This leads to a large gap in academic achievement by socioeconomic background even before children start school. Preschool attendance has been shown to decrease these gaps.[35]

Middle-class parents may also feel more comfortable interacting with children's teachers, in their schools, and may be more likely to advocate for them there.[36] While some find this positively influences children's outcomes,[37] others suggest that there are no positive effects to increased parental involvement on children's educational outcomes once other factors are considered.[38]

Family-Level Resources: Social Capital

A final theory is that children benefit from the social capital provided by relationships with parents with more advantages. Parents with advantaged social backgrounds are more likely to have attended college themselves than those with less-advantaged ones and thus are more able to give children advice about how to proceed through school. They may know more about the process of getting to college than parents who have not attended college themselves. Parents then transmit this information to children. In this way, parents are able to provide their children with reliable and personalized information about schools and colleges. Parents may also be more likely to access information from friends, coworkers, and others. Often, parents with more resources have larger social networks of "loose ties" that can provide them with varied information.[39]

Parents with more advantages are also more likely to interact with children's teachers and be more involved in their school education. We know from the sociologist James Coleman and his colleagues that the more parents interact with teachers and other parents, the more closure there is in a community.[40] Closure is when families know one another—parents know the parents of their children's friends. Closure is beneficial because children gain support, information, and supervision from tightly knit social networks. Children in communities with closure are less likely to get away with bad behaviors—they are more carefully monitored, and they may feel more responsibility to their community or network members.

Neighborhoods and Peers

Closure also exists in neighborhoods. Neighborhoods are yet another setting in which children find themselves for portions of their days. There are a number of ways we can imagine that neighborhoods influence children. Coleman talked about the supervision and support that neighbors in tightly knit communities provide to resident children.[41] Lareau wrote about the information that parents could gather about schools by bumping into teachers at neighborhood grocery stores or events. Parents in middle-class neighborhoods were more likely to meet teachers than those in working-class neighborhoods because teachers often live in middle-class neighborhoods themselves.[42] William Julius Wilson discussed the importance of having employed role models in neighborhoods so children learn the right norms regarding work and work habits.[43] We can also imagine that wealthier neighborhoods have better parks and opportunities for extracurricular and summer activities, and are closer to grocery stores that offer more nutritious and less expensive food than corner markets.[44] Students who live in less-advantaged neighborhoods may be exposed to violence and crime that could affect their ability to get to schools and concentrate when there. Research also suggests that the effects of living in disadvantaged neighborhoods persist over several generations. When both grandparents and parents live in high-poverty neighborhoods, children's cognitive ability scores are more than a half a standard deviation below children whose parents and grandparents have not lived in poverty.[45]

While some studies have found evidence that the type of neighborhood that children live in affects educational outcomes[46] and others have found an association between frequent residential mobility and negative school outcomes,[47] still others have shown that when poor children move to better neighborhoods there is little effect on their academic outcomes. In a housing mobility experiment called Moving to Opportunity (MTO), families were given vouchers to move to less-segregated, less-poor neighborhoods. Children in families who used their vouchers to make these moves did not experience significant academic gains in their new neighborhoods.[48] There may be several reasons for this. One is that the disruption of a move has a short-term negative consequence on children's academic outcomes.[49] Children lose friends and neighborhoods and have to rebuild them in a new place. These short-term disruptions may mask gains that show up much later. Another possibility is that much of the literature on neighborhood effects on children's academic outcomes overestimates the effect by not accounting for many of the other important differences between families who are living in high-poverty neighborhoods with high levels of mobility and those who are not.[50]

Children's neighborhoods also influence the types of peers they have (though neighborhood and school peers may be different groups). Children who perceive that parents, teachers, and peers do not expect them to achieve academically may create subcultures in which academic achievement is not valued. In a classic study in the sociology of education, Jay MacLeod describes how a group of low-income teenagers living in a housing development in Boston (whom he calls the "Hallway Hangers") develops an oppositional stance toward education because they do not see it as a viable path to upward social mobility.[51] In another classic, Paul Willis's *Learning to Labor*, he finds that working-class male students in Britain valorize blue-collar labor and purposely disrupt school relationships, creating a subculture that contributes to their academic failure.[52] More recently, Karolyn Tyson shows that students get ridiculed for high academic achievement more often in schools that have a larger proportion of students from less-advantaged socioeconomic backgrounds.[53]

Where Do Schools Fit In?

Research has shown that children come to schools differently equipped to participate—this could be due to individual differences that correlate with socioeconomic status (like health), to home environments that reflect different levels of resources, parental time and attention, stimulation, and varied values, traditions, expectations, and norms, or to neighborhoods and peers that differ between more- and less-socioeconomically-advantaged students.[54] Likely, it is due to some combination of these—though the exact combination is hard to determine. Students begin school with these differences that may lead to varying academic outcomes, and they go through with these same differences: after school and in summer they spend time in their neighborhoods, at home, and with peers. Early differences in academic preparation lead to cumulative disadvantages in later academic outcomes: early differences in preparation lead to more difficulty in achieving high grades and test scores, and these losses become harder and harder to make up as a student advances through school.[55] Others have described the concept "cumulative advantage," which suggests that early advantages make it easier to gain later on, that is, those with better preparation find it easier to gain resources and other advantages that promote learning and academic achievement over time.[56] Do schools exacerbate, ameliorate, or not affect these initial gaps in academic outcomes at all? Why is it so hard to determine if and how schools affect achievement gaps?

The two paradigms described in the previous chapter, functionalism and conflict theory, view the role of schools in reinforcing inequality differently. Functionalism attributes inequality in school achievement to extraschool factors. Children come to school better or worse prepared based on their family background. They make friends with either high or low achievers and this reinforces their differences in achievement. Students with fewer advantages to begin with may not have good role models outside of schools. However, according to functionalists, schools themselves (ideally) do not contribute to these inequalities. Students are treated the same ways regardless of their social background. The types of curricula to which students are exposed and the grouping of students are seen as neutral, or, in the best-case scenario, initial inequalities are minimized. Students are taught the same material regardless of their backgrounds, which should give their "innate" ability a chance to express itself.

The conflict perspective contends that differences between and within schools reinforce and perhaps even magnify inequalities across students. Further, they argue that schools treat students differently as a result of a child's ascribed characteristics. The ways a child behaves and a teacher's preconceived notions of the child affect expectations of that student—not simply her or his pure ability. One reason that students can have different educational experiences is that they attend schools that are quite different. The tables at the beginning of this chapter show that those students attending schools with higher concentrations of poverty tend to have less-qualified teachers with higher teacher turnover, for example. The second way that schools can affect students differently is by treating students differently according to their social background when students attend the same school. Ability-grouping and differentiated course-taking have been found to relate to students' social background and to provide very different learning environments based on the groups to which students are assigned. Those within the conflict paradigm then provide reasons to believe that schools at best maintain and, at worst, exacerbate gaps in outcomes by socioeconomic inequality.

Although policy-makers and the public at large also seem to believe that schools are a source of inequality in academic outcomes (or, at least, if they did a better job they could shrink gaps between children), much of the sociological research on school effects finds very modest effects of schools on gaps in academic outcomes by socioeconomic background. Decades ago, the sociological research community was surprised by the results of the famous *Coleman Report* that suggested that family background differences accounted for most of the differences in outcomes for students, with very little attributable to schools (except for black students in segregated schools for whom integrated schools would improve outcomes).[57] Writing in the 1970s, Christopher Jencks and colleagues also found that school quality, defined as differences in resources like teacher experience, class size, and the composition of the school, did little to explain gaps in academic outcomes by socioeconomic background.[58] These findings were confirmed in the 1990s.[59] Even within the past five years, scholars like Sean Reardon have shown that the gaps in academic outcomes by socioeconomic background remain remarkably similar throughout students' school years. They neither grow nor shrink appreciably.[60]

For many, this does not seem intuitive. Students spend so much of their time in schools, and much of their learning is done in schools. And indeed researchers do find some aspects of differences between schools that matter for children's outcomes. For example, qualitative evidence shows that wealthier schools have more guidance counselors that can provide advice and information to students about college choice, application, and financial aid.[61] While there is debate about how much teacher certification matters, teachers with masters' degrees and schools with less teacher turnover are associated with better student outcomes and are more likely to be found at schools with more-advantaged student bodies.[62] However, though it may seem to some that more resources (like new textbooks, science equipment, computers, and so on) should improve student outcomes, there is debate about the extent to which this is actually true.[63]

Social researchers have also looked at the extent to which students are treated differently based on their socioeconomic status within the same schools. Decades ago, researchers found that children were tracked into lower- and higher-ability groups differentially according to socioeconomic background.[64] They argued that this led to different learning environments and "self-fulfilling prophecies." A self-fulfilling prophecy means that if a student is labeled "low ability," that student will, in time, become "low ability" whether or not she or he started out that way. To give an example, a girl mistakenly gets put in the low-ability group (her test scores are the same as those in the high group). Because she is in the low-ability group, she does not learn as much as quickly as those in the high-ability group and perhaps devotes less attention to her studies, believing she is "low-ability." After five years in elementary school, she has not learned as much as those in the high-ability group, and now is considered low-ability on tests, compared to her high-ability peers. Survey research from a study called High School and Beyond found that students who were assigned to higher tracks experienced greater gains in math achievement than those in lower tracks in schools with little mobility across tracks.[65]

In past decades, in high schools particularly, ability-grouping had generally been characterized by tracking. Some students were placed in college preparatory or advanced tracks, some were placed in basic tracks, some were placed in vocational tracks. Because of these negative effects of tracking, though, "tracking" was largely replaced with much more fluid course choices.[66] Students are now mostly able to choose from different levels of ability: college preparatory, honors, Advanced Placement, or other types, but they can do so differently by subject. With more ability to freely choose courses, some students may choose to take honors-level English and college preparatory math, while others may decide to take Advanced Placement calculus and college preparatory biology. One rationale for allowing more flexibility is that students are not labeled according to a single track or grouping, but instead can show strengths in some areas, and perhaps not others.

Allowing students more flexibility in course choices does not necessarily eliminate socioeconomic differences across students, however. First, math course placement is very important for student outcomes—more important than taking advanced courses in other subjects, and students from more-advantaged socioeconomic backgrounds are more likely to take advanced math courses. Second, students with more socioeconomic advantages do enroll in more honors or Advanced Placement courses than students with fewer resources.[67] Not only do students with resources enroll in Advanced Placement courses at higher rates than those with fewer when they are in the same schools; those schools that serve a wealthier student body offer more Advanced Placement courses to begin with. One reason for the discrepancy between middle-class and poorer students is that middle- and upper-middle class parents know about these courses and advocate for their children to enroll in them and for schools to offer more of them. This creates an "information gap" between wealthier and less-wealthy students that contributes to stratification by socioeconomic status.[68]

While there are arguments that schools provide mechanisms for more-advantaged students to maintain these advantages, through schools with more highly-qualified teachers, more teacher stability, and more guidance counselors, and through opportunities for taking Advanced Placement and International Baccalaureate courses, there is also compelling research showing that schools shrink gaps between students by socioeconomic status during the school year. This research finds that gaps between students by socioeconomic background grow smaller during the school year, but increase again over the summer. The implication is that students' family background and other characteristics influence students less while they are in school and so drive less inequality in learning.[69]

All of these findings seem to conflict: some say schools matter for inequality, others say they don't. Why is there so little agreement? One answer may be in how we measure socioeconomic status, differences between schools, and gaps in academic outcomes. Is socioeconomic status best measured gradationally or continuously or are there distinct differences between groups? For example, is there a difference between those marked as "poor" by federal definitions (or by taking advantage of free or reduced price lunch) and those who are not? Or do students receive roughly similar gains to each addition to their parents' income or education? Are there large differences between schools that have high-poverty populations and other schools, or between those with very advantaged populations and all other schools (as research now seems to suggest)? Or does each increasing concentration of poor or wealthy students influence student outcomes in roughly the same ways?

"Learning" and gaps in learning have been measured in a variety of ways as well. One could look at a measure of test scores at a single point in time, as NAEP scores are often presented. Or one could look at learning rates, as much of the research on the summer learning gap does. Rates are often measured at the beginning and end of a particular period or of several periods, so they may explore how students compare at the beginning of a period and how they compare at the end. Those who study summer learning argue that the length of the period matters: measuring learning only during the school year gets at school effects better than when a year includes both the academic year and summer, when students are not in school. Some have argued that researchers should look at "impact," the difference between the learning rates of groups during the school year and during the summer, to see how much schools are influencing gaps that are due to family background and other nonschool factors.[70]

Much of the debate about how learning and learning gaps are measured stems from researchers' desire to separate the effects of family background from the effects of schools. How easy is it to do this? How do we separate out students' experiences outside of schools (that are related to socioeconomic background) from those that occur in schools (and are related to socioeconomic background)? Often decisions about where students go to school and what courses they take in those schools are strongly related to socioeconomic background, in ways that make them hard to separate. It may also be that the specific mechanisms that are used to distinguish students (whether grade retention, tracks, or taking particular courses) matter little. As those in the conflict paradigm might theorize, families with advantages will find ways of differentiating themselves, regardless of the school's structure—perhaps by segregating themselves across schools or in "schools within schools," in "gifted" programs, or in other specialized programs, or by taking different courses that are marked as "special" like AP or IB. Though the forms of differentiation may change, families with advantages will maintain their positions through them.

Finally, it could be that schools simply do not have enough influence to erase gaps whose roots are in other contexts: individual, family, neighborhood, or peer (or others). Those who study summer learning gaps argue that schools cannot "catch up" after gaps have grown during the summer.[71] Maybe with longer school days or years, schools could increase their influence and reduce such gaps, which is consistent with ideas functionalists might have about schools and socioeconomic inequality. Despite the persistent influence of family background, though, reformers often charge schools with reducing these gaps, without necessarily providing ways to minimize inequalities in other aspects of children's lives related to family background that affect school achievement (health, housing, extracurricular and summer activities, and others).

The tables and figures in this chapter show that experiences in schools, what may be considered akin to "learning opportunities," and school outcomes differ by whether students come from more- or less-socioeconomically advantaged families. Even though overall test scores and college enrollment have increased for everyone and dropout rates have decreased, regardless of family socioeconomic status, gaps in these indicators between students remain fairly constant across time. Explanations for these differences emphasize different factors—individual-level ones like health or inherent ability, or family resources like financial, cultural, or social capital, or different neighborhood and peer environments, which provide different opportunities for and challenges to achievement. In the end, there is mixed evidence about how schools influence gaps in academic outcomes, with some compelling studies that suggest that, overall, school minimize the gaps, but these gaps persist because schools cannot make up for differences in socioeconomic background that occur in non-schooling hours. In the next chapter, I provide similar tables and figures that show differences across race and ethnicity and English-language ability. Here, I show the extent to which students of different races and ethnicities are in different schooling environments. Then, I explore differences in academic outcomes by race and ethnicity and explanations for those outcomes. Finally, I wonder about the role of schools in these outcomes. Research suggests that while schools may diminish inequality by socioeconomic background, they actually may increase inequalities by race.[72]

5 Inequality by Race and Ethnicity, Immigrant Status, and Language Ability

In the previous chapter, I described how socioeconomic background was related to educational experiences and outcomes. In this chapter, I look at the same aspects of inequality, but shift to racial and ethnic inequality in America's schools. Should schools provide equal resources to children of all races and ethnicities? Should they ensure equal outcomes by race and ethnicity? And if we agree they should, can they? What are some explanations for racial and ethnic inequality in schools, and what role do schools play in maintaining, shrinking, or increasing gaps between groups? Again, I am going to focus on two aspects of schooling. The first is how educational experiences and learning opportunities differ between schools based on their racial compositions. The second is how educational outcomes may differ by race and ethnicity.

First, we might ask: What is "race"? Sociologists typically conceive of race as a socially constructed designation for people, a categorization. Often it is based on one's appearance or heritage. Meanings, images, and practices get ascribed to racial categories. Beliefs about how people should act based on their racial category (or gender or sexual orientation as well) are called "stereotypes." Racial categories and their meanings are not fixed, but change over time and by place. Racism occurs when stereotypical ideas or preconceptions about a group are used in such a way as to keep a group from attaining resources or power. In this sense, segregation of schools was a racist practice.

Racial classifications have varied throughout US history. In this chapter, I use the crude contemporary racial categorizations Asian American, black, Hispanic (any race), Native American, and white, non-Hispanic, when possible, with greater ethnic detail in some cases. These categories mask much variation. For example, the category Asian Americans sometimes includes Hawaiian and Pacific Islanders, a group much different in history and contemporary profile from Chinese, Koreans, or Asian Indians. The categorization "Asian American" refers to those from many different countries, with varied histories and cultures—Cambodia, China, India, Japan, Korea, Laos, Pakistan, the Philippines, Thailand, Vietnam, and others. Black refers to blacks with many generations in the United States (African Americans), as well as Haitian, Dominican, Caribbean, and African blacks. Hispanics include those from Mexico, Central America, South America, and Spain, some of whom have recently immigrated and some of whom have been in the United States for many generations. Native Americans or American Indians include indigenous groups from all regions of the United States, including Alaska.

For most of this chapter, these racial classifications refer to children with only one racial identification, but for a growing number of children, one racial category does not adequately capture their racial identity. Children who have parents of different race and ethnic groups are a growing population.[1] I briefly describe the research done thus far on their educational experiences.

A SHORT HISTORY OF EDUCATION AND RACE AND ETHNICITY

The history of race relations in education in this country is largely the history of how the United States dealt with the education of black students. How other groups were treated varied by geography and time of immigration. The treatment of blacks in this country was far more universal and systematized. The historical time line of the education of blacks in the

United States can be roughly divided into four parts. The first is from the first settling of the country—in the 1600s and 1700s—to 1865. This can be characterized generally as "no education." Education for slaves was considered dangerous for slave owners. Educated slaves could converse with one another through letter writing over great distances—possibly increasing the odds of an uprising. Learning to read would introduce slaves to new ideas—about liberty and freedom—ideas that would threaten plantation owners' control over them. Further, simply being in school meant time away from work. Slave owners wanted slaves working for them, not reading and writing. So, during slavery, education was considered dangerous and too time-consuming for slaves. There are exceptions to this—some masters were "enlightened" and allowed (or even encouraged) slaves to read and write. Many free blacks were able to get some kinds of education—though mostly through informal means like apprenticeships and tutors. Slaves taught one another to read and write secretly in the few hours they had in their days.[2]

The next block of time can be characterized as "segregation." Slaves were freed during the Civil War. The brief period in which blacks enjoyed more political and social freedoms after the war was called reconstruction. By the late 1800s, though, Jim Crow laws created new limitations on the freedom of blacks, including restrictions on voting and segregation in schools and other public areas. In 1896, segregation was deemed constitutional according to the court case *Plessy vs. Ferguson*. Plessy, one-eighth African American, had refused to ride in the "colored" section of a train. The Supreme Court found that laws that mandated separate spaces for black and white Americans were not unconstitutional. Segregated facilities were deemed legal as long as the separate facilities had equal resources. This case justified the logic of "separate but equal" facilities. This segregation, largely in the South, that was enforced through Jim Crow laws is called de jure segregation—segregation according to the law. In the North, though, there were fewer explicit laws mandating segregation. In the North, school segregation was largely due to the geographic separation of races. Because blacks tended to live in one part of a city and whites in another, some schools would be primarily black and others primarily white. This is called de facto segregation.

Blacks weren't the only minority in segregated schools at this time. In California, schools were created for the children of Filipino, Japanese, and

Chinese immigrants who came to work in agriculture and mining. Asian students were designated "Mongolian" and separate schools for Mongolians were established in 1902.[3] A group of Chinese immigrants to Mississippi were considered black and sent to black segregated schools.[4] Whites didn't know where to put them in their racial hierarchy, so they decided "not white" must be "black." Mexican and other Hispanic students were also placed in segregated schools in California and Texas.

From 1954 on, there is "desegregation." Desegregation began in earnest with the landmark court case *Brown vs. the Board of Education of Topeka, Kansas* (1954). The decision in this court case overturned the *Plessy vs. Ferguson* decision. This historic decision made de jure segregation, or segregation that is based on law, unconstitutional based on the argument that separate schools could not provide equal resources to their students. The ruling was based on the fourteenth amendment to the Constitution, which states "no state shall make any law which shall deprive a person of life, liberty, or property without due process nor deny to anyone with in its jurisdiction equal protection under the law." Title VI of the 1964 Civil Rights Act gave the federal government the means to withhold federal funding from schools that were segregated. Title VI states that no person because of race, color, or national origin can be excluded from or denied the benefits of any program receiving federal assistance. Schools practicing de jure segregation were cut off from government Title I funding (intended to increase resources for schools with many students in poverty), and schools that did not achieve "racial balance" were threatened with a loss of federal funding. School desegregation, especially in the South, sped up after the passage of this act.[5]

Segregation was considered unlawful for Hispanic Americans for a different reason. Supreme Court judges argued in *Mendez vs. the Westminster School District* (1946) that the special educational needs of Hispanic children mandated that they attend integrated schools. It was argued that in segregated schools children were speaking Spanish too much and this impeded their ability to learn English quickly.[6] Native Americans also attended segregated schools. From 1875 to 1928, children were removed from their families and taken to boarding schools where they would be taught to assimilate into "white" culture. This attempt was unsuccessful for many attendees, though, and some of these same schools have become places to learn and celebrate Native American heritage.[7]

Numerous policies were attempted to integrate schools, including merging urban and suburban districts, allowing interdistrict transfers of black students to primarily white schools and white students to primarily black schools, and student reassignment and busing. During this time, many magnet schools were established in order to retain and attract white students in urban, segregated school districts.[8] A magnet school is a publicly funded school that attracts students based on the special characteristics of that school. Some may be for the performing arts, and some may specialize in leadership training, while others may specialize in rigorous math and science programs. Students have to apply to these schools. Generally, these schools achieve a mix of racial groups, and often many resources go to the "best and brightest" that attend these schools.

Reassignment, or "forced" desegregation, was attempted in many places through busing students from primarily black schools to predominantly white schools within the same district. Perhaps the conflicts that erupted over busing in Boston are the most famous example of tension over the issue. Black students often had to ride for an hour (or sometimes more) on a bus to get to their desegregated school. Many students found the experience alienating—apart from being difficult to get to, students felt they weren't wanted by the other students in the school. Minority students felt isolated and misunderstood in mostly white schools. Further, as more minority students were bused to predominantly white schools, more and more white parents fled to schools in the suburbs or took their children out of public schools and sent them to private schools.[9]

All of these policies intended to desegregate schools were met with opposition, and in 1974, the Supreme Court decided in *Milliken v. Bradley* that schools could not be forced to integrate if there was no intent to keep them segregated. While racial segregation in schools declined during the 1970s and 1980s, more cases like *Milliken* were brought to the Supreme Court in the 1990s. During the 1990s, it was clear that no longer was the condition of segregation unconstitutional, merely the intent. De jure segregation was relatively easy to combat with this criterion. If there is a law which states that students should be segregated, it is easy to show that segregation is intentional. De facto segregation, though, was much harder to combat. If students are just going to school in the neighborhoods in which they live, how do you know separation by race is intentional? After these court decisions, desegregation became harder to enforce.[10]

Even some of the few successful efforts to desegregate like intradistrict transfer programs and the aggregation of urban and suburban districts have largely been underutilized or dismantled. One landmark Supreme Court decision in 1971, *Swann v. Charlotte-Mecklenburg Board of Education,* held that students from the city could be bused to schools in the suburbs and vice versa. This decreased segregation in the schools in Charlotte-Mecklenburg. In 2002, though, the Supreme Court reversed this decision and, since then, segregation in Charlotte-Mecklenburg schools has increased.[11]

De facto segregation, the segregation of students because they live in different neighborhoods, became much more entrenched as white students fled urban neighborhoods, perhaps in part to avoid attending desegregated schools. Leaders of suburban counties and townships limited the construction of certain types of residences, particularly multifamily dwellings, which restricted the supply of affordable housing for lower-income and minority families. Policies such as these maintain segregation through de facto means—through what are perceived to be families' housing "choices."[12]

The final end of this timeline is called "second-generation segregation." School segregation has been increasing since the 1980s, although there may be some evidence that is leveling off.[13] Second-generation segregation also refers to racial segregation that is due to practices within schools. Ability-grouping and differential course-taking also separate students within schools by race. This occurs when white and Asian students are disproportionately found in honors or AP classes, and blacks and Hispanics are found in regular or vocational tracks or even in special education classes. Jonathan Kozol noticed that a majority of the special education students in a predominantly white school in the Bronx were black, and he wondered how children of color might be affected by this separation from other students.[14]

It is hard to determine whether segregation both across schools and within them is intentional. Segregation that is intentional is illegal, according to the Supreme Court, but segregation that happens for other reasons (students live in different places, students test into programs differently) is not. In 1990, in Selma, Alabama, parents protested the differential tracking of racial groups in schools. They argued that it was intentional. When a black superintendent, Norward Roussell, attempted to increase the numbers of minority students in a college preparatory track in the school, he was immediately fired.[15]

Decades ago, Ray Rist also explored second-generation segregation or unequal treatment within schools. He noted the propensity for black students to receive harsher punishments than whites who committed the same offenses, even among those with similar histories of offenses.[16] This has been noted more recently by Ann Arnette Ferguson and many others who observed that black boys, in particular, are punished more frequently than other students.[17] Students may also segregate themselves within schools—hanging out with same race peer groups.[18]

Many researchers have argued that there are negative consequences of racial segregation in schools. Proponents of affirmative action in university admissions argue that students should be exposed to diverse groups of people.[19] You learn from people with different ideas—black, white, Hispanic, and Asian. Learning to value diversity and being able to interact with those who are racially or culturally different are skills that all students will need in an increasingly diverse workforce and as globalization brings people from different places into contact more frequently.[20]

However, for minority students, there may be more negative consequences of segregation in schools. There is evidence that teachers have lower expectations of black and Hispanic students than they do of white and Asian students, and this may affect students' expectations of themselves.[21] Further, for minority students, segregation can lead to less "cultural capital," which is valuable for the types of careers that have historically been occupied by whites, and to less social capital, which may aid in getting such careers. Whites may have stronger social networks connected to colleges and jobs, and they may also have accurate and reliable information about jobs and colleges. Contact with whites connected to the mainstream may aid minority groups' access to information.[22]

Finally, there are resource differences. Segregated schools of minorities tend to be located in poorer neighborhoods. Schools have less money to buy equipment, run arts and music programs, repair buildings, and provide new materials and other amenities. Students in these schools may not have the same opportunities to learn as whites have.[23]

Even though there are many negative consequences of segregation overall, in some cases segregation may be beneficial. Blacks around the country enroll in exclusively black or minority charter schools. Black students attend Historically Black Colleges or Universities (HBCUs). Some students in these schools report feeling more comfortable in and in control of their environments. These are schools in which white children cannot dominate discussions. Other students want to preserve cultural traditions. For example, Native Americans fought for the right to school children in Navajo culture during the 1960s. This resulted in the founding of the Rough Rock Demonstration School in 1966. In 1972, the Indian Education Act required that federal money be used to develop programs to teach and preserve Native American traditions and the Office of Indian Education was created. In 1975, tribes were given the right to run their own schools on tribal land by the Indian Self-Determination and Education Assistance Act.[24]

This history of segregation has affected the typical school experiences and learning opportunities of students of different races and ethnicities in the United States. The following tables show how segregated schools are currently and how that affects exposure to students of other races. Throughout the rest of the chapter, I show differences in school poverty composition and teacher experience across the schools that children of different races and ethnicities attend.

SCHOOL EXPERIENCES

Segregation and Exposure

When children begin school, they enter very different environments according to their race or ethnicity. Table 5-1 shows the segregation of minority, public, primary school students from white students in the most- and least-segregated metropolitan areas in the United States for 2008–2009. Although segregation in schools had declined in the 1970s and 1980s, it increased again dramatically in the 1990s. Since about 1998, though, similar to racial residential segregation, there is some evidence that school racial segregation has declined.[25] Despite this recent decline, it is still quite apparent in many schools across the nation. As in the

Table 5-1   Dissimilarity Scores for the Metropolitan Areas with the Highest and
Lowest Segregation of Minority Group Students from White Students in
Public Schools, 2008–2009

Highest Dissimilarity Indices

BLACK-WHITE		HISPANIC-WHITE		ASIAN-WHITE	
Chicago, IL	82.3	Los Angeles, CA	73.4	Baton Rouge, LA	63.7
Milwaukee, WI	81.2	Springfield, MA	73.0	New York, NY	58.0
New York, NY	80.7	New York, NY	71.2	Greensboro, NC	56.4
Detroit, MI	80.2	Boston, MA	70.2	Detroit, MI	55.4
Cleveland, OH	80.1	Hartford, CT	69.7	New Orleans, LA	54.3
Youngstown, OH	77.4	Cleveland, OH	69.0	San Francisco, CA	54.2
Syracuse, NY	77.2	Chicago, IL	68.6	Buffalo, NY	53.9
Cincinnati, OH	76.9	Milwaukee, WI	68.2	Lansing, MI	53.9
Springfield, MA	75.1	Providence, RI	67.6	Birmingham, AL	53.5
Indianapolis, IN	74.3	Allentown, PA	66.9	Los Angeles, CA	53.5

Lowest Dissimilarity Indices

BLACK-WHITE		HISPANIC-WHITE		ASIAN-WHITE	
Lakeland, FL	25.2	Honolulu, HI	24.2	Palm Beach, FL	24.9
El Paso, TX	27.9	Palm Bay, FL	30.8	Sarasota, FL	25.0
Honolulu, HI	31.6	Raleigh, NC	32.7	Colorado Springs, CO	25.1
Boise, ID	33.4	Virginia Beach, VA	34.1	New Haven, CT	27.0
Albuquerque, NM	34.6	Lakeland, FL	34.3	Las Vegas, NV	27.7
Modesto, CA	35.5	Augusta, GA	36.1	Tucson, AZ	27.8
Raleigh, NC	35.7	Jacksonville, FL	36.2	Oxnard, CA	28.0
Greenville, SC	38.1	Colorado Springs, CO	37.9	El Paso, TX	28.5
Las Vegas, NV	39.1	Akron, OH	38.5	Charleston, SC	28.6
Santa Rosa, CA	39.3	Toledo, OH	38.6	Albuquerque, NM	28.9

SOURCE: Nancy McArdle, Theresa Osypuk, and Dolores Acevedo-García, *Segregation and Exposure to High-Poverty Schools in Large Metropolitan Areas: 2008–09*, Diversitydata.org special report, Analysis of National Center for Education Statistics, Common Core of Data, 2008–09, published in 2010, table 3, http://diversitydata.org/Publications/school_segregation_report.pdf.

Table 5-2   Percentage of Students in Schools with 75% or More Minorities and
75% or More Whites by Race and Ethnicity, 2008

	75% or More Minority	*75% or More White*
White	3.7%	63.1%
Black	53.1%	8.4%
Hispanic	58.7%	7.6%
Asian/Pacific Islander	34.3%	18.4%
American Indian/Alaska Native	29.7%	23.3%

SOURCE: National Center for Education Statistics, *Status and Trends in the Education of Racial and Ethnic Minorities*, 2010, table 7.4, http://nces.ed.gov/pubs2010/2010015/tables.asp.

previous chapter, segregation is measured here with dissimilarity scores. Dissimilarity values over 60 are considered high; those between 30 and 60 are considered moderate, and those below 30 are considered low. A dissimilarity value of 100 would indicate complete segregation. From the table below, we see that many of the nation's large metropolitan areas have dissimilarity scores for blacks and whites and for Hispanics and whites over 60. For many cities, scores are over 70 and some, for blacks and whites particularly, are in the 80s. That means that over 80% of white or black students would have to change schools for there to be the same racial representation in each school as there is in the metropolitan area as a whole. For Asians and whites, segregation is less stark, with most of the highest dissimilarity scores under 60. The least segregated metropolitan areas show dissimilarity scores between 20 and 30. These cities are moderately sized, often with proportionately small populations of particular minority groups.

Table 5-2 shows the percentage of students of different races and ethnicities who attend predominantly white and predominantly minority schools, which may be another way to think about segregation. Fewer than 4% of whites attend schools with high concentrations of minorities (75% or more), while a majority attend schools with high concentrations of whites (again 75% or more). A majority of black students attend schools that predominantly comprise minorities, and less than 10% attend schools

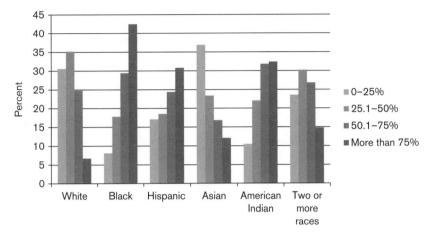

Figure 5-1. Percent of Students by Race and School Percentage Eligible for Free and Reduced Price Lunch by Quartiles, 2011–2012.

SOURCE: National Center for Education Statistics, *Digest of Educational Statistics,* 2013, table 216.60, https://nces.ed.gov/programs/digest/d13/tables/dt13_216.60.asp.

with mostly whites. Hispanics are the most likely to attend predominantly minority schools and the least likely to attend predominantly white schools, while Asian Americans and American Indians are less likely to attend predominantly minority schools, and more likely to attend predominantly white ones.

School Poverty

Black and Hispanic students are much more likely to be in high-poverty schools compared to whites. This is shown in figure 5-1. Only 6.7% of white students, both elementary and secondary, attend schools with over 75% of the student body eligible for free or reduced price lunch. This is compared to 42.5% of blacks, 30.8% of Hispanics, and 32.4% of American Indians. Asian Americans (not including Pacific Islanders) and multiracial students fare a little better with only 12.1% and 14.8%, respectively, attending the highest-poverty schools. White students and Asian Americans are the most likely to be attending low-poverty schools (with less than 25% eligible for free or reduced price lunch) at 30.6% and

Table 5-3   Average Teacher Experience and Percentage with Fewer Than Three Years
of Teaching Experience by School Racial Composition, 2007–2008

	Average Years of Teacher Experience	Percent of Teachers with Fewer Than 3 Years of Teaching Experience
White Enrollment of 50% or More	14.1	10.0%
Black Enrollment of 50% or More	13.1	12.9%
Hispanic Enrollment of 50% or More	12.4	15.4%
Asian Enrollment of 50% or More	12.5	15.7%
American Indian Enrollment of 50% or More	13.1	13.8%

SOURCE: National Center for Education Statistics, *Status and Trends in the Education of Racial and Ethnic Minorities*, 2010, table 9.2, http://nces.ed.gov/pubs2010/2010015/tables.asp.

36.9%, followed by multiracial students (23.6%), Hispanic (17.1%), American Indian (10.5%), and black students (8.1%). As mentioned in chapter 4, school poverty is closely related to resources and teacher qualifications. Lower-poverty schools may have fewer resources, may have fewer sources of reliable and personalized information about higher education, and may have peer cultures that are less likely to promote college-going.

Teacher Experience

Teachers at schools that serve large minority populations have less experience generally, and are less likely to be retained. Table 5–3 shows that schools with white enrollments over 50% have teachers with over 14 years of experience on average, with about 10% who have fewer than three years of teaching experience. Teachers at schools with majority black or American Indian enrollment have about one year less teaching experience on average, and those with majority Hispanic or Asian American enrollment have almost one and a half fewer years of experience. A higher proportion of less-experienced teachers are also found at these schools, with almost 13% and over of the teachers having less than three years teaching experience.

Table 5-4   Average Number of Students per Teacher by Percentage of Students Who Are a Racial or Ethnic Minority

School Racial Composition	15 or Fewer	16-20	20-25	26 or Greater
0–25% Minority	70.5%	21.9%	5.1%	2.6%
26–50% Minority	65.1%	25.6%	5.6%	3.7%
51–75% Minority	57.2%	29.8%	10.2%	2.9%
Over 75% Minority	59.3%	24.3%	11.2%	5.1%

SOURCE: Author's calculations using National Center for Education Statistics Schools and Staffing Survey 2011–2012. Computation by NCES PowerStats Version 1.0.

Class Sizes

Class sizes also appear to vary by school racial composition, with greater numbers of students per teacher as the minority concentration of a school grows. Table 5–4 shows that while most schools have 15 students or fewer per teacher on average, classes with 20 to 25 students per teacher and with 26 or more students per teacher are more likely to be found in schools with more minorities. For example, 11.2% and 5.1% of schools with over 75% minorities have between 20 or 25 or 26 or greater students per teacher, respectively. For those schools with minority concentrations at 25% or below, only 5.1% have 20 to 25 students per teacher and 2.6% have 26 or greater students per teacher. It is worth noting, again, though that research has not definitely demonstrated that class size matters a lot for student achievement.[26]

STUDENT OUTCOMES

Similar to the last chapter, I separate out student experiences in schools (their learning opportunities) from their outcomes. And, as in the last chapter, this ordering is not meant to imply that different learning experiences necessarily result in different educational outcomes by race and ethnicity. After presenting differences in educational outcomes, I will discuss theories about why they exist and ideas about how schools are implicated in either perpetuating or ameliorating gaps between races and ethnicities.

Educational Expectations

As in the previous chapter, although educational expectations may not necessarily be perceived as outcomes, they are frequently talked about as "causes" of outcomes or at least as factors that shape educational outcomes in important ways, so I want to present some figures describing them by race and ethnicity. Unlike socioeconomic background in the previous chapter, this figure shows that students' expectations about future education in high school by race are quite similar, especially at younger ages. Figure 5–2 shows that the years of education that black students expect are similar to the years expected by whites, especially at younger ages. Black students expect about 15.6 years of education in eighth grade, as do whites. That is a little less than a completed bachelor's degree (which is about 16 years of education), on average. Asian Americans' educational expectations are the highest, with 16.2 years expected, or more than a bachelor's degree on average. Hispanics' expectations are lower at about 15.2 years.

Researchers have presumed that the educational expectations of minorities in the United States should be lower than those of whites, given the different educational experiences of minority students (particularly those that attend predominantly minority schools) and their different educational outcomes. Some have argued that experiences with discrimination lead black and Hispanic students to lower their educational expectations as a reaction to perceptions of blocked opportunities. Black and Hispanic students perceive, these researchers argue, that they will not have the same opportunities as whites to advance, and so set their sights lower.[27] Other researchers, though, find that black students have high aspirations and expectations in spite of perceptions of achievement. Roslyn Mikelson calls this the "attitude-achievement" paradox. Blacks have very favorable views of education as a means to mobility, while still being aware of individual experiences with discrimination.[28] Jay MacLeod similarly found in his ethnography of students living in a housing project in Boston that the black students had much more faith in education, and consequently more optimistic expectations for educational advancement,

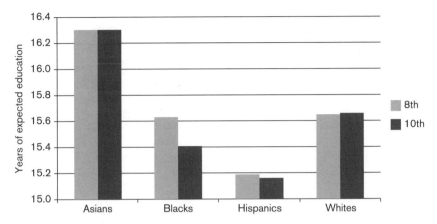

Figure 5-2. Years of Expected Education by Race or Ethnicity, National Educational Longitudinal Study, 1988–1990.

SOURCE: Kao, Tienda, and Schneider (1996).

than the white students living there.[29] Others have argued that, starting with W. E. B. DuBois and Booker T. Washington, blacks have looked to education as a means to dignity and mobility in a society that discriminates against them.[30]

Other researchers have found evidence for the "blocked opportunities" theory, though. Black and Hispanic students' educational expectations decline from eighth to tenth grade, while, on the whole, those of Asians and whites do not.[31] This suggests that they become more discouraged about their chances to achieve higher levels of education the older they get—suggesting that as students experience more discrimination or learn about others' experiences of discrimination, they adjust their expectations.

GPA and Grade Retention

Despite similar educational expectations, grade point averages, or GPAs, show fairly stark differences by race. GPAs are usually measured on a scale from 0 to 4.0. A 2.0 is approximately a C average, 3.0 is a B average, and a 4.0 is a perfect A average. Figure 5–3 shows the GPAs of high school graduates over selected years drawn from the National Center for

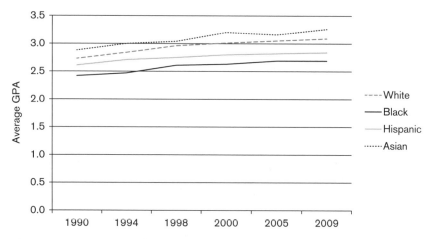

Figure 5-3. Average GPA of High School Graduates by Race and Ethnicity, Select Years, 1990–2009.

SOURCE: US Department of Education, Institute of Education Sciences, National Center for Education Statistics, High School Transcript Study (HSTS), various years, 1990–2009, found on *The Nation's Report Card*, www.nationsreportcard.gov/hsts_2009/race_gpa.aspx.

Education Statistics's High School Transcript Study. It shows small growth in the gap in GPAs by race and ethnicity over time, even as all GPAs have increased. Asian Americans have an average GPA around 3.2 in 2009, with whites following at a little over 3.0. Next are Hispanics with an average GPA around 2.8 in 2009, followed by blacks with a GPA of around 2.6.

It follows from looking at GPA differences that there are differences in retention in grades by race and ethnicity. In a study looking at grade retention from 1994 through 2009, whites had the lowest retention rates, followed by Hispanics, and then blacks (Asians were not included in their study).[32] In the lower grades, particularly first grade, the retention rates are highest for all groups. These rates fall over the years, with a small increase in ninth grade. While all race and ethnic groups follow these patterns, gaps between race and ethnic groups in these rates are found at all levels. About 5.4% of non-Hispanic, white first graders are retained in grade the following year followed by 6.9% of Hispanics. The black retention rate for first graders is 8.7%. These rates drop to between 1% and 2%

Table 5-5   Retention Rates by Grade and Race and
Ethnicity, 1994–1995 through 2009–2010

Grade	Non-Hispanic Whites	Blacks	Hispanics
1st	5.4%	8.7%	6.9%
2nd	1.8%	3.0%	2.4%
3rd	1.3%	3.8%	2.1%
4th	1.2%	2.5%	2.0%
5th	1.2%	2.0%	1.5%
6th	1.3%	2.1%	2.0%
7th	1.7%	3.5%	2.3%
8th	1.6%	3.1%	2.2%
9th	2.2%	4.1%	4.2%
Total	2.0%	3.8%	2.8%

SOURCE: Warren, Hoffman, and Andrew (2014): table 2.

for whites until ninth grade when they are a little over 2%. For Hispanics, rates are mostly a little over 2%, climbing to over 4% in ninth grade. For blacks, though, rates range from over 2% to over 3%, reaching a little over 4% in ninth grade. (See table 5–5.)

NAEP and SAT Scores

Both the National Assessment of Educational Progress (NAEP) scores and SAT scores vary according to race, with the same patterns observed. The NAEP scores, measured on the y-axis of the figure, show Asian Americans with the highest math scores, followed by whites, Hispanics, and then blacks. Although Asians and whites have converged at times, and blacks and Hispanics have converged at times, gaps between the Asians and whites and blacks and Hispanics have persisted, staying about the same in magnitude over time. (See figure 5–4.)

The National Assessment of Educational Progress (NAEP) reading scores show a different pattern from the math scores, however. Big gaps in reading scores by race in 1980 became much smaller by 2012. On reading

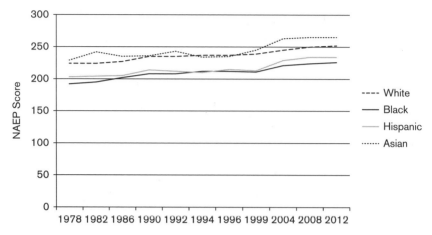

Figure 5-4. Math NAEP Scores at Age 9 by Race, 1978–2012.

SOURCE: US Department of Education, Institute of Education Sciences, National Center for Education Statistics, National Assessment of Educational Progress (NAEP), 1978, 1982, 1986, 1990, 1992, 1994, 1996, 1999, 2004, 2008, and 2012, Long-Term Trend Mathematics Assessments, http://nces.ed.gov/nationsreportcard/lttdata/report.aspx.

tests, whites maintain an advantage, though Asian Americans' scores are quite close. The average scores of Hispanics and blacks are also quite close on reading tests. (See figure 5–5.)

Average SAT scores also show gaps across races. Whites score highest on critical reading, followed by Asian Americans, American Indians, Hispanics, and blacks. On both math and writing SAT tests, Asian Americans score highest, followed by whites, American Indians, Hispanics, and blacks. (See table 5–6.)

Special Education and Course-Taking

Not only are there differences in GPAs and test scores, which may be consequential for high school graduation and continuation to college; research has also found that black students particularly are more likely to be placed in special education programs and remedial classes in schools, and less likely to be identified as gifted.[33] Table 5–7 shows the percentage of students served under the Individuals with Disabilities Education Act

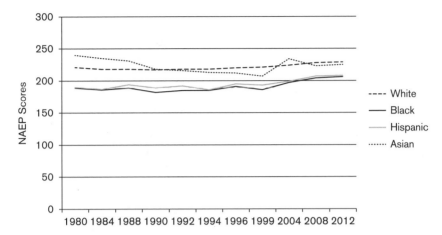

Figure 5-5. Reading NAEP Scores at Age 9 by Race, 1980–2012.

SOURCE: US Department of Education, Institute of Education Sciences, National Center for Education Statistics, National Assessment of Educational Progress (NAEP), 1971, 1975, 1980, 1984, 1988, 1990, 1992, 1994, 1996, 1999, 2004, 2008, and 2012, Long-Term Trend Reading Assessments, http://nces.ed.gov/nationsreportcard/lttdata/report.aspx.

Table 5-6 Critical Reading, Math, and Writing SAT Scores by Race, 2011–2012

Race	Reading	Math	Writing
White	527	536	515
Black	428	428	417
Mexican American	448	465	443
Puerto Rican	452	452	442
Other Hispanic	447	461	442
Asian	518	595	528
American Indian	482	489	462

SOURCE: US Department of Education, National Center for Education Statistics, *Digest of Education Statistics,* 2012 (NCES 2014–015), 2013, chap. 2, https://nces.ed.gov/fastfacts/display .asp?id=171.

Table 5-7   Percentage of Students Aged 3–21 Served by the Individuals with Disabilities
Education Act by Race and Disability Type, 2011–2012, and Percentage of
Students Identified as Gifted and Talented by Race, 2006

	White	Black	Hispanic	Asian	American Indian	Two or More Races
All disabilities	13.4	15.3	11.5	6.3	16.2	12.6
Autism	1.1	0.8	0.7	1.1	0.6	1.0
Developmental delay	0.8	0.9	0.6	0.5	1.4	1.3
Emotional disturbance	0.8	1.3	0.4	0.1	1.0	0.9
Hearing impairments	0.2	0.1	0.2	0.2	0.2	0.1
Intellectual disability	0.8	1.5	0.7	0.4	1.0	0.7
Multiple disabilities	0.3	0.3	0.2	0.2	0.4	0.2
Orthopedic impairments	0.1	0.1	0.1	0.1	0.1	0.1
Other health impairments	1.8	1.7	0.9	0.4	1.6	1.6
Specific learning disabilities	4.4	5.9	5.0	1.5	6.8	3.9
Speech or language impairments	3.0	2.4	2.6	1.8	3.0	2.8
Traumatic brain injury	0.1	0.1	#	#	0.1	0.1
Visual impairments	0.1	0.1	0.1	#	0.1	#
Gifted and Talented	8.0	3.6	4.2	13.1	5.2	NA

SOURCES: National Center for Education Statistics, *Digest of Education Statistics: 2013*, table 204.50, https://nces.ed.gov/programs/digest/d13/tables/dt13_204.50.asp; National Center for Education Statistics, *Digest of Education Statistics: 2010*. NCES 2011–015, 2011, table 49, https://nces.ed.gov/programs/digest/d10/tables/dt10_049.asp?referrer=list.

by race and type of disability. Overall, blacks and American Indians are the most likely and Asian Americans are the least likely to have recognized disabilities. Hispanics and multiracial students are less likely to receive special services for disabilities than whites. Looking specifically at type of disability, the table shows that blacks are most likely to be classified as having emotional disturbances and intellectual disabilities at higher rates than other race or ethnic groups. American Indians are more likely to be recognized as having developmental delays, and they also have high rates of specific learning disabilities. Whites and Asians are most likely to be classified as having autism. Across other types of disabilities, rates are similar across race and ethnic groups.

It is difficult to separate out the factors that may influence how students get classified with particular disabilities. Medical tests may confirm some of these diagnoses, but often the judgment of professionals and the advocacy of parents are important. Medical conditions like hearing and orthopedic impairments may be less open to subjective judgment than diagnoses of emotional disturbances and intellectual impairment. It is hard to discern why there are more differences by race and ethnicity in the diagnoses of these more subjective conditions. At the other end of the spectrum, table 5–7 also shows the percentage of students who are designated as gifted and talented by race. About 8% of whites students are classified as gifted and talented compared to 3.6% of black students, 4.2% of Hispanics, and 5.2% of American Indians. Asian Americans exceed white's rates, with 13.1% identified as gifted and talented.

White and Asian American students are more likely to take AP, IB, or other advanced courses than blacks or Hispanics. When Karolyn Tyson investigated the reasons for this, she found that black students were not encouraged to do so by teachers and black students were afraid of doing badly in these courses.[34] She also found that the fewer students of color in these classes, the less comfortable black students felt taking them. This has improved over time, however. Table 5–8 shows that although white students make up about 61% of students in public schools in 1999 and about 56% in 2008, they still represented more than 67% and 61%, respectively, of AP test-takers in those years. The difference is more dramatic for Asian American students, who make up less than 5% of the public school population in all years. They represent over 11% of test-takers. Blacks, who are about 17% of the public school population, and Hispanics, whose representation has grown from about 16% to over 21% during these years, compose from 4.5% to 7% of test-takers and from 9.2% to 13.6%, respectively. Their presence among test-takers is less than among the public school population as a whole. The same is true for American Indians, who were about 1.2% of the population during this time.

The table does show, though, that over time the representation of both blacks and Hispanics has grown dramatically. The numbers of blacks taking AP exams increased by almost 250%, while Hispanics' numbers

Table 5-8   Racial Composition of Students Taking Advanced Placement Courses, 1999–2008, and Percentage Change over Time by Race

Year	White	Black	Hispanic	Asian American	American Indian
1999	65.0%	4.5%	9.2%	11.1%	0.5%
2000	67.5%	4.8%	10.0%	11.5%	0.5%
2001	66.9%	4.9%	10.5%	11.3%	0.4%
2002	66.6%	5.0%	10.8%	11.2%	0.4%
2003	66.1%	5.1%	11.4%	11.2%	0.5%
2004	65.0%	5.3%	12.0%	11.2%	0.5%
2005	63.7%	5.7%	12.4%	11.3%	0.5%
2006	62.2%	6.0%	12.7%	11.2%	0.5%
2007	62.2%	6.5%	13.1%	11.3%	0.5%
2008	61.4%	7.0%	13.6%	11.5%	0.5%
% change 1999–2008	113.1%	249.9%	233.7%	133.5%	147.1%

SOURCE: National Center for Education Statistics, *Status and Trends in the Education of Racial and Ethnic Minorities,* NCES 2010–015, 2010, table 14a, http://nces.ed.gov/pubs2010/2010015 /tables/table_14a.asp.

increased by 233%. In comparison, the numbers of white and Asian American test-takers increased by 113% and 135%, respectively.

Taking advanced math courses has been shown to be a strong predictor of enrollment in college and the type of college in which a student enrolls.[35] Precalculus and calculus are both advanced math courses that high school students may opt to take. Figure 5–6 shows that almost 50% of Asian students and over 30% of white students take precalculus compared to a little over 20% and less than 20% of Hispanic and black students. Almost 30% of Asian American students take calculus and little over 15% of white students do also, compared with less than 10% of American Indian, Hispanic, and black students.

School Discipline

While not a typically measured and reported educational "outcome," school disciplinary actions may affect other educational outcomes and a

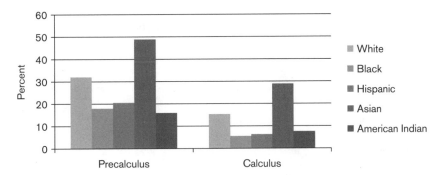

Figure 5-6. Percentage of Students of Different Races Who Take Precalculus or Calculus, 2005.

SOURCE: National Center for Education *Statistics, Status and Trends in the Education of Racial and Ethnic Minorities,* NCES 2010-015, 2010, table 13a, http://nces.ed.gov/pubs2010/2010015 /tables/table_13a.asp.

student's life chances. Time spent suspended or expelled likely influences grades, test scores, educational expectations, and maybe even high school graduation and continuation into college. Students who are disciplined more—either because they have more serious behavioral issues or because teachers (who are predominantly white) interpret behaviors of students of color as threatening more so than those of white students—may become discouraged about their prospects in school. They may spend less time in school, put less effort into their studies and get lower grades and test scores, and may drop out more frequently. Attention has been drawn to disproportionate rates of school discipline faced by some students of color, particularly boys.[36] Table 5-9 below shows the racial and ethnic composition of those students receiving various forms of school discipline during the 2011-2012 school year. To read this table, the percentage receiving a particular form of school discipline, say, in-school suspensions, should be compared to the overall percentage enrolled in schools. If the number is much greater, then students in that racial and ethnic group are overrepresented among those being punished. If the percentage is lower, than students in that group are underrepresented.

Table 5-9 shows that whites and Asian Americans are underrepresented among those who receive all forms of discipline. White students

Table 5–9 Percentage of Students Receiving Various Types of School Discipline by Race and Ethnicity in 2011–2012

	Whites	Blacks	Hispanics	Asians	Native Americans	Multiracial
Overall enrollment	51%	16%	24%	5%	0.5%	2%
In-school suspension	40%	32%	22%	1%	0.2%	3%
Single out-of-school suspension	36%	33%	23%	2%	2%	3%
Multiple out-of-school suspensions	31%	42%	21%	1%	2%	3%
Expulsion	36%	34%	22%	1%	3%	3%

SOURCE: US Department of Education Office for Civil Rights, *Civil Rights Data Collection: Data Snapshot: School Discipline,* Issue Brief No. 1, March 2014, www2.ed.gov/about/offices/list/ocr/docs/crdc-discipline-snapshot.pdf.

make up 51% of the student body (in 2011–2012), but they received only 40% of in-school suspensions, 36% of single out-of-school suspensions, 31% of multiple out-of-school suspensions, and 36% of expulsions. Asians make up 5% of students and received only between 1% and 2% of all school suspensions and expulsions. Hispanic students and multiracial students appear to be represented among those receiving various punishments proportional to their overall enrollment. Hispanics make up about 24% of all students and receive anywhere from 21% to 23% of the different forms of school discipline. Multiracial students are about 2% of all students and make up about 3% of those being disciplined in schools. Blacks and Native Americans are generally overrepresented among those being disciplined. Blacks compose 16% of the student population but account for 32% of those receiving in-school suspensions, 33% of those receiving a single out-of-school suspension, 42% of those receiving multiple out-of-school suspensions, and 34% of those who are expelled. While they account for only 0.5% of the student population, Native Americans make up 2% to 3% of those receiving out-of-school suspensions or expulsions.

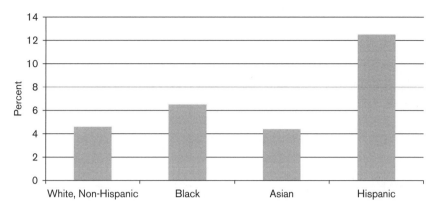

Figure 5-7. Percentage of 15–24 Year Olds Not Enrolled in Schools with No Degree by Race, 2011.

SOURCE: Jessica Davis and Kurt Bauman, *School Enrollment in the United States: 2011 Population Characteristics,* 2013, table 1, US Census Bureau.

Dropout

Differences in educational outcomes likely operate cumulatively: disappointing grades may lead to worse test scores, which may lead to disengagement from school, for example. Figure 5–7 shows that there are racial and ethnic differences in the likelihood of dropping out of school. This figure shows the percentage of youths aged 15 to 24 who are not enrolled in school and who have not attained a high school degree. Asians have the lowest rate of dropout at 4.4%, with whites following at 4.6%. The rate for blacks is above 6%, while the rate for Hispanics is above 12%.

College Enrollment

Figure 5–8 shows the percentages of those 14- to 24-year-old high school graduates who have enrolled in or completed some college by race from 1999 to 2013. Asian Americans have the highest rates of college enrollment overall, with over 80% to as high as almost 92% of high school graduates enrolling in or completing some college. This is followed by whites. About 70% or more of white high school graduates over the years enroll in

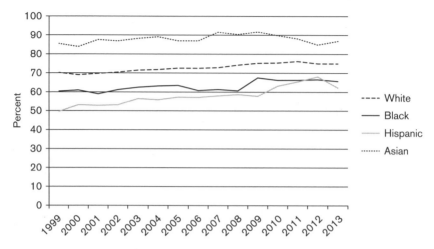

Figure 5–8. Percentage of 14- to 24-Year-Old High School Graduates Who Have Enrolled in or Completed Some College.

SOURCE: US Census Bureau, Current Population Survey Historical Data, table A-5a, www.census .gov/hhes/school/data/cps/historical/index.html.

or complete some college. Blacks and Hispanics follow, with from 50% to over 60% enrolling in or completing college. Although initially Hispanics seemed to enroll at the lowest rates, they have caught up to the enrollment rates of blacks. Gaps across racial groups have generally gotten smaller over the last 14 years, as other racial groups have caught up to Asian Americans, but the gap between blacks and whites has stayed about the same at about 10 percentage points.

EXPLANATIONS FOR DIFFERENCES IN OUTCOMES BY RACE AND ETHNICITY

Although gaps in educational outcomes have gotten smaller in NAEP reading test scores and in college enrollment over time, gaps in GPA have increased slightly, while math test score gaps have remained the same. The tables and figures above show current marked differences in students' grades, SAT scores, course-taking, rates of school disciplinary actions, and high school dropout by race and ethnicity. As with socioeconomic background, we can identify several different contexts where students might experience differences by race and ethnicity that could lead to these outcomes: at the individual level, in families, in neighborhoods, in peer groups, and, finally, in schools.

Individual-Level Explanations

Some have proposed that groups have different innate levels of intelligence. Richard Herrnstein and Charles Murray in their controversial book *The Bell Curve* suggested that racial and ethnic groups can be ranked, placing Asians highest on the continuum. They argued that there were both genetic and environmental causes for these differences.[37] However, other researchers argue that there are few reasons to suspect that genetics account for much of the differences, as there is much more genetic variability within racial groups than between them. Others criticized this book and others like it for not recognizing that IQ test results vary dramatically for the same groups over time, and others charged that the main claims of the book were not adequately supported by the data they used.[38]

Researchers who look at individual-level explanations have also focused on motivations to achieve educationally. These researchers look at students' own educational expectations. As shown in figure 5–2 earlier in this chapter, there are some differences across students, but these differences can only partially explain the racial differences across groups in outcomes. High educational expectations do seem to contribute to the high educational attainment of Asian Americans compared to other groups, though they may not completely account for differences in all educational outcomes.[39] However, educational expectations cannot account for the educational outcomes of blacks and Hispanics. Blacks have educational expectations (at least the attainment of a four-year degree) that are close to or equal to those of whites. When researchers account for educational expectations, the differences in outcomes between blacks and whites grow even larger.[40]

Another explanation reflects an individual's psychological reaction to how society perceives a racial or ethnic group. Psychologists have suggested that how students perceive they will be judged as members of a minority group matters. "Stereotype threat" occurs when students become anxious

that their test performance will reflect other members of their racial or ethnic group or gender.[41] When black and white students are asked to identify
their races prior to taking a test, black students score worse than white students. These differences are not so pronounced when students are not asked
to identify their races. Steele suggests that when black students identify
their race, they are reminded of the stereotypes about blacks that suggest
they are lower-performing. Students believe that they will be judged according to their race, and this places pressure on them to succeed, which produces anxiety. While the psychological reaction to testing is at the individual
level, it is important to point out that black students' anxiety is a result of
stereotypes that are held by the larger society.

Family

Explanations that focus on family differences across race and ethnic
groups often emphasize either "structure" or "culture." Structural explanations explain differences according to the financial resources available to
families. Certainly having higher incomes and more wealth allows families to buy educational resources and opportunities for children. Families
with resources can buy more books, computers, Internet access, museum
passes, and concert tickets, can afford to travel, and can buy other educationally enriching experiences. Families with higher incomes and wealth
may be able to afford homes near public schools that they consider higher
quality. Families such as these may also be more likely to perceive that
they will be able to afford to pay college tuition.

Indeed, there are stark differences in the income profiles of students by
race and ethnicity. Though there is variability across ethnic groups, Asian
Americans as a whole tend to have the highest median incomes, higher
even than whites (though this is not true of Southeast Asians, and Chinese
and Korean families also have higher rates of poverty than whites). Whites
who are not Hispanic are typically next, followed by Hispanics. For example, in 2013, Asian American households had a median income of $67,065.
Whites followed with a median income of $58,270. Hispanics had a
median income of $40,693 and blacks' median household income was
$34,598.[42] Native Americans had a median income slightly above blacks
at $36,252.[43]

Even when accounting for these differences in income, racial and ethnic differences in outcomes do not disappear.[44] Income differences do explain some of the differences between these groups, but not all of them. Some researchers argue that income provides an incomplete picture of the resources available to families for providing advantages to children. They contend that wealth must also be considered, because wealth is important for buying homes near good schools, for paying tuition, and as collateral for loans. As stark as income differences are between blacks and whites, wealth differences are even greater. In 2014, white households had a median net worth of $140,900, compared to $11,000 for blacks and only slightly more ($13,700) for Hispanics.[45] While differences in wealth have not been as thoroughly studied as differences in income, there is evidence that wealth differences do explain part of the difference between blacks and whites in educational achievement through differences in the "cultural capital" to which children are exposed. Children with more wealth go to museums more, and have more exposure and cultivation in music and the arts.[46]

Differences in family resources may also lead to differences in access to reliable information and other types of social capital. Families' sources of information about "good" schools, "good" colleges, and their application procedures, as well as scholarships and financial aid to pay for college tuition, may be influenced by both their incomes and their own educational experiences. Families tend to be in networks that are similar to themselves socioeconomically, so those who have family, friends, neighbors, and coworkers with more advantages may have better information than those whose friends have fewer resources. Family members are themselves often the best sources of information, and parents who have achieved higher education may be more able to help their own children strategize and plan for high achievement that leads them to colleges and universities, particularly prestigious ones. Asian American and white parents tend to have higher educational levels than blacks, Hispanics, or Native Americans, and their higher educational levels may influence how well they are able to provide information and advise their children. Current data from the Census Bureau show that in 2014, 35.7% of non-Hispanic whites had completed bachelor's degrees or more education, compared to 22.3% of blacks and 15.3% of Hispanics. Asian American parents had the highest rates of bachelor's degree completion, with 52.4% of those over 25 having one.[47]

Differences in resources cannot account for educational outcomes across all groups, generally. Other explanations focus on other family-level explanations like the parenting practices of different racial and ethnic groups. For example, researchers have suggested that black parents read to and speak to children less than white parents and believe in stricter discipline.[48] Differences in parenting practices (reading and ways of speaking to children) before school begins, as well as differences in the use of center-based preschools, contribute to race and ethnic gaps in preparation for kindergarten and first grade.[49] Black parents are said to be more authoritarian than authoritative, that is, they have stricter rules and there is less room for discussion and negotiation about them. Children do not participate as much in family decision-making. While these differences may have some effect on children's achievement, researchers have also noted than first-generation Asian American parents are also described as "authoritarian," and Asian Americans have very high educational achievement compared to whites.[50]

Finally, at the family level, researchers contend that racial, ethnic, and immigrant groups may have different cultural values that lead to different educational outcomes. Researchers looking at Asian Americans suggest that because many groups come from countries with Confucian traditions, they are well suited to the hard work and delayed gratification that result in high educational achievement.[51] Other researchers complicate this explanation, though, suggesting that South Asians, for example, do not come from such traditions.

The appearance of the term "model minority" as a way to describe Asian Americans was in 1966 in a *New York Times* article by the sociologist William Peterson. It appeared at a time when black and Hispanic activists were demanding equality of opportunity in education and other arenas. Stephen Steinberg suggests that this term implied that if minorities worked hard and had the "right" values, they could succeed in the United States. The term "model minority" was used to counter the argument that US institutions, like education, were not affording opportunities for minorities to succeed in the United States.[52]

Mexican American families have been characterized as being "familistic," that is, they value obligations to one another over individual achievement. It has been said that this leads to decreased educational achievement among Mexican Americans, as family responsibilities take precedence over schooling. However, researchers find that first-generation Mexicans express the most familistic values, while having the highest achievement among Mexican-origin students.

Finally, dating back decades, blacks and other poor minorities have been charged with maintaining a "culture of poverty." This term was famously used in a report issued by Senator Daniel Patrick Moynihan in 1965, though Moynihan based his ideas on those of the anthropologist Oscar Lewis.[53] While Senator Moynihan explicitly associated this culture with blacks, suggesting that high rates of female-headed households and the lack of employed males led to few role models for children and a culture that did not value educational achievement, decades later William Julius Wilson would attribute this "culture" to a lack of economic opportunity that resulted in an underclass that was defined more by economic position than by position in a racial and ethnic hierarchy.[54]

Scholars, and particularly scholars of color, fought the notion that black families did not value education. Throughout US history, blacks and other people of color fought hard to attain the same access to education that whites had. Blacks faced overt discrimination and threats of violence to attend schools and to integrate schools. Surely, families would not have made these sacrifices if they did not value education.[55]

Neighborhoods and Peers

Racial segregation in the United States is stark, particularly between blacks and whites. Where a student lives affects not only what school she or he attends, but also access to grocery stores, health clinics, parks, extracurricular and summer activities, and other amenities. Neighborhoods may be dangerous for students or places where children can gather to play. William Julius Wilson famously argued that it was the effects of concentrated poverty that mattered for neighborhood residents,[56] but predominantly black neighborhoods have fewer neighborhood amenities and are perceived to be more dangerous than other types of neighborhoods, even predominantly white neighborhoods with residents of similar socioeconomic backgrounds. Researchers have found that black-white test score gaps are higher in more racially segregated cities,[57] though some argue that it is racial segregation in schools and not in neighborhoods that matters most.[58]

Peer explanations for differences in educational outcomes often focus on how minority students collectively make meaning of their experiences in a society in which they may face disadvantage and discrimination. John Ogbu and others after him have argued that "involuntary" minorities, those from groups that were unwillingly brought to or incorporated into the United States, have judged their chances for mobility in the United States—for getting a good education and stable, high-paying jobs—against those of the majority dominant group throughout most of US history, whites. They use whites as their "reference group," and find that their chances at success are lower than those of whites. Because of this, Ogbu argues that groups like blacks, Native Americans, and Hispanics who were brought to or incorporated into the United States unwillingly become discouraged and form "oppositional cultures" that define "whiteness" as undesirable. Those who behave like or aspire to be like whites are labeled and teased.[59] He and his colleague Signithia Fordham report that black students who do well in school, speak non-black English, and listen to certain types of music fear being teased for "acting white." Those students who could do well at school try to hide their success by either deliberately doing poorly, being athletic, or acting like a class clown. Their research was conducted in a predominantly black school in Washington, DC.[60]

Other researchers have argued that the fear of being labeled as "acting white" is more complicated, however. For example, Prudence Carter finds that those students who are able to navigate both black and white cultural territories are most successful. Based on her research in Yonkers, New York, she notes that students often do not exclusively confine themselves to "black" or "white" styles of speaking, dress, music, or other tastes and behaviors, but can use either depending on the situation. These students are "cultural straddlers" when they are speaking to teachers or other authority figures and when they are speaking to peers. "Switching codes" between white and black types of speech or tastes and preferences in this way allows these students to relate to teachers, counselors, and coaches, while also affording them the social support of their predominantly black and Hispanic peer groups. Students who could not easily move between the two styles were more likely either to be teased as "acting white" or to be unable to relate to teachers and other adults in school.[61]

Many researchers have found little evidence for an "oppositional culture" among blacks and Hispanics, instead finding some optimism and faith in education as a mechanism for advancement.[62] Karolyn Tyson points out that in many schools, all students, white, black, and Hispanic, are afraid of being labeled "nerdy" if they overachieve academically compared to their peers. This "overachievement" becomes racially labeled when schools seem to systematically exclude blacks and Hispanics from academically rigorous course placements. Academic achievement is not labeled racially when black and Hispanic students are well represented among the high-achieving students in a school.[63] Angel Harris finds that black students who feel positive about their racial identity and black students who perceive that discrimination may be an obstacle to their success actually do better in school than those who negatively perceive their black identity or who don't recognize discrimination as a challenge in their lives.[64]

Schools

As in the previous chapter, it seems that there could be many reasons why Asian, white, black, Hispanic, and Native American children perform differently in schools that do not necessarily have to do with schools themselves. There may be differences in individuals' reactions to society-held stereotypes, differences in family resources or cultures and values, differences in neighborhood resources, and differences in relationships with neighbors and peers. Researchers that argue that schools play a meaningful role in maintaining or even exacerbating differences by race and ethnicity, those who may subscribe to the conflict paradigm's view of schools, suggest that there are not only differences between schools, but also differences in how students are treated within the same schools, by race and ethnicity. Some of the family-level explanations for educational gaps by race and ethnicity do not simply focus on the family and its norms, values, and cultural and financial resources; they also begin to touch on the school's role in how these differences become meaningful in schools.

The first part of this chapter focused on how students of color may be concentrated in schools with other students of color, which are also likely to have higher concentrations of students in poverty. These schools have higher teacher turnover and, on average, teachers have fewer qualifications than schools that are whiter and wealthier. Highly segregated, predominantly minority schools are associated with worse educational outcomes than those that are less segregated, and researchers have found that minority students perform better in integrated schools.[65]

Other sociologists contend that there are differences in the ways that students are treated within schools that implicate schools in maintaining gaps in educational outcomes. Some researchers argue that differences in family cultures and values are not recognized or respected by schools. Angela Valenzuela, for example, suggests that Mexican American students face "subtractive schooling" in the United States. They are used to caring, family-like relationships with teachers from experiences with schooling in Mexico. When teachers do not respond in the same ways in the United States, some students withdraw and lower their expectations.[66] Still other researchers borrow the term "cultural capital" to suggest that black and other minority students do not have the styles of speech, styles of dress, or tastes in music and art that predominantly white teachers in schools consider valuable.[67] This lack of white "cultural capital" disadvantages students of color who do not have it. Annette Lareau suggests, though, that students of color can have very high levels of cultivation and cultural capital, which can be used to their advantage, although these students must still cope with discrimination.[68]

Teachers may hold different expectations for students based on their races, for example. Teachers may hold lower expectations of black and Hispanic students, and students perceive that those expectations are lower.[69] On the other hand, Asian American students report that they feel pressure from the sometimes unrealistically high expectations that teachers hold for them.[70] These differences in expectations become self-fulfilling prophecies, such that students attempt to match their academic performances to that which is expected of them. These differences in expectations are, in part, reflected in their course-taking patterns. Schools that had more diverse, academically rigorous programs have been found to have fewer racial stereotypes about student academic ability.

Student discipline has also been unevenly applied across race, as shown in table 5–9 in this chapter. Black boys and young men are subject to more, and more severe, punishment than students of any other race. Black students, but boys particularly, are more likely to receive detention, suspension, or expulsion than any other race or ethnic group except Native Americans. This is attributed to stereotypes that society holds of black men as criminals or gang members, as aggressive and violent. Interruptions to students' schooling, like detentions or suspensions, affect the time they spend in classes learning. They also influence a student's perceptions of him- or herself and his or her relationships to authority figures. Students learn to mistrust authority, believing that they will always be judged as suspicious and a potential criminal.[71]

Gaps between children of different socioeconomic groups tend to shrink during the school year and widen over the summer, suggesting that schools equalize some of the differences between children that result from socioeconomic position.[72] However, gaps in test scores between blacks and whites increase during their time in school, even for those who enter school with roughly the same set of skills.[73] Not only are schools unable to compensate for the uneven sets of skills that black and Hispanic students have upon entering kindergarten, but differences between black and whites students in fact grow over time spent in school. It is likely that differences in achievement by race and ethnicity are a messy combination of individual, family, neighborhood, and school factors. Research suggests, though, that schools may not ameliorate, and may even exacerbate, some of these differences.

IMMIGRANT STUDENTS

As I discussed in chapter 2, one reason for the universalization of public schooling was as a response to increasing immigration. Children from very different cultures and countries had to be taught "American" values, norms, and behaviors, like the value of democracy. Public schools, especially in diverse places like New York City, were supposed to "Americanize" immigrant children, to teach them similar cultural values and traditions as those of the whites already living in the country. This, it was thought, would promote a cohesive society, a society that shared values. A successful immigrant then was thought to be successful when he or she had learned these values. When immigrants valued hard work—the "Protestant Ethic"— they would be successful in schools. Social researchers argued that the more successfully students assimilated into US society, the more successful they would be in school.[74]

"Assimilation" occurs when immigrants adopt the values, norms, behaviors, and traditions of the societies into which they migrate. Along with this cultural assimilation comes educational and economic assimilation. The better immigrants fit in to a society, the better grades they get and the more education they achieve, and then the better the jobs they get, along with higher incomes. In this sense, the more assimilated, the more immigrants come to resemble the dominant group, in the case of the United States, native-born whites.

Historians cite two examples of immigrants whose assimilation contributed to their success in the United States. Irish and Italian immigrants came to the United States with low levels of schooling. Education was not universal or even that common in Italy or Ireland during the nineteenth century. Most immigrants were farmers looking for labor in the United States. Historians cite examples of Irish and Italian parents not understanding the need for children to attend schools in the United States. Often the labor of the child was more important to the immigrant family, and families would pull their children out of school to go to work. Authorities were at odds with parents in trying to educate children. After a generation or so, Irish and Italians accepted the prominent role of education in the United States, and these children then got better grades and stayed in school longer, becoming indistinguishable in educational outcomes from other white ethnic groups.[75]

There were some groups, though, that were initially more successful than whites—these groups did not just equal whites' success in schools and in the workforce; they surpassed whites' achievement. The educational and occupational success of Jewish and Asian immigrant students was initially thought to be because these cultures had similar values to US culture. Both Jewish and Asian students were said to have values that resembled the "Protestant Ethic," that is, both Jewish and Asian students were described as valuing hard work and delaying gratification.[76]

There is some evidence to support this idea that immigrants, coming from a different culture, retain ideas from that culture. If the culture values education, then the immigrant retains that value in the United States. Research shows that the more "assimilated" an Asian American student is, the more closely that student's grades and educational achievements resemble those of whites. First-generation Asian American students have higher grades, higher achievement test scores, and higher educational ambitions than whites. Third-generation students resemble whites more. Black immigrants and children of immigrants have higher educational achievement than native-born blacks in the United States.[77]

These observations led social researchers to discuss "segmented assimilation." They argue that although some groups may come to resemble whites in terms of educational and economic achievement, it is often more desirable for the members of a group to retain their cultural heritage, particularly if they live in communities where native-born members of that group are more disadvantaged than native-born whites. Thus group members would become educationally and economically assimilated, but not culturally assimilated—that is why it is called "segmented assimilation."[78]

Table 5–10 shows results from a study called the Children of Immigrants Longitudinal Study, conducted by Alejandro Portes and Ruben Rumbaut. This study follows a sample of junior high school students through their high school years, from 1992 to 1996. The sample was drawn from three cities: San Diego, Miami, and Fort Lauderdale, all places with high levels of immigration. The table does not include a representative sample of all children of immigrants in the United States; so, for example, Koreans, Japanese, and African immigrants are not well represented in these areas. Children of immigrants can be born in the United States to immigrant parents or they themselves may have immigrated as young or even older children. The table shows that outcomes vary dramatically by the ethnicity or place of origin of immigrant groups. Asian children of immigrants tend to have the highest GPAs, with Chinese at the top. Dominican children of immigrants appear to have the lowest grades. However, Hmong children of immigrants have the lowest expectations for advanced degrees, followed by Mexicans. Chinese have the highest proportion expecting an advanced degree, followed by Jamaicans and Cubans. Finally, when we look at the percentage of those in the sample who had dropped out of school by their senior year of high school, Cubans had the highest percentage, followed by Mexicans and Nicaraguans, and Hmong and Chinese had the lowest.

Table 5-10   GPA, Expectation of an Advanced Degree, and Dropout by
Ethnicity, 1992–1996, for Children in the Children of
Immigrants Longitudinal Study

	GPA in 1995	Expects an Advanced Degree	Dropped Out by 1995
Chinese	3.65	64.3%	0%
Vietnamese	3.03	48.1%	5.5%
Filipino	2.86	44.5%	4.2%
Hmong	2.65	6.0%	3.8%
Jamaican	2.39	54.2%	6.8%
Mexican	2.25	24.9%	8.8%
Nicaraguan	2.21	49.5%	8.8%
Cuban	2.20	50.9%	10.1%
Haitian	2.12	54.9%	6.2%
Dominican	1.96	31.3%	5.6%

SOURCE: Ruben G. Rumbaut, "Coming of Age in Immigrant America," *Research Perspectives on Migration* 1, no. 6 (1998): 1–14, table 4, http://carnegieendowment.org/files/rpm/rpmvol1no6.pdf.

There are a number of possible reasons for the achievement differences between immigrant and white, native-born students, and for differences between immigrant groups. Immigrants may have a number of advantages working in their favor. The first is called "self-selection." Those immigrants who come to the United States may come because they are able to get good jobs. That is one of the criteria for legally immigrating to the United States—you can get citizenship if an employer sponsors you. Generally, employers who are willing to sponsor immigrants want highly skilled workers, so they'll be likely to sponsor scientists, professionals, or others with highly valued skills. Consequently, adults who immigrate tend to be highly skilled people with a good prospect of getting a job and high levels of education. Those most different from their less-educated peers in their home countries may be the most successful.[79]

Immigrants may also retain some cultural values that help them achieve once they are in the United States. For example, Asian American students and their parents place a high value on hard work and persistence, as well as getting good grades.[80] Immigrants may live together in ethnic communities or enclaves. We know from James Coleman and his work on social capital that tightly knit communities provide supervision and support for youths.[81] Immigrant communities may not simply be functional communities, tied together because they live in the same area; they may also value communities because they share the same cultural traditions, norms, and beliefs. Students from these communities may feel accountable to them and supported by them. They may be closely supervised and there may be a lot of information sharing among community members. Min Zhou and Carl Bankston find this in their study of the Vietnamese immigrant community in New Orleans. They show that students who identify themselves more as Vietnamese and less as American do better in school. Further, students who speak Vietnamese and take part in Vietnamese traditions achieve more. Zhou and Bankston argue that this "segmented assimilation" helps students achieve because students, through their ethnic identification, tie themselves to the Vietnamese community. By doing so, they get the support, information, and supervision from the community.[82]

Another reason for the high educational achievement of immigrants has been labeled "immigrant optimism."[83] "Voluntary minorities," who come to a country willingly for political or economic reasons, compare themselves to peers who did not migrate, and may see themselves as fortunate. They believe they have better opportunities to succeed educationally and economically in the country to which they immigrated. Children of immigrants may be aware of the sacrifices that parents have to make in order to get them educated in the United States and may work hard so as not to disappoint them.[84]

There are also challenges that immigrants face when coming to the United States that may affect their educational achievement. One of the main challenges may be difficulty with English. In 2012–2013, about 9.2% of public school students were classified as English Language Learners, or ELL.[85] ELL students, perhaps not surprisingly, score lower in reading on national assessment exams like the NAEP. For example, in 2013, ELL fourth graders scored 187 on average, compared to 225 for those who are not designated ELL. Only 7% were at or above proficient, compared to 37% of non-ELL students. In eighth grade, ELLs scored 225 on average compared to 268 for non-ELL students. The same is also true for math scores. ELL students scored 25 points lower in fourth grade and 41 points lower in eighth grade on average on math NAEP tests in 2012–2013.[86] The high school graduation rate for ELL students was 61.1% nationally in 2012–2013, according to a government press release, compared to an overall graduation rate of 81.4% across all students.[87]

Those classified as ELL are deemed to need special language support in schools. Often these students take different classes from those who are English-proficient and much of their educational time is spent learning English. For some, English difficulties slow learning, and for others, less proficiency speaking English may be mistaken for low ability. Standardized tests are hard to take if you do not know English, and grades may be lower than they should be given the talent or ability of the test-taker.[88] Some research shows, though, that differences in outcomes by ELL status disappear after accounting for students' individual and family characteristics like parental education and family income.[89] For students who are not necessarily ELL, but are proficient in their or their parents' native languages, there may be benefits. Bilingual students may have access to social capital from English-speaking peers and support from their non-English-speaking parents and communities.[90]

Immigrants who are unfamiliar with the dominant culture in the United States may feel lonely and isolated in schools, and immigrant students may not have the same sources from which to gain information as white, native-born students or their native-born peers. Some immigrant students may also have lower family incomes, less wealth, and lower parental education compared to native-born whites and immigrant students from other groups. Immigrants from Mexico, for example, often occupy jobs in agriculture or in service work that are not highly skilled and do not pay well. Immigrants who come as political refugees, as Vietnamese, Cambodians, Lao, Hmong, and Nicaraguans did, may not have the same levels of education as US natives. Often political refugees are given government asylum and aid. These immigrants may have a difficult time finding jobs that utilize their skills (perhaps farming skills, rice-growing, and so on). Political refugees may also have experienced a great deal of trauma in escaping from their home countries. This may interfere with learning. Further, refugees may have spent time in camps before immigrating to the United States and lost years of formal schooling waiting to immigrate.

There may also be cultural differences across immigrant groups that affect educational outcomes. Research shows, for example, that Vietnamese youths in Boston drop out of high school less than whites, while Lao and Khmer students drop out more. Some argue this may be because in Vietnam, there is more adherence to a Confucian culture that emphasizes hard work over talent and ability, whereas in the predominantly Buddhist value system of the Khmer and Lao, children's fates may be considered predetermined.[91] If a child does not do well in school, that child was not fated to be a scholar. Mexican families are often said to have high degrees of "familism," meaning that Mexican immigrants may place high value on the survival of the family, sometimes at the expense of individual achievement. Mexican students may have more responsibilities to their families, like getting a job to contribute economically or watching siblings or doing housework. These commitments may interfere with academic pursuits.[92] Cultural misunderstandings may also occur when the dominant culture does not understand the minority culture and vice versa. US teachers may emphasize critique and argumentation in academic work. In some cultures, it is considered impolite to make eye contact or challenge teachers in any way. Teachers may interpret this as rude, disinterested, or simply not intelligent behavior.[93]

What is clear from table 5–10 is that the race or ethnicity of an immigrant matters. Racial differences among immigrants are prominent. How immigrant students get "racialized," that is, the racial groups into which they get placed in the United States, seems to matter a great deal in their future educational trajectories.[94]

MULTIRACIAL STUDENTS

Very little research to date has been done that explores the educational outcomes of multiracial students, but it is a growing population that may deserve more attention in the future. When educational outcomes of multiracial children have been explored, researchers generally find that students score between their single-race peers. For example, children who identify as both Asian and white have average GPAs that fall above whites but below those of single-race Asians. Students with biracial black-white identities score below white students, on average, but above single-race black students. However, this same research tends to find that biracial students also have more behavior problems, experience depression and isolation more often, and feel less connected to their schools, though these relationships vary based on the racial identities of the students and the racial compositions of the schools.[95] Whether and how growing numbers of multiracial students influence racial categories and how changes in racial categories may affect gaps in educational achievement are questions to explore in the future.

In the next chapter, I look at how educational outcomes differ by gender. This chapter presents a different picture from that which has been painted in this chapter—initial disadvantages women faced in educational experiences have been followed by educational achievement that in many ways exceeds that of men. Discussion of gender differences in education are now largely focused around two topics: whether boys are disadvantaged by their educational experiences and why boys and men are more likely to pursue Science, Technology, Engineering, and Mathematics (STEM) fields.

6 Inequality by Gender and Disability

In this chapter, I focus on how educational experiences differ by gender and, to a lesser extent, sexual orientation and gender identity, and on differences by disability status. The previous two chapters have looked at how students' experiences differ by race and ethnicity and socioeconomic background both across different schools and within the same schools. Although there has been a history of gender segregation across schools, which I will review, for the most part, contemporary public education finds boys and girls distributed similarly across schools, so most differences in treatment between boys and girls occur when they are in the same schools.

Girls generally do better in school than boys. They get better grades, score about equally and sometimes higher on reading and math ability tests, drop out of school less, and enroll in college more than boys. The different experiences of girls and boys in schools have led to what some researchers call a "boy crisis" in schools.[1] The roots of this crisis may be in how the behaviors of boys and girls are taught and reinforced differently, with girls' behavior ultimately reaping more academic rewards. Teachers may perceive boys as more troublesome and dangerous (especially the behaviors of black boys), regardless of their actual behavior, and punish boys more severely, leading them to become discouraged. Despite their achievements, though, girls do tend to take fewer advanced math and science courses in high school and, in part because of this, are not found in Science, Technology, Engineering, and Math, or STEM, fields as often as boys are. Although there is little research to date on sexual orientation and achievement, studies find that lesbian, bisexual, gay, queer, and transgender students are bullied more and report mental health problems at a higher rate than teens who identify as heterosexual. Disability status also seems to matter for children's educational outcomes, and it is difficult to separate out how much outcomes are due to actual differences in ability, to stigmas attached to disability statuses, or to other factors related to disability status.

First, I want to define a few terms. Sex is the categorization (male or female) that is based on biological and physiological differences. Gender is a social category (often masculine or feminine) that describes attitudes and behaviors that are associated with biological distinctions by sex. Sexism is the different valuation of one sex over another. Gender is constantly being defined and renegotiated in society with different roles and responsibilities being defined as "masculine" or "feminine," and with different understandings of how one's gender identity may be defined— whether in binary categories (male and female) or with other designations that allow for more fluidity across categories (male, female, transgender male, transgender female, gender queer, and so on). The adoption of many of these terms in more mainstream institutions like public schools and universities is relatively recent and presents interesting challenges to the ways that people believe that gender corresponds to particular roles, responsibilities, and behaviors.

Schools in the United States have primarily seen gender as consisting of two categories—male and female—and they have historically privileged male over female students. For example, in the 1700s in the New England colonies, female students were thought to need separate and particular skills for their roles in adult life—mainly the domestic arts of sewing, cooking, raising children, and teaching religion. Reading, writing, and arithmetic were taught to females usually so that they could better teach religion to their children.[2] More privileged females may have been taught music, art, or literature in order to better entertain upper-class guests. Few years of schooling were seen to be required to teach these skills, so schooling for most young girls who attended school was done in Dame Schools, which only lasted a couple of years. In other regions of the country, like the South, more elite girls were taught sporadically by governesses or tutors or in convent schools.

During this time, boys were also not regularly schooled, and those who did attend school went to the same Dame Schools for only a few years to learn reading, writing, and math or had more regular tutoring from governesses. Some boys were allowed to continue schooling after Dame Schools in town schools, while girls were not. This did not change until the late eighteenth century. Elite boys, though, attended private schools for much longer, usually to learn classic subjects like Latin and Greek. Elite universities only admitted men for these studies.

When public schools expanded, they first served boys. At the same time, private academies educating elite boys proliferated. One of the first of these for girls, the Young Ladies Academy of Philadelphia, was founded in 1787. This academy taught girls the same subjects as boys learned in private academies, with all male teachers. The numbers of academies founded for the serious education of girls grew, but it wasn't until 1826 that larger numbers of girls were allowed to attend the growing numbers of public high schools.[3]

Women were not admitted into higher education until 1803 (at the Bradford Academy), usually into their own sex-segregated academies. Oberlin College became the first coeducational institution, with men and women taking classes together, in 1832. It was shortly after this in 1834 that the sex-segregated but very prestigious Seven Sisters Colleges (Barnard, Bryn Mawr, Mt. Holyoke, Radcliffe, Smith, Wellesley, Vassar) were founded. These colleges were intended to mirror the Ivy League educations of male students at places like Harvard, Yale, Dartmouth, and Princeton.

In the years that followed, as education expanded, more and more institutions for girls' and women's education opened, and more institutions began admitting women. This expansion of women into education was halted briefly, though, after World War II. The GI Bill signed in 1944 provided tuition assistance and living expenses for veterans to attend universities and vocational education or to complete their high school educations. Women left positions in the labor force that they had occupied during World War II and also fewer enrolled in university studies as the nation as a whole moved toward younger ages of marriage and younger ages at which women gave birth to their first children. During these years after World War II, the years that would produce the "Baby Boom" generation, discourse around women's roles (particularly middle- and upper-class, white women) focused on being good wives and mothers.

Though many universities were coeducational before the 1950s and 1960s, the civil rights movement and other movements of the 1960s reignited discussion about equal opportunities and treatment for women in education and in the labor force. The women's movement of this time was focused on equal rights for men and women in all arenas. In part due to this new social awareness of the still-existing inequalities between men and women, prestigious Ivy League universities like Harvard and Princeton opened their doors to women in 1969. Very few single-sex male institutions exist today. One of the last to admit women was the Virginia Military Institute, or VMI, which was sued for discrimination in 1990 and ordered to admit women. It did so in 1997.

The women's movement and the growing agitation against inequality between the sexes also led to the passage of Title IX in 1972. It mandated that women receive equal treatment in all aspects of education, including not only sports, as it is most famously known for, but also in nine other areas of education such as access to higher education, career education, education for pregnant and parenting students, employment, learning environment, math and science, sexual harassment, standardized testing, and technology. (See figure 6–1.)

Figure 6–2 shows the percentages of women and men aged five to 19 enrolled in schools in the United States from 1850 to 1990. From this figure, you see that although women were less likely to be enrolled from about 1850 to 1900, from 1900 on women and men are about as likely to be enrolled in school. In 2013, a greater percentage of girls were enrolled in schools, particularly between ages 14 to 19.[4] So, although women were considered disadvantaged relative to men in terms of enrollment before 1900, it appears that, at least in terms of enrollment, women in the past few years are experiencing an advantage over men.

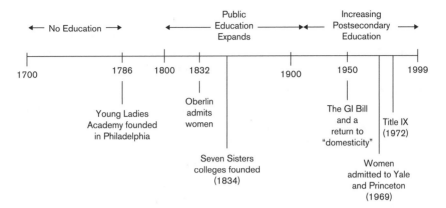

Figure 6-1. A Timeline of Chosen Events in the Education of Women.

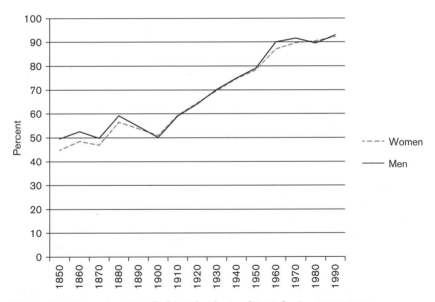

Figure 6-2. Percentage Enrolled in Schools, Aged 5–19, by Sex, 1850–1990.

SOURCE: National Center for Education Statistics, *120 Years of American Education: A Statistical Portrait*, 1993, table 2, US Department of Education.

From figure 1–2 in chapter 1, which showed the eventual educational attainment of men and women over 24 years old in 2014, we saw that women are slightly overrepresented among those who have some college, associate's degrees, and master's degrees. Men and women appear to be equally likely to have bachelor's degrees, but men are more likely than women to hold professional or doctoral degrees. Contemporary trends seem to suggest that women are not as disadvantaged as they have been historically compared to men, and, in some cases, they are experiencing educational advantages in attainment. The next sets of tables and figures may provide some clues about why this occurs. How do girls and boys compare in their experiences with grades and test scores, course-taking, school discipline, high school dropout, and enrollment in college? While this chapter provides a snapshot of some of these differences and a brief overview of some explanations for them, Thomas DiPrete and Claudia Buchmann provide a much more thorough treatment of gender differences in education and explanations for them in their recent book *The Rise of Women: The Growing Gender Gap in Education and What It Means for American Schools.*[5]

EDUCATIONAL EXPECTATIONS

First, I present the educational expectations of male and female students. Educational expectations reflect both a student's desire for a particular level of education and their assessments of being able to attain that level. Aspirations refer to the desire to attain a particular level of education without regard for the obstacles that may prevent students from achieving it. Educational expectations are typically better predictors of how much education students will actually attain than their aspirations.

Figure 6–3 shows that female high school seniors have higher educational expectations than males. Males are better represented among those with expectations to attain a high school degree or less, to complete some college, and to attain a bachelor's degree only, while females are more likely to expect a graduate or advanced postbaccalaureate degree. Over 40% of females expect this, compared to less than 30% of males.

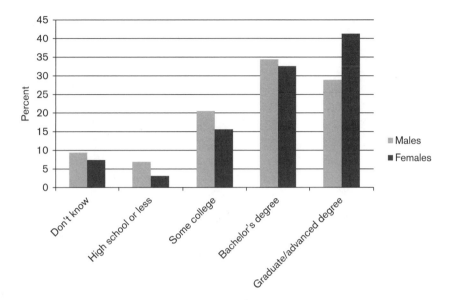

Figure 6-3. Educational Expectations of High School Seniors by Sex in 2004.

SOURCE: Institute for Education Sciences, US Department of Education, *Issue Tables*, "Postsecondary Expectations and Plans for the High School Senior Class of 2003-04," NCES 2010-170rev, 2010, table 1, https://nces.ed.gov/pubs2010/2010170rev.pdf.

GRADES AND GRADE RETENTION

Researchers speculate on why girls get better grades than boys. Some suggest that grades reflect subjective judgments about behavior and work habits, as well as academic talent, and girls are socialized to have behavior that is more compatible with what teachers value.[6] Others suggest that girls are socialized to want to please teachers and others, so they work harder.[7] GPAs may also be higher because girls are less likely to take academically risky courses, like advanced math or science courses that might jeopardize their good grade point averages, as we show in the following section. Figure 6-4 shows that girls do indeed have higher GPAs than boys, and this pattern has been consistent over time, occurring even before women were more likely to enroll in college than men. That gap has remained at about .20 of a point.

Perhaps not surprisingly, given their higher grade point averages, girls are also less likely to be retained in a grade. Table 6-1 shows the rate at

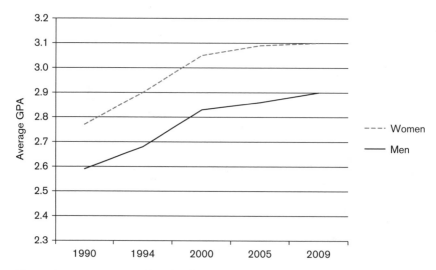

Figure 6-4. Average GPA of High School Graduates by Sex, Select Years, 1990–2009.

SOURCE: US Department of Education, Institute of Education Sciences, National Center for Education Statistics, High School Transcript Study (HSTS), various years, 1990–2009, found on *The Nation's Report Card*, www.nationsreportcard.gov/hsts_2009/gender_gpa.aspx.

| | *Table 6-1* | Retention Rates by Grade and Sex, 1994–1995 through 2009–2010 |

Grade	Girls	Boys
1st	5.9%	6.5%
2nd	1.9%	2.2%
3rd	1.6%	2.0%
4th	1.5%	1.5%
5th	1.3%	1.4%
6th	1.5%	1.9%
7th	1.8%	2.3%
8th	1.6%	2.2%
9th	2.2%	3.5%
Total	2.2%	2.6%

SOURCE: Warren, Hoffman, and Andrew (2014): table 2.

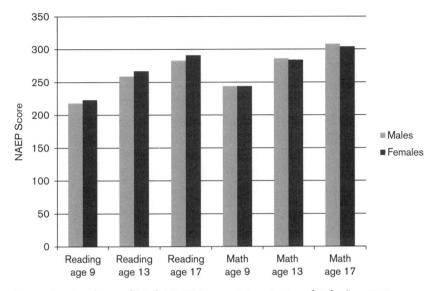

Figure 6-5. Reading and Math NAEP Scores at Ages 9, 13, and 17 by Sex, 2012.

SOURCE: National Center for Education Statistics, NAEP Data Explorer, http://nces.ed.gov /nationsreportcard/lttdata/report.aspx.

which girls and boys are retained in each grade from 1994–1995 through 2009–2010. Although both girls and boys have high retention rates at grade one, boys' are more than half a percentage higher than girls'. Rates are much more similar from second through sixth grade, and then the gap between boys and girls begins to grow again, such that by ninth grade, boys are more than one percentage point more likely than girls to be retained. Overall, the result is that about 2.2% of girls experience retention at some grade level compared to 2.6% of boys.

TEST SCORES—NAEP AND SAT

While much has been made about "innate" ability differences by sex, there appears to be little evidence that there are large gaps. Girls are commonly thought to be better at verbal skills—reading and writing—than boys. Figure 6-5 shows that girls do score slightly higher than boys on National

Table 6-2   Average Critical Reading, Mathematics, and
Writing SAT Scores by Sex, 2013

	Females	Males
Critical Reading	494	499
Mathematics	499	531
Writing	493	482

SOURCE: College Board, *2013 College-Bound Seniors: Total Group Profile Report*, 2013, http://media.collegeboard.com /digitalServices/pdf/research/2013/TotalGroup-2013.pdf.

Assessment of Educational Progress (NAEP) tests, but not by a large amount. Girls appear to maintain this slight advantage throughout their school years. Math scores show a different pattern, though. Girls and boys, at age nine, initially score about even on NAEP math tests (at least in 2012). However, boys gain more advantage as they go through school, with the largest gap between boys and girls occurring at age 17. It is puzzling that this gap grows as time goes on. One wonders how much of this has to do with how boys and girls are treated within schools and how much occurs in families and peer groups as students grow older.

Unlike NAEP scores, the SAT scores shown in table 6–2 show larger advantages for males in mathematics and a slight advantage, though very small, for males in critical reading. In 2013, for instance, males scored 499 on the critical reading SAT, while females scored 494. In math, the gap was larger, with males scoring 531 on average, compared to females scoring 499. Only in writing did females experience an advantage with a score of 493, compared to males' 482.

SPECIAL EDUCATION AND COURSE-TAKING

Boys and girls may be disproportionately represented in some classes based on perceptions of their abilities. For example, boys may be more likely to be identified as having disabilities and, because of that, may be placed in separate classes for all or part of some school days, or receive

Table 6–3   Sex Composition of Students Aged 6–12 and 13–17 Served by the
Individuals with Disabilities Education Act by Disability Type, 2003

	Age 6–12		Age 13–17	
	MALE	FEMALE	MALE	FEMALE
All disabilities	67%	33%	66%	34%
Autism	83%	17%	85%	15%
Emotional disturbance	80%	20%	77%	23%
Hearing impairments	56%	44%	52%	48%
Intellectual disability or developmental delay	56%	44%	56%	44%
Multiple disabilities	65%	35%	57%	43%
Specific learning disabilities	67%	33%	66%	34%
Speech or language impairments	66%	34%	62%	38%
Visual impairments	57%	43%	53%	47%

SOURCE: Kris Zorigan and Jennifer Job, *Gender in Special Education,* Learn NC, University of North Carolina School of Education, www.learnnc.org/lp/pages/6817#noteref1.

supplemental services. Table 6–3 shows the sex composition of those identified with particular types of disabilities in 2003. The table shows that, even though boys and girls are roughly half each of the school population, boys make up about two-thirds of those with identified disabilities. The differences between boys and girls are greatest for those disabilities that might require more subjective judgments: emotional disturbances and specific learning disabilities, for example. The differences are smallest for hearing and visual impairments, which may be the most straightforward to assess. In addition to those with identified disabilities, schools also create special education plans for students who are identified as gifted or talented, usually through a battery of IQ and other tests, through assessments of teachers, parents, and other adults, and often in consultation with school psychologists. At this end of the spectrum, girls are slightly overrepresented compared to boys, with 7.0% of elementary schools girls in such programs compared to 6.3% of boys in 2006.[8]

Although girls are less likely to have identified disabilities that might require remediation and are more likely to be identified for gifted and

Table 6-4 Percentages of Females and Males Taking Advanced Math and Science
Courses by Course Type and Year, 1982–2004

	Females	*Males*
Precalculus		
1982	4.5%	5.1%
1992	11.4%	10.5%
2004	20.1%	17.6%
Calculus		
1982	5.3%	6.6%
1992	10.3%	11.2%
2004	13.5%	14.7%
Chemistry I or Physics I		
1982	15.1%	14.7%
1992	29.8%	24.3%
2004	36.8%	29.8%
Chemistry I and Physics I		
1982	4.4%	7.6%
1992	12.0%	12.5%
2004	16.6%	18.2%
Chemistry II, Physics II, or Advanced Biology		
1982	14.9%	14.3%
1992	14.1%	14.5%
2004	18.8%	18.0%

SOURCE: National Center for Education Statistics, Institute for Education Sciences, *Advanced Mathematics and Science Coursetaking in the Spring High School Senior Classes of 1982, 1992, and 2004: Statistical Analysis Report.* NCES 2007–312. (Washington, DC: US Department of Education, 2007), figures 3 and 19.

talented programs, they are also less likely to be represented in some of the most challenging, advanced classes. Women are not as well represented as men in the Science, Technology, Engineering, and Math (STEM) fields, despite their overall better performance in schools and scores on the NAEP and SAT, which are equal or close to men's. One reason for their later underrepresentation in these fields may be that girls and boys make different choices about classes in high school. Table 6–4 uses data from the high school transcripts of three cohorts of tenth graders that

Table 6–5   Percentages of Females and Males Taking Advanced Placement Courses by Course Type, 2011

	Females	Males
Humanities	54.8%	45.2%
Math/Physical Sciences	45.6%	54.5%
Foreign Language	61.5%	38.5%
Biology	54.1%	45.1%
Computer Science	15.9%	84.1%
Social Sciences	50.8%	49.2%

SOURCE: Krista D. Mattern, Emily J. Shaw, and Maureen Ewing, *Advanced Placement® Exam Participation Is AP® Exam Participation and Performance Related to Choice of College Major?*, Research Report 2011–6, College Board, 2011, https://research.collegeboard.org/sites/default /files/publications/2012/7/researchreport-2011–6-ap-participation-performance-major-choice .pdf.

completed high school in the 1980s, 1990s, and 2000s. It shows that, although girls are more likely than boys to take precalculus as their highest math course, boys are more likely to complete calculus. Girls are more likely to complete chemistry I or physics I as their most advanced science courses, while boys are more likely to take both. However, girls are more likely to complete chemistry II, physics II, or an advanced biology course than boys, though the difference is small. Although more students overall are opting to take advanced math and science courses over time, the differences in enrollment between boys and girls have remained stable over the decades.

Women are also unequally represented among math and science Advanced Placement courses, though they are better represented among other types of Advanced Placement courses. Table 6–5 shows the sex composition of the AP course-takers for a sample of students entering four-year universities in fall 2006. Of those who took AP math or physical science courses, less than half were women. The difference between men and women is most dramatic for computer science AP classes. In this sample, only 15.9% of those taking such classes were women. However, for biology, foreign languages, and humanities AP classes, women are

Table 6-6   Percentage of Students Receiving Various Types of School Discipline by Sex in 2011–2012

	Boys	Girls
In-school suspension	67%	33%
Single out-of-school suspension	68%	32%
Multiple out-of-school suspensions	72%	28%
Expulsion	74%	26%

SOURCE: US Department of Education Office for Civil Rights, *Civil Rights Data Collection: Data Snapshot: School Discipline,* Issue Brief No. 1, March 2014, www2.ed.gov/about/offices/list/ocr/docs/crdc-discipline-snapshot.pdf.

overrepresented compared to men. Social science AP classes seem to have the most equal representations of men and women.

DISCIPLINARY ACTIONS

Table 6–6 shows that boys are more likely to be subject to various types of school discipline compared to girls. While boys and girls roughly make up about 50% each of the school population, boys received 67% of in-school suspensions and 68% of single suspensions, and are 72% of those who are suspended multiple times. Almost three-quarters of those who are expelled from school are boys.

Researchers speculate on the reasons for these differences. Girls and boys may be socialized differently at home, in schools, and by peers such that girls learn and are rewarded for behavior that does not challenge authority, while boys may be taught that behaviors that challenge authority are "masculine."[9] Teachers may expect boys to be less well behaved, may notice boy's behavior more than girls, and may punish it more often. Regardless of the causes, the increased likelihood of punishment may discourage boys from high academic achievement and from continuing their education in high school or beyond. Researchers have noted that school discipline presents an example of how "intersectionality" happens in schools: black boys appear to experience disproportionately more school

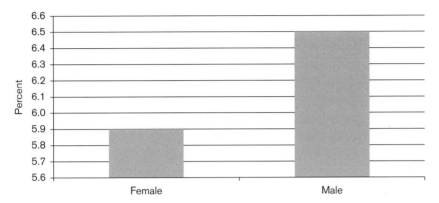

Figure 6-6. Percentage of 15-24 Year Olds Not Enrolled in Schools with No Degree by Sex, 2011.

SOURCE: Jessica Davis and Kurt Bauman, *School Enrollment in the United States: 2011 Population Characteristics*, 2013, table 1, US Census Bureau.

punishments than white boys and black girls. Scholars argue that black boys and men are more likely to be perceived as "dangerous" and "threatening" and that leads school officials to both notice and interpret behaviors as "menacing."[10]

DROPOUT AND COLLEGE ENROLLMENT

In part due to differential treatment and experiences, or worse performance in school, young men appear to drop out of school and not complete high school degrees more than young women. Figure 6-6 shows that 6.5% of 15- to 24-year-old males were not enrolled in school and had not completed a high school degree in 2011, compared with 5.9% of females.

Even among those eligible for college—those who had completed high school degrees—women were more likely to enroll in college than men, although that has not always been the case. Male high school graduates were more likely to enroll in or complete some college up until 1980, when the situation reversed. Currently, almost 70% of women high school graduates ages 14 to 24 enroll in or complete some college compared to a little over 60% of men. (See figure 6-7.)

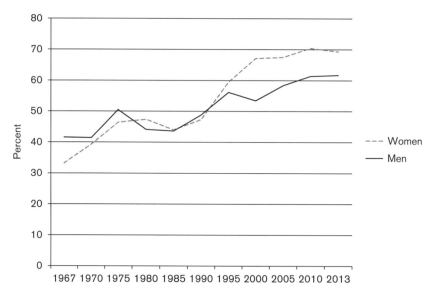

Figure 6-7. Percentage of 14- to 24-Year-Old High School Graduates Who Have Enrolled in or Completed Some College, Selected Years, 1967–2013.

SOURCE: US Census Bureau, Current Population Survey Historical Data, table A-5a, www.census .gov/hhes/school/data/cps/historical/index.html.

EXPLANATIONS FOR GENDER DIFFERENCES IN EDUCATION

Unlike children of different races or socioeconomic backgrounds, children of different genders attend pretty much the same types of public schools with few differences in access to resources, good teachers, and similar peers. Where boys and girls may differ is in how the individual character-istics that are associated with the gender roles they adopt are taught and rewarded or punished by families and schools. While some believe, as the former Harvard president Larry Summers famously suggested, that boys and girls show innate differences in preferences for particular toys or activities, other researchers focus on how girls and boys are influenced or socialized to have different preferences and behaviors.

Some researchers find differences in the ways that children are social-ized within families.[11] How mothers and fathers in traditional, heterosexual families divide labor outside and within the household influences children's beliefs about their appropriate gender roles.[12] Mothers who work outside the home have been reported to have daughters who want to work outside the home,[13] and parents' occupational expectations—whether they follow traditional gender stereotypes or expect nontraditional jobs— are highly associated with children's own expectations and eventual choices.[14] There may be differences in the roles and responsibilities that children are assigned within the home that are gender-based, particularly among immigrant and nonwhite ethnic groups. For example, Hmong teenage girls are expected to marry early and take care of their spouse's family, while girls may also assume more responsibility for childcare and other jobs in Mexican families.[15] Sometimes this different treatment limits the amount or type of education that girls seek, but for other recently immigrated families, traditional gender roles lead to tighter control of girls than boys. This then leads to higher achievement for girls, as in the case of Vietnamese in New Orleans.[16] In Nancy Lopez's study of Dominican, West Indian, and Haitian adolescents, girls expected to get and attained much more education than their male peers because they perceived that they would likely have to support themselves and possibly their children without the help of a spouse. This motivated girls to complete education and to major in practical fields in which they would be likely to find stable employment, like nursing.[17]

Schools also send messages to girls and boys about appropriate preferences, behaviors, and roles according to gender. Karin Martin describes how children are taught gendered behaviors as early as preschool. She finds that girls are more often reminded of their dress (to pull up tights, sit and play so as not to show underwear) than boys. Girls are more often told to use soft voices. Girls also are reminded to sit properly so as not to take up much space more than boys, and are often more discouraged from rambunctious play. Girls are more likely than boys to have behaviors redirected with specific instructions (for example, "stop yelling and come over here to help me pass out snacks").[18] The behaviors that girls are taught are often those that teachers reward (or at least punish less often) in schools. Students who are able to sit quietly and control their voices are perceived to be better students and, to the extent that elementary school teachers' assessments are particularly subjective, may be rewarded with better grades. This may be one reason that researchers identify a "boy problem" in schools, in which boys get disciplined more, have lower grades, and drop out more than girls. Boys may not be taught or have the same types of behavior reinforced in early schooling.

Ideas about "masculinity" and "femininity" may also be reinforced by students' peer groups, and by the peer cultures of schools more generally.[19] C.J. Pascoe talks about how masculine behaviors are reinforced by the term "fag" in American high schools. Boys use the term not to apply to those who identify as gay, but rather to police the masculinity of their peers. "Fag" is used to describe behaviors among straight boys that are not perceived as masculine.[20] Work in England by Paul Willis describes the very masculine identities reinforced by working-class peers.[21]

Schools may reinforce differences between genders that are learned and experienced in homes and in peer cultures. One more obvious way they may do so is through the formal curriculum. Boys and girls in coeducational schools often learn about the great men of history. Women who enter into history books like Betsy Ross or Florence Nightingale are noted for the feminine-type activities they perform—one as a seamstress and the other as a nurse, two traditionally feminine activities. Students may read books by male authors. In young children's literature, male and female characters fill different roles. Though there has been much effort to change the stereotyping in children's literature, often girls need to be rescued more than boys and boys more often do the rescuing. Students learn less about women's contributions to history, and traditional women's roles are stressed in history and literature. Women and men begin to see these differences in division of labor as natural or normal.

There are also ways that the informal or hidden curriculum influences students' ideas about appropriate gender roles. One is in the number of male and female role models students have, and in the division of labor between men and women in schools. Elementary and middle school teachers (approximately 81% in 2013, according to the Bureau of Labor Statistics)[22] are predominantly women, as are teachers' aides. Men are better represented higher in the school hierarchy. About half of school principals are men.[23] The lesson is that the higher the prestige, status, and pay of a position, the more likely it is to be occupied by a man. Men are the bosses or supervisors. One study suggests that children who attend schools with women principals have fewer gender stereotypes.[24]

Schools also reinforce gender segregation. Barrie Thorne shows how teachers often separate students into lines by gender. School chores may be gendered (who waters plants versus who carries milk cartons). Tables and desks may be arranged by gender. Playground activities are segregated by gender, with boys often occupying more space in fields for sports, while girls occupy smaller amounts of space nearer to schools for smaller games like hopscotch. Separation between boys and girls gets reinforced when girls chase boys and boys avoid them, and when girls are accused of having "girl germs" or "cooties." Thorne finds that even among teachers who consciously do not separate children by gender, very few intervene when students do so themselves. This separation is perceived to be "normal" or "natural," such that neither teachers nor students are critical of it.[25]

In high school, segregation into different activities in which identities are formed may become more important, as may peer opinion. For boys, athletics may be an important source of pride, prestige, and friendship, or they may be a source of pain and ostracism. Masculine identities are often formed on sports teams—"jocks" are often the most popular kids. "Masculine" attributes are thought to be taught and honed on sports teams—aggressiveness, competitiveness, self-confidence, teamwork, endurance, and notions of playing by rules and fair play.[26]

For girls, often athletics is not their main source of popularity (though this may be changing in large part because of Title IX). The most popular girls are often those girls who support male athletics. These supportive roles include managing male athletic teams or cheerleading. For girls, emotion may play a bigger role in their popularity. Identities are formed through connections with other people, with friends or cliques, or with boyfriends.[27]

DIFFERENCES IN STEM

Girls and boys begin to plan different futures for themselves in high school. And, in doing so, they plan different academic courses. Another way in which boys and girls differ is in the courses they choose to take in high school. Despite being lower-performing (getting lower grades), boys are more likely than girls (of the same ability levels) to take college preparatory classes. Girls take fewer elective math and science courses than boys. This is a puzzle for researchers.

Some have suggested that there are gender differences in spatial orientation and spatial reasoning abilities—whether genetic or taught differently to babies—that account for boys' preferences to study math and science.[28] Others, though, focus on how environmental differences shape these seemingly natural preferences. Parents may encourage different tastes and behaviors for boys and girls, for example. Teachers and peers may do the same. Ideas about the innate talents of boys for math and science (and girls for reading and writing) may lead to an orientation toward males in word problems. Sports may be used as examples in these problems, for instance. Boys, because of preconceived notions about their abilities, may have greater exposure to math both outside and inside schools. Ideas that boys may be more academically talented than girls have been studied in experiments in which researchers found that when students were asked to identify their genders before taking tests, girls performed worse than when they were not asked to identify as female. Researchers speculate that asking students to identify as female reminds them that their performance will be judged compared to males, which creates heightened performance anxiety and leads them to do worse on tests.[29]

It may be that career aspirations for girls are different from those of boys, though girls may get the same or better grades than boys. Girls may more often plan careers that will accommodate a family.[30] There may also be fewer role models for women in STEM fields than there are for men. Mentors provide contacts and information, are people to model behavior upon, and are people that show students that "people like them" can succeed. For women, it may be important to know that other women have "made it," and that therefore they can too.[31] In addition, teachers may use sex-typed examples of the professions. Doctors and scientists may always be pictured as men. Teachers may use the male pronoun when referring to doctors and the female pronoun when referring to nurses. Men are praised and called on more in class, and these patterns may be more likely to be observed more in classes that are taught by men, like math and the sciences.[32]

Table 6-7   Field of Bachelor's Degree for Bachelor's Degree Holders Aged
              25–39, 2009

Field	Percent Female
All Fields	*54.7*
Computers, Mathematics, and Statistics	30.6
Biological, Agricultural, and Environmental Science	52.9
Physical and Related Sciences	39.6
Psychology	74.9
Social Sciences	50.7
Engineering	20.1
Multidisciplinary Studies	60.7
Business	48.8
Education	78.5
Arts, Humanities, and Other	58.5

SOURCE: Julie Siebens and Camille L. Ryan, *Field of Bachelor's Degree in the United States: 2009: American Community Survey Reports. ACS-18,* United States Census Bureau, US Department of Commerce, 2012, table 2, www.census.gov /prod/2012pubs/acs-18.pdf.

These differences in preferences for STEM fields continue in college. Table 6–7 shows big differences in the majors of recent bachelor's degree recipients by sex. Women made up 54.7% of all bachelor's degree recipients between 25 and 39 years of age in 2009. If the percentage of women in a field exceeds 54.7%, women are overrepresented in that field. If it is lower, they are underrepresented. The table shows women are most underrepresented in engineering, with only 20% of engineering bachelor's degrees having been earned by women. This is followed by computers, mathematics, and statistics, with a little over 30% of degrees earned by women, and then physical sciences and related fields with a little under 40% achieving these degrees. Women are overrepresented most dramatically among those earning education degrees, with nearly 80% of education bachelor's degrees going to women. Women are also more likely to received degrees in psychology. About 75% of psychology bachelor's degrees go to women. Men and women are more equally represented in biology, the social sciences, and arts and humanities generally. The representation of women among doctoral degree recipients is very similar to their representation among bachelor's degree holders.[33]

SEXUAL ORIENTATION, GENDER IDENTITY, AND EDUCATION

Very little research has been done on how academic experiences differ by sexual orientation. Certainly, students who have expressed nonheterosexual and nonconventional gender identities have faced severe bullying and have felt isolated from other students. These students have been more likely to experience depression and are more likely to attempt and commit suicide.[34] School peer cultures have been shown to privilege masculine behaviors and ridicule those who do not conform through the use of terms to connote gay identity like "fag."[35] However, recently students with nonconforming gender and sexual identities have received more acceptance. Struggles over transgender students' right to use the bathrooms appropriate for their gender identity and to be included in social functions like proms as their chosen identities are more common in the media. For example, on March 5, 2015, National Public Radio aired a story called "Transgender Students Learn to Navigate School Halls" that described some schools' attempts to address issues of gender identity early as a way to create comfortable and safe spaces for non-gender-conforming students.[36]

ABILITY DIFFERENCES AND EDUCATIONAL EXPERIENCES

Students may also experience different academic environments because of physical, emotional, social, or learning disabilities. Before and into the early 1970s, students who were labeled as having a disability would often not be educated in public schools. These students were not guaranteed the right to public education and would be educated either in homes by parents or in institutions. Initial efforts were made to accommodate students with disabilities in public schools, but these were spotty and not well enforced. For example, in the late 1950s and early 1960s, federal monies were provided for training for teachers of students with disabilities and for the production of materials geared toward deaf, blind, and mentally challenged students. The Elementary and Secondary Education Act of 1965 provided states with grants to educate students with disabilities. It was not until 1975, though, with the passage of Public Law 42–142, the Education for All Handicapped Children Act, that public education would be guaranteed for children with disabilities. The most current version of this law, which changed names in 1990, is the Individuals with Disabilities in Education Act, or IDEA. Prior to the amendments of IDEA, students with such disabilities were concentrated in separate classrooms so that they might receive more specialized services. However, starting in the 1990s with IDEA, schools have moved from this model to one of inclusion of students with disabilities in the general curriculum and classrooms. Students who have recognized disabilities often spend all or part of their days in classrooms with students without such designations. Students are often granted additional support in the form of aides or supplemental services outside of the classroom. Individual Education Plans (IEPs) are developed for students with recognized disabilities so that their needs may be better met. Plans are made to identify and provide for children early, even before school begins, and to accommodate their transitions to adulthood. Consistent with the No Child Left Behind Act of 2001, schools must report on and be accountable for the progress of students with disabilities. As a result of these measures, more students with disabilities are graduating now than ever before.[37]

Students with disabilities, though, may struggle not only because of their disability, but because of the label. Students with disabilities may be assessed with alternative testing requirements, and there may be confusion over who can and should be provided with these alternatives. There is often confusion about the rights and responsibilities of schools of choice like charter schools to students with disabilities, though such schools are not legally allowed to exclude children with disabilities.

Table 6–8 shows that students with recognized disabilities do indeed score lower on math and reading NAEP scores and are more likely to drop out of school—about twice as likely as students without disabilities. The reasons for these differences are likely complex and could include the nature of the disability, teachers' and parents' lowered expectations,

Table 6-8   NAEP Average Math and Reading Scores at Age 9 in 2012 and Percentage
of 16–24 Year Olds Not Enrolled in School and without a High School
Degree

	No Disability Status	Disability Status
Math NAEP aged 9 in 2012	247	216
Reading NAEP aged 9 in 2012	225	183
Percentage of 16 to 24 year olds not enrolled in school and without a high school diploma in 2009	7.5%	15.5%

sources: National Center for Education Statistics, Institute of Education Sciences, Generated with the NAEP Data Explorer, June 11, 2015, http://nces.ed.gov/nationsreportcard/lttdata /report.aspx; and US Department of Education, Institute of Education Sciences, *Trends in High School Dropout and Completion Rates in the United States: 1972–2009*, Compendium Report, 2011, table 6.

the stigma of the label faced by the student, and learning environments that may differ from those of students without recognized disabilities.

While there are differences in students' school experiences by gender, sexual orientation, and nonconforming sexual orientations and gender identities, as well as by recognized disabilities, students are rarely segregated across schools. Students may be treated differently within schools because of these distinctions, and so in some ways, these differences between students are not like those between students of different socioeconomic or racial and ethnic backgrounds. Students with different amounts of resources and students of different racial or ethnic backgrounds often go to very different types of schools, leading to different types of inequality between them.

The next chapter explores inequality in schools internationally. How does the United States compare to other nations? Does the experience of other nations suggest that inequality is "natural" or "normal"? To what extent might differences in school's purpose and organization influence inequality in other nations? Can the United States learn anything from the experiences of other countries?

7 Educational Inequality in Other Nations

The previous three chapters have shown varying degrees of inequality by socioeconomic background, race and ethnicity, and gender in schools in the United States. We have asked the questions: What can schools do about this? Are these inequalities largely due to inequalities in other facets of students' lives? One way we may be able to gain perspective on educational inequality in the United States and its causes is to look to other nations. How much inequality in educational outcomes across socioeconomic background and gender do other nations experience? How might the organization of and ideology behind their schooling contribute to differences between nations?

The globalization and internationalization of education have led to greater similarities across schools worldwide, generally. Over time schools across the globe are becoming more alike.[1] These similarities affect educational inequality within nations. For example, one way that educational systems across nations are similar is that they all have experienced the expansion of access to schooling. While primary schooling is nearly universal for the world's young children, secondary school is fast approaching this ideal. The next frontier in school expansion is at the tertiary level. Access to postsecondary schooling is growing at a faster rate than primary or secondary schooling, mostly because only small proportions of the population attend postsecondary schools.[2]

A second way that globalization and internationalization have affected inequality in schooling is by promoting declining gender gaps in educational access across nations. Gender inequality has been an ideal within most individual nations' education systems, and it is explicitly expressed by international organizations like the United Nations. This ideal has become institutionalized in school practices, and is spreading worldwide. Another growing similarity among schools across the globe is the importance of merit in achieving educational success. Part of the ideology accompanying mass education is that students should be judged on merit rather than social background; thus they should be given the same tools to allow meritocratic processes to sort them. As education systems become less national and more international in character, struggles between social classes within nations have less force to shape education than the powerful international and institutional ideology of meritocracy. Despite this growing belief in meritocracy, though, a fourth trend that scholars note is the greater influence that parents' socioeconomic background has on school outcomes for children. As nations further develop their education systems, the quality of institutions tends to improve and become more uniform. As the quality of institutions within a nation becomes less variable, institution quality has less influence on variation in individual students' outcomes. Variation across socioeconomic background becomes more important.

Since scholars have argued that globalization and internationalization lead to similarities in education systems across the world, is inequality in US education that different from what is found in other nations? Is the United States part of the larger global movement toward greater gender equality but growing socioeconomic inequality in educational outcomes? Or is the United States more of an exception compared to other nations? In this chapter, I am going to place the US education system in an international context. How does educational inequality in test scores compare to that found in other countries? What are some structural and organizational differences between education in the United States and education in other countries that may influence inequality? Do the purposes of education differ in other places, and if so, how? And how might this affect educational inequality?

Scores from tests like the Program for International Student Assessment, or PISA, and the Trends in International Math and Science Study, or TIMSS, are publicized frequently, and often these are used to compare the quality of education across nations. Scholars, like Linda Darling-Hammond, suggest that these test scores reflect both educational *quality* and educational *inequality*.[3] Shown in table 7-1, the latest PISA results from 2012 show the United States close to or below the mean in math, reading, and science for the 65 nations that are included in the PISA testing. These results are interpreted to suggest that the United States is not keeping up with other countries, that the United States is not educating students in science and math particularly in the best ways, and that the United States cannot compete with the education systems of Singapore, Taiwan, Korea, Japan, and, more recently, Finland.

The most recent (2011) TIMSS results present a somewhat different picture. I present table 7-2 to show the differences in eighth grade math scores across countries. The TIMSS also reports differences in fourth grade math and fourth and eighth grade science scores across countries. The table shows Korea and Singapore with the highest mean scores. Finland is ranked eighth. The United States is just below Finland, but ahead of Great Britain, Australia, Sweden, and Norway. On TIMSS tests, the United States is among the top scoring countries, rather than below the median of the group.

Linda Darling-Hammond in her book, *The Flat World and Education*, suggests that these scores very much reflect educational inequality, rather than educational quality necessarily.[4] She contends that if education were improved for those who score the lowest—those in the poorest schools with the fewest resources—then the average score of the United States would be more comparable to those of the top-scoring nations. Darling-Hammond argues that quality and inequality are inextricably intertwined. The United States cannot raise its quality, as measured by PISA or TIMMS scores, until it deals with the inequality in the education system. As I will show in this chapter, those countries with higher overall scores on these achievement tests also tend to have smaller differences by family income,

Table 7-1   Mean Math, Reading, and Science Scores and Percentages of Low and
High Math Achievers by Country, PISA, 2012

	Mean Math Score	Share of Low Math Achievers	Share of High Math Achievers	Mean Reading Score	Mean Science Score
OECD average	494	23.1%	12.6%	496	501
Shanghai-China	613	3.8%	55.4%	570	580
Singapore	573	8.3%	40.0%	542	551
Hong Kong-China	561	8.5%	33.7%	545	555
Chinese Taipei	560	12.8%	37.2%	523	523
Korea	554	9.1%	30.9%	536	538
Macao-China	538	10.8%	24.3%	509	521
Japan	536	11.1%	23.7%	538	547
Liechtenstein	535	14.1%	24.8%	516	525
Switzerland	531	12.4%	21.4%	509	515
Netherlands	523	14.8%	19.3%	511	522
Estonia	521	10.5%	14.6%	516	541
Finland	519	12.3%	15.3%	524	545
Canada	518	13.8%	16.4%	523	525
Poland	518	14.4%	16.7%	518	526
Belgium	515	18.9%	19.4%	509	505
Germany	514	17.7%	17.5%	508	524
Vietnam	511	14.2%	13.3%	508	528
Austria	506	18.7%	14.3%	490	506
Australia	504	19.7%	14.8%	512	521
Ireland	501	16.9%	10.7%	523	522
Slovenia	501	20.1%	13.7%	481	514
Denmark	500	16.8%	10.0%	496	498
New Zealand	500	22.6%	15.0%	512	516
Czech Republic	499	21.0%	12.9%	493	508
France	495	22.4%	12.9%	505	499
United Kingdom	494	21.8%	11.8%	499	514
Iceland	493	21.5%	11.2%	483	478
Latvia	491	19.9%	8.0%	489	502
Luxembourg	490	24.3%	11.2%	488	491
Norway	489	22.3%	9.4%	504	495
Portugal	487	24.9%	10.6%	488	489
Italy	485	24.7%	9.9%	490	494
Spain	484	23.6%	8.0%	488	496

Russian Federation	482	24.0%	7.8%	475	486
Slovak Republic	482	27.5%	11.0%	463	471
United States	**481**	**25.8%**	**8.8%**	**498**	**497**
Lithuania	479	26.0%	8.1%	477	496
Sweden	478	27.1%	8.0%	483	485
Hungary	477	28.1%	9.3%	488	494
Croatia	471	29.9%	7.0%	485	491
Israel	466	33.5%	9.4%	486	470
Greece	453	35.7%	3.9%	477	467
Serbia	449	38.9%	4.6%	446	445
Turkey	448	42.0%	5.9%	475	463
Romania	445	40.8%	3.2%	438	439
Cyprus	440	42.0%	3.7%	449	438
Bulgaria	439	43.8%	4.1%	436	446
United Arab Emirates	434	46.3%	3.5%	442	448
Kazakhstan	432	45.2%	0.9%	393	425
Thailand	427	49.7%	2.6%	441	444
Chile	423	51.5%	1.6%	441	445
Malaysia	421	51.8%	1.3%	398	420
Mexico	413	54.7%	0.6%	424	415
Montenegro	410	56.6%	1.0%	422	410
Uruguay	409	55.8%	1.4%	411	416
Costa Rica	407	59.9%	0.6%	441	429
Albania	394	60.7%	0.8%	394	397
Brazil	391	67.1%	0.8%	410	405
Argentina	388	66.5%	0.3%	396	406
Tunisia	388	67.7%	0.8%	404	398
Jordan	386	68.6%	0.6%	399	409
Colombia	376	73.8%	0.3%	403	399
Qatar	376	69.6%	2.0%	388	384
Indonesia	375	75.7%	0.3%	396	382
Peru	368	74.6%	0.6%	384	373

SOURCE: Data are from Snapshot of Performance in Mathematics, Reading, and Science, PISA 2012 Results in Focus, OECD, www.oecd.org/pisa/keyfindings/PISA-2012-results-snapshot-Volume-I-ENG.pdf.

NOTE: Low achievers refer to those who scored below level 2. High achievers are those who scored in level 5 or 6.

Table 7–2   Selected Mean Math Scores of Eighth
Graders by Country, TIMSS, 2011

Education system	Average score
TIMSS scale average	500
Korea, Rep. of	613
Singapore	611
Chinese Taipei-CHN	*609*
Hong Kong-CHN	*586*
Japan	570
Russian Federation	539
Israel	516
Finland	514
United States	**509**
England-GBR	507
Hungary	505
Australia	505
Slovenia	505
Italy	498
New Zealand	488
Kazakhstan	487
Sweden	484
Ukraine	479
Norway	475
Armenia	467
Romania	458
United Arab Emirates	456
Turkey	452
Lebanon	449
Malaysia	440
Thailand	427
Tunisia	425
Chile	416

SOURCE: International Association for the Evaluation of
Educational Achievement, Trends in Mathematics and Science
Study (TIMSS), 2011, http://nces.ed.gov/timss/table11_3.
NOTE: Places in italics are not entire nations. They are either
cities within nations, or, in the cases of England, just one part of
Great Britain.

suggesting less inequality in school experiences and potentially less inequality in adult outcomes.

One difficulty in comparing educational inequality internationally is in figuring out how to measure it. There are few data that allow for good international comparisons. The United Nations Educational, Scientific, and Cultural Organization, or UNESCO, summarizes information from the PISA exams across nations and across various indicators like wealth, gender, and rural/urban residence. Not all countries provide data on all measures, but below I provide a sampling of some countries with more educational inequality and some countries with less educational inequality than the United States on two educational outcomes: achieving basic proficiency in reading and in math at the upper-secondary level. Data for these comparisons come from the 2012 PISA. To make comparisons with the United States, I select five countries with higher levels of inequality and five with lower levels to show the extent of inequality and also the variety of countries and regions in these groups. Generally, the United States falls somewhere in the middle of the distribution when countries are ranked according to their levels of inequality, usually a bit above the median. For example, of the 70 countries reporting wealth inequality in basic math proficiency, the United States ranked forty-ninth (from most to least inequality). So, while inequality between rich and poor, males and females, and rural and urban residents is certainly not the worst in the United States, there are also places where it is better. I will provide an educational profile of two of these cases at the end of the chapter.

Figure 7–1 shows the percentage of those who are in the poorest income quintile (lighter bars) who achieved basic proficiency in reading compared to those in the richest quintile (darker bars). Some countries have low levels of proficiency overall, like Peru, Tunisia, and Jordan. These countries also experience the highest levels of inequality between richest and poorest. The United States generally has a high percentage of its richest students achieving proficiency (92%), only slightly lower than Singapore (95%) and Korea (94%) and a bit greater than Germany (91%) and Finland (89%). However, the poorest students in the United States fare worse, with about 77% achieving reading proficiency, compared to 84% in Singapore, 85% in Germany, 89% in Finland, and 91% in Korea. Countries

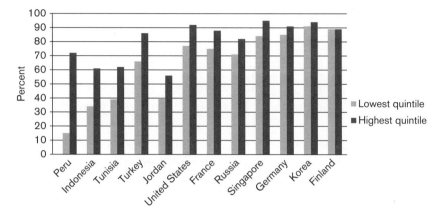

Figure 7-1. Inequality among Those Who Achieved Basic Proficiency in Upper Secondary Education in Reading for Selected Countries, Poorest Compared to Richest Quintile, 2012.

SOURCE: World Inequality Database on Education, UNESCO, www.education-inequalities.org/.

like Russia and France have a smaller gap between rich and poor, but this is largely due to the lower percentage of the richest students achieving basic proficiency.

Figure 7–2 shows the percentage of those who are in the poorest income quintile (lighter) who achieved basic proficiency in math compared to those in the richest quintile (darker). Some countries have low levels of proficiency overall, like Peru again and, to some extent, Malaysia and Greece. New Zealand and the United States experience similar levels of both proficiency and inequality, with about 88% of the lowest quintile achieving basic proficiency and 96% of the highest. This results in a gap between the richest and poorest of about eight percentage points. Other countries have both higher levels of proficiency overall and lower levels of inequality. Austria, Ireland, and Australia have anywhere from 91% to 93% achieving proficiency in the lowest quintile and 96% and 98% in the highest. Gaps here are four to seven percentage points. Korea and the Netherlands do even better, with 96% of the lowest quintiles achieving proficiency and 98 % to 99% of the highest, resulting in gaps between the richest and poorest of only two to three percentage points.

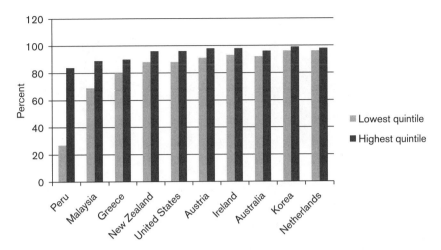

Figure 7–2. Inequality among Those Who Achieved Basic Proficiency in Upper Secondary Education in Math for Selected Countries, Poorest Compared to Richest Quintile, 2012.

SOURCE: World Inequality Database on Education, UNESCO, www.education-inequalities.org/.

In figure 7–3, I show gender inequality in achieving basic reading proficiency in upper-secondary school, according to the 2012 PISA. For all of the countries on which UNESCO reports, females have an advantage over males. That advantage is greatest in Jordan, where 68% of females have achieved basic proficiency but only 31% of males have. Other examples of places with a large female advantage include Thailand and Sweden. Even Finland has a slightly larger gender gap than the United States, but it should also be noted that a higher percentage of both males and females achieve basic reading proficiency there than in the United States. The United States falls near the middle of the distribution of countries with 90% of females and 79% of males achieving basic proficiency, for a gap of 11 percentage points. Countries that have smaller gender gaps in reading proficiency tend to have a greater percentage of males who achieve proficiency. In New Zealand, for example, although the same percentage of females achieves proficiency as in the United States (90%), a slightly higher percentage (80%) of males do. In Singapore and Korea, 87% and

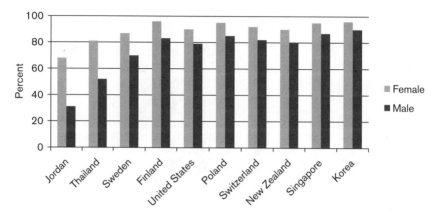

Figure 7-3. Inequality among Those Who Achieved Basic Proficiency in Upper Secondary Education in Reading for Selected Countries, Females and Males, 2012.
SOURCE: World Inequality Database on Education, UNESCO, www.education-inequalities.org/.

90% of males achieve basic reading proficiency, resulting in gender gaps of eight and six percentage points.

Figure 7–4 shows the percentages of males and females in selected countries who have achieved basic math proficiency in upper-secondary school, according to PISA 2012 results. There are a few countries in the dataset where males outperform females, like Costa Rica and Croatia, but for the most part, where there are gaps between the percentages achieving proficiency in math, females have the advantage. This can be seen in Sweden and Thailand. For many other countries, though, the genders have achieved parity. In the United States, 93% of both males and females have achieved basic proficiency in math, and in Japan, Poland, Vietnam, and Canada, those percentages are 97% for both males and females.

In both figures, figure 7–5 and figure 7–6, I show inequalities in reading and math proficiency in selected nations according to whether students attend school in rural or urban locations. Inequality between rural and urban schools in the United States is quite low compared to other nations, though there is some. About 79% of rural students in the United States achieve basic reading proficiency compared to 82% of urban students.

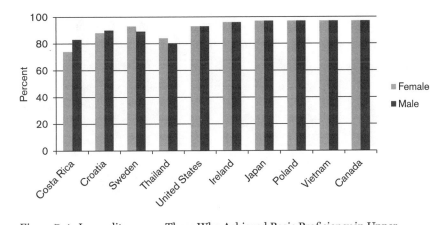

Figure 7-4. Inequality among Those Who Achieved Basic Proficiency in Upper Secondary Education in Math for Selected Countries, Females and Males, 2012.

SOURCE: World Inequality Database on Education, UNESCO, www.education-inequalities.org/.

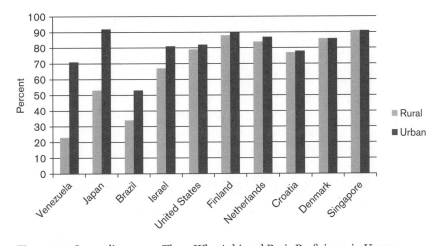

Figure 7-5. Inequality among Those Who Achieved Basic Proficiency in Upper Secondary Education in Reading for Selected Countries, Rural and Urban Students, 2012.

SOURCE: World Inequality Database on Education, UNESCO, www.education-inequalities.org/.

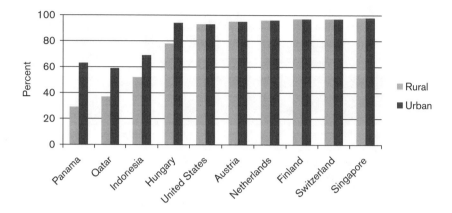

Figure 7-6. Inequality among Those Who Achieved Basic Proficiency in Upper Secondary Education in Math for Selected Countries, Rural and Urban Students, 2012.

SOURCE: World Inequality Database on Education, UNESCO, www.education-inequalities.org/.

Few nations have much smaller gaps—Finland and the Netherlands have similar gaps of about two to three percentage points, while there is almost no gap between rural and urban students in Croatia, Denmark, and Singapore. In Singapore, this is not surprising, since only a very small portion of this small nation-state could be considered rural. There are substantial gaps in other countries, though, in nations with both large and small rural populations. The largest gap between rural and urban students is in Venezuela, though the gap in Japan is also very large. In math, the results are similar. There are large gaps in math proficiency in countries like Panama, Qatar, Indonesia, and Hungary, but no gaps in the United States and nations like Austria, the Netherlands, Finland, Switzerland, and Singapore.

There are many other educational outcomes on which one could compare inequality across nations. For example, UNESCO collects data on preschool education rates, the percentage of adolescents who are not in school, the percentages of students who have never been to school, literacy, the transition to secondary schooling, mean years of schooling, and other things. Unfortunately, UNESCO only has data for the United States on PISA scores, so for comparability to the United States, I have only presented those above. UNESCO also collects information on dimensions in which inequality could be manifest like language spoken at home, ethnicity, and religion, but not consistently for all countries. Again, for comparison with the United States, there is only information on income quintile, gender, and rural/urban residence.[5]

WHAT ACCOUNTS FOR HIGH OR LOW EDUCATIONAL INEQUALITY?

The reasons that educational outcomes in a country are more or less unequal are likely a result of many different factors. The wealth and development of countries affect the amounts and types of resources they can devote to schools, and the culture and values of a nation may influence the ways it organizes its educational system(s). Underlying ideas about collectivism, individualism, fairness, competition, and other values may influence how students get guided or sorted into different parts of the educational system. Nations may have different ideas about how schools connect to the larger labor market, which influence how they structure education. In this chapter, though, I suggest some organizational and curricular differences between countries that might influence educational inequality within them. I end with two different cases, countries in East Asia (China, Taiwan, and Japan) and then Finland, to provide examples of countries where educational inequality is less than it is in the United States.

National Differences

Internationalization has led to a greater degree of decentralization of education in many countries, but the extent of centralization versus decentralization remains one major difference in the organization of educational systems across nations. A high degree of centralization occurs when one institution, usually the national government, has strict control over the functioning of schools in a country. For example, in some countries, government ministries control public preschool, elementary and secondary school, and postsecondary education. They may also strictly supervise private education institutions. These government ministries can control which students go to which schools, through exams or applications. They control personnel, perhaps directly hiring and firing teachers or assigning teachers to various schools in different parts of the country. They may directly control the training and professional development of teachers through government-run or affiliated teacher-training colleges. They may provide incentives to become a teacher, through subsidized or free tuition at postsecondary teacher-training universities or other institutions. They may control the curriculum, such that students in a nation are taught the same subject matter with the same materials, and they may control assessment with national examinations. Finally, they allocate funding to schools. Funding comes from government revenue and is distributed according to how government ministries see fit. Some examples of highly centralized educational systems are Finland, Greece, and Vietnam.

An educational system is highly decentralized in cases where national governments have less control over schools. Personnel decisions, teacher training, curricular matters, assessments, and decisions about funding may not be carried out by agencies at the federal level or may be left to private institutions. The United States is arguably among the most decentralized educational systems. The federal government exerts little control over schooling decisions. Its powers are limited to distributing or withholding funds from Title I that provide resources for schools serving high-poverty populations. Important decisions about education—particularly about funding—are left to states and local school districts. Personnel decisions are made at the local level, as are many curricular decisions (though efforts have been made to standardize curricula within states and even federally with the promotion of the "Common Core," to be discussed in the next chapter). Despite the mandate to test from the No Child Left Behind Act, states use their own assessment instruments and make their own determinations about which schools meet accountability standards and which schools do not. And curricular materials and assessments are not often developed by national or state offices or by local teachers, but rather created by private organizations and corporations (some for-profit, others not) like Pearson, the College Board, the Educational Testing Service, and a variety of textbook, curriculum development, and assessment companies. This decentralization is one reason why it has been so difficult to promote policies like desegregation in schools in the United States.

When comparing centralized versus decentralized systems, it may seem that decentralized systems have less means to create equal conditions in schools. Researchers note that when institutions are decentralized, there is no central body monitoring funding, personnel, admissions, curricula, or assessment. Schools may receive very different amounts of funding per student, as they do in the United States, based on state and local revenues (especially if tax bases and rates differ dramatically by place). Talented teachers may be drawn to places where the pay is higher—typically those places that have more revenue. Governments that do not have official policies toward the inclusion of ethnic minorities or women are less able to ensure and enforce equal representation of these groups in particular schools. Advantaged (wealthier, majority race) parents may choose to live in areas served by these resource-rich schools, further contributing to inequality. However, inequalities based on political party or affiliation may be weakened. When governmental elites—for example, members of particular parties—have a lot of influence, centralization can lead to children of these elites reaping educational advantages like admission to particular schools.[6]

Other national differences that may matter include the wealth or general development of a country. Researchers have long found that there is a relationship between how economically developed a country is (which is often measured by gross domestic product) and how universal its education is.[7] More developed countries tend to have education provided at younger and older ages—often with fully funded or subsidized preschools, and elementary and secondary schools. Some nations even provide partially or fully subsidized postsecondary education. This relationship is not without exception, though. The United States, one of the most economically developed nations, does not provide universal access to preschool, nor are its subsidies for postsecondary education high compared to other nations. More developed nations tend to extend education to all groups in society—girls, minorities, the poor, and those living in rural or remote locations.

While this association has been observed, there is some question about whether development "causes" more education or more education "causes" development. Certainly the greater national revenue that comes from increasing economic development can be used to fund schools more equitably, though this does not have to be the case necessarily. It is also possible that nations invest in education, particularly in the education of the least advantaged of its citizens, as a strategy for increasing workplace productivity, thereby increasing economic development.

Other differences that may have consequences for educational inequality in a country, and are related to development, are the geography and urbanization of a nation. Highly urbanized countries, those that rely less on agriculture, may expand educational institutions to train their industrial workforce. At lower levels of education, emphasis on job-related skills may involve more mathematical, scientific, and practical skills, and this may decrease educational inequality in outcomes between groups in schools. However, at higher levels of education, as more poor and disadvantaged students remain in schools, initial inequality in test scores may grow. When secondary schools include not just the socially advantaged or talented youths, differences in achievement scores between groups may increase.

The geography of a country may also play a role in educational inequality in some nations. Countries with remote regions that are difficult to travel to or that have large minority populations living in those regions (many with different languages or cultural traditions from the majority members of the nation) may face barriers to providing education and maintaining educational quality in these places.

Countries also have a variety of cultural traditions and values borne from very different histories. It is difficult to say how these values, beliefs, and traditions influence the educational systems of countries, particularly the levels of inequality that are seen. Much has been made of the Confucian tradition of many nations like China, Korea, Taiwan, and Vietnam. Confucian ideology promotes strict hierarchy and relations of authority, values effort over ability, and elevates the role of the scholar in society. In traditionally Confucian societies, the highest aspirations were to become a scholar, to pass the highest level of examinations. Those who did would be publicly celebrated with lavish parties thrown in villages and their names would be inscribed on tablets documenting all who passed such exams. More importantly, the highest government posts were reserved for such scholars. In the Confucian tradition, there are no social barriers to pursuing scholarship, but likely those who had privileges (did not have to farm to sustain themselves) were more likely to be able to become scholars.

It is unclear how countries' values and traditions may matter for education. As far back as Max Weber, some have argued that Protestant values and ethics promote educational and occupational success. The ability to work hard and delay gratification is said to lead to better educational success, and thus predominantly Protestant countries may differ from others. It is difficult, though, to relate these values and traditions to specific features of educational systems and to associate these differences with educational inequality. Countries may specifically value egalitarianism. In these cases, this value may lead to lower educational inequality as subsidies are provided for education or education is provided for free by the state. This may happen in communist or more socialist countries. It may also be an explicit part of national policy, as it is in Finland.

School Organization

Nations also differ in the ways that they organize schooling, for example, by which grades are compulsory and how and when students are organized into different groups. Some nations have mandatory kindergarten and even preschool. Others divide education into two sections in the elementary years (lower and higher groups). Some have middle schools or junior high schools. Others divide secondary levels into lower and higher groups. There may be only one division between elementary and secondary education. Some children are in the primary levels until age 10, others until 12 or 13. Education is compulsory until age 18 in some countries (for example, the United Kingdom) and as low as age 11 in others (for example, Haiti).

Nations also vary in how they organize children within schools, whether it is by tested ability or whether children learn in mixed-ability groups, or some combination of both. In Finland, children begin their educations in mixed-ability groups and remain so until secondary school. In other places, children are separated by tested ability earlier. In Germany, for example, students are tested and placed into different schools by seventh grade. In the United Kingdom, the sorting of students does not occur until well into secondary schooling. There is some evidence to suggest that the earlier tracking occurs, the more educational inequality there is in academic outcomes.[8]

School calendars and days may also be organized differently across nations. The United States typically has the longest continuous break (summer vacation), originally conceived so that students could use that season to help on family farms. Other nations offer more but shorter breaks throughout the school year. In the United States, students typically spend about 943 hours per year in school. Chilean students spend more time in schools (at over 1000 hours), while Russia is low at 470 hours.[9] Researchers in the United States suggest that time spent in schools (and not on extended breaks) ameliorates inequalities by socioeconomic background.[10]

Teacher qualifications, training, and pay may also differ across nations. Teachers may receive either free or subsidized training based on government policies, as they do in Finland. Degree programs may be stratified in different ways so that teachers receive different types of qualifications. Postgraduate degrees (like master's degrees) may be required for secondary school teachers, while two- or four-year programs suffice for preschool or primary school teaching. Finally, teacher pay varies across nations. Standardized to US dollars, a primary school teacher with the minimum training may make as little as $11,000 in Poland or Hungary, or as much as $60,000 or $70,000 in Switzerland or Luxembourg. In the United States, the starting salary for a primary school teacher is about $38,000, which is above the average for many countries. Highly qualified senior teachers with a lot of experience can expect to make about $56,000 in the United States, which is again above average for most countries. However, in Korea, similar teachers can expect to make over $76,000, and in Germany $79,000. In Poland, these experienced teachers make as little as $22,000 on average.[11] In the United States, primary school teachers make about 66% as much as other similarly educated workers. In other countries, like Korea, Spain, and Portugal, they make more. In most countries, they earn salaries close to other similarly educated workers.

Another difference between schools is in their exam structures and what exams are used for. Right now, the United States has no national examinations. Whether students are promoted into high school or the types of high schools that they attend do not depend on exam scores (except in the case of magnet or private schools). The same is not true of children in other countries. National exams may determine who goes to an academic high school, who goes to a vocational high school, or who goes to high school at all. Because national exams are so important, the curriculum of some elementary and middle school classrooms is concerned with scoring well on these exams. While the United States does not require examinations to sort students into different types of public secondary education, there have been criticisms that exams to assess students have pushed US schools into focusing too much on exams at the expense of other topics (arts and music, for example). Schooling systems that sort children into different types of schools (vocational or university-bound, for example), like Germany, show higher levels of inequality in outcomes and lower levels of mobility.

Although it is not part of the public school system formally, many nations' public education systems operate alongside what have been called "shadow education" institutions. These may also be called "cram schools." The equivalent in the United States may be tutoring services like Kumon, Kaplan, or Khan Academy; however, in some countries, like Vietnam, Korea, Singapore, and others, students may spend another several hours in these schools, primarily to prepare for exams that sort them into different secondary schools or for national exams that determine their secondary school or postsecondary placement. These are services that students must pay for. Many of these academies employ public school teachers, who are eager for extra income. It is not hard to imagine that the more a country relies on shadow education services that parents must pay for, the more likely it is that the educational outcomes will differ between those who can afford such services and those who cannot. There is debate, though, about how much shadow education like extra tutoring or cram schools actually improves students' educational outcomes. Some studies find it produces a significant improvement, while others find little to none.[12]

It may be helpful to take a more detailed look at education systems that appear more meritocratic and have been held up as models for other nations, including the United States. Over the past several decades, the United States has looked to East Asia for examples of more successful educational systems. Seeing stark differences in achievement scores, particularly between the United States and Japan, the researchers Harold Stevenson and James Stigler decided to investigate why it might be that East Asian children were outperforming Americans.[13] They studied schools in the United States, Japan, Taiwan, and China in an attempt to explain why East Asian kids perform better than US students. It has also been noted that students in these countries have smaller differences in their math and reading achievement scores than students in the United States.

Stevenson and Stigler considered many explanations for these differences in scores, but here I focus on ones that may impact inequality among students. One difference is that Americans have longer vacation times—they spend roughly half of the days of the year in school, while Asian students spend about two-thirds. Another large difference between Asian and American schools is in the level of federal control. Asian schools are funded by the government, and thus there are not large disparities between the funding levels of schools in one area compared to another. Further, the government controls the goals of education, sets the standards, and creates the curriculum. The government also maintains control over the measurement standards—administering and evaluating students according to national exams. This can be contrasted to the US system, in which school districts control much of the standards, evaluation, and curriculum formation. Funding is largely determined by the community or neighborhood in which the constituent children reside.

Stevenson and Stigler also note that Asian children are more likely to work in groups than American children and that Asian children are not grouped by ability at young ages. All students in a particular group work together. Privileges and responsibilities belong to the group, not just the individual.

Another explanation for differences in inequality in outcomes between Asian and US schools is that cultural values about education differ. One of these differences is in beliefs about effort and ability. Stevenson and Stigler consistently find that Americans are more likely to believe that ability determines their scores in school, while Asian students are more likely to think that hard work is the key to school success. This has been shown in studies of Asian Americans as well.[14] Many researchers attribute this belief, in part, to Confucianism, a philosophy which urges that if you work hard, you can improve yourself. This belief influences parents too. Figure 7–7

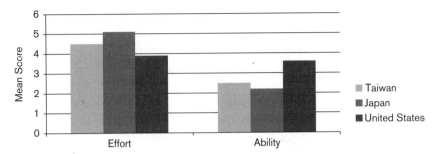

Figure 7-7. Mean Scores for Agreeing That Effort versus Ability Is the Most Important Factor in Children's Academic Success by Country.

SOURCE: Stevenson and Stigler (1994).

NOTE: The vertical axis measures the mean on a seven-point Likert scale, where 1-complete disagree and 7-complete agreement.

from Stevenson and Stigler's research shows that mothers in the United States are more likely to agree that ability differences are primarily responsible for children's academic success, while in Japan and Taiwan, mothers are more likely to agree that effort is most important. You can imagine how this may influence children—those who believe their scores can change will work harder. Those who believe they do not have the innate ability to succeed academically will not try. If early differences in achievement that may be related to socioeconomic background and academic preparation are attributed to "innate" ability, those from less-privileged backgrounds who are less academically prepared may become discouraged.

Another country whose educational system has been held up as a model of exceptional quality and equity is Finland. The country underwent very conscious educational reforms after World War II. The Finnish system comprises comprehensive basic education until tenth grade, at which time students are sorted into upper general secondary school or upper vocational secondary school. From upper general secondary school, students are prepared to enter university. From upper vocational secondary schools, they can enter polytechnic postsecondary education.

Finnish students score among the highest on the PISA math tests, and Finland also has some of the lowest variance in test scores. There are several attributes of the educational system in Finland that may account for this, but, according to Pasi Sahlberg, the most important among these is respect for the teaching profession.[15] Sahlberg argues that Finnish culture has always had great respect for teachers. Because of this, entry into post-secondary teacher education programs is highly competitive. Teachers in primary and secondary schools are required to have master's degrees, and there is close collaboration between education schools and policy-makers and practitioners. Teachers make about the average salary of teachers in the OECD countries, but their salaries rise as they get more experience, not as a result of merit pay. Teachers at higher levels of education get paid more than those who teach in basic education.

More than salary, though, Sahlberg argues, it is the autonomy of teachers that affords more success to students. Teachers spend less time in the classroom than the average in OECD countries, and more time working together and in professional development. Teachers are encouraged to also be researchers and are given time to work on policies and practices that improve student performance. Teachers' and, to a large extent, students' success is not judged by test performance. Indeed, students are tested very little until they reach tenth grade.

There are other features of Finnish schools that may contribute to student success and low inequality. Preschool is universal, early grades are devoted more to socialization than to academics, and there is little stigma associated with being retained in a grade, as about a third of Finnish students are. Sahlberg argues that flexibility in teaching and learning and, as opposed to current reforms in the United States and other North American and European countries, less, not more, standardization and testing are key. He argues that the public trusts schools to be providing the best education for students, and does not need to continuously assess them to be sure.

There are some who are skeptical that these reforms would work in the United States or other large, heterogeneous countries.[16] Finland has a small but robust economy, led by a few large technology companies primarily. The standard of living in Finland is high and income inequality is already quite low, compared to other countries. The small population is concentrated in a few urban areas, and it is mostly racially and ethnically homogenous. There are few immigrants compared to other countries in Europe. Skeptics contend that educational reforms are easier to adopt in countries with these conditions.

What can we learn from these two cases, countries in East Asia and Finland, where education is of high quality (at least as measured by test scores), but there is low inequality? It is difficult to tease apart what matters most—is it cultural values, respect for and education of teachers, professional autonomy, more or less standardization of curriculum and testing? Does it have to do with the economic conditions of the countries? Does it have to do with how funding is distributed and the involvement of national governments in policy-making for schools?

It is difficult to know for certain, and more research could be done looking at observable factors that distinguish between school systems characterized by low or high inequality. The United States has attempted to implement a number of reforms throughout its history that were aimed at increasing quality or decreasing inequality. Sometimes these two goals have coexisted, and sometimes the effects of concentrating on one have exacerbated the other. For example, policies to increase school quality may have detrimental effects on school inequality, unlike what appears to be the case in East Asia and Finland. In the next chapter, Jessica Brathwaite and I review some of these reform movements and specific policies, concentrating on how they may have influenced school inequality in the United States across the last several decades.

8 Education Reforms and Inequality

Jessica Brathwaite and Kimberly Goyette

Throughout this book, we ask: Can schools reduce inequality? In this chapter, we look at some of the ways school reform efforts have tried to address inequality and how focusing on other goals for education has affected inequality. Throughout this chapter, we may also ask whether changes in school policies are enough. Can changes in schools alone reduce the gaps between rich and poor and between minority and nonminority students?

Early chapters have shown that schools have a variety of socialization and stratification goals: to prepare students for their adult roles, to sort them into different positions in the public and private spheres, to provide skills necessary for the workforce, to teach values that are integral to forming students' identities, and others. Attempts to improve on one or more of these goals may have consequences for others and, particularly, for school inequality. This section looks at reform efforts starting in the nineteenth century, focusing first on the rise of assessment and accountability in state and federal policy and then on the movement to make schools behave more like the private sector through programs and policies that increase school choice and alternative teacher certification. While these movements are not necessarily separable in practice (testing increased as school choice was promoted), we separate them here conceptually. One strand of reform focused on increasing accountability, which was thought to minimize gaps between students of different socioeconomic groups and races and ethnicities by mandating that districts and schools report them and, as a result, make plans to address them. Another strand focused on promoting "choices" and increasing public education's resemblance to and reliance on the private or philanthropic sector. Increasing student options and options for teacher certification was thought to remove inefficiencies in public education that contributed to low quality in schools with few resources. By increasing choice, school inequality should decrease as racial minority and poor students choose higher-quality options for themselves. In each section, we discuss whether these two strands of reform did indeed have their intended effects on school inequality.

THE RISE OF ASSESSMENT, ACCOUNTABILITY, AND STANDARDS

Common Schools and the Progressive Era

While public schools date back to the seventeenth century, the first *system* of public schools was established in 1837 by Horace Mann in Massachusetts. This first public education system was created as a mechanism for social mobility to ensure that all youth have equal access to a basic liberal arts education. This common school movement was an attempt to improve cohesion and equity in response to the escalating friction between religious groups and between social classes.[1]

As reviewed in chapter 2, public schools expanded nationwide throughout the first half of the twentieth century due to changes in immigration, the implementation of child labor laws, and a decline in agricultural work. As rural agricultural labor declined, manual and administrative labor attracted families to cities. The age for compulsory education rose during this time period, which also increased the number of school-aged children in cities.[2] The Fair Labor Act of 1938 restricted child labor, creating more time for children to attend school. Increased immigration from Europe brought even more youth with varied needs and goals.[3]

Considering the new and diverse public school population, the traditional liberal arts high school curriculum was deemed outdated and irrelevant for the large number of students who would not continue their education through college. Progressive reformers promoted the idea that schools were responsible for creating a competent work force. Progressive reformers tailored the high school curriculum to match the skills required in the labor market, by offering courses in typing, economics, home economics, cooking, business, and management.[4] This differentiated education was considered to be the most efficient way to provide a socioeconomically diverse American youth with the wide array of skills needed in the work force.[5] This differentiated education is the birth of modern-day tracking, where students are assigned to vocational or college preparatory tracks during their high school careers. During the progressive era, schools were held accountable for creating a skilled labor force.

Administrative progressivism was also part of school reform during this time. Previously local municipalities had control over school decisions, but administrative progressives sought to centralize decision-making in those who were considered to be experts and intellectuals.[6] These power elites would make curriculum decisions at the state level to standardize learning. This centralized leadership made it necessary to standardize the measurement of student outcomes. Testing was considered as a cost-effective and systematic way to measure student learning.[7]

Civil Rights and International Defense

Concerns over the academic and technological preparation of American youth also increased the need for testing and measuring schools. The advance of the Cold War and the launch of Sputnik in 1957 created public hysteria that Russian students were better academically prepared than American students, and that American students lacked the math, science, and engineering knowledge necessary to improve US technological and defense systems. As a result, the National Defense Education Act (NDEA) was passed in 1958 by President Dwight Eisenhower, and it provided federal funding for the study of these subjects.[8]

While there was a national focus on increasing technical skills and student performance, demographic changes and internal migration led to an emphasis on equity under the civil rights movement. During the 1950s and 1960s, large numbers of African Americans moved from the South to the

North, and urban schools were flooded with poor and minority students. White families fled urban centers, relocating to the suburbs. This led to concentrated poverty in inner cities, as jobs and the white middle-class tax base exited the city. Urban cities became known as urban ghettos, and inner-city poverty became a focal point of education and social policy.

As reviewed in detail in chapter 5, in 1954, schools were desegregated as a result of *Brown v. The Board of Education of Topeka, Kansas.*[9] The civil rights era introduced major federal investment in ensuring equal access to education for all races, for all socioeconomic groups, and regardless of disability status. Black activists fought for improvements to urban schools, for equal access to a high-quality curriculum, and for increases in the number of black educators.[10]

In 1960, Vice President Lyndon Johnson made mention of improving schools for low-income students in his conception of the "Great Society."[11] In 1965, the Elementary and Secondary Education Act (ESEA) was passed to provide funding for impoverished schools, through a program called Title I. The Head Start program was also created in this year to provide a quality preschool education to low-income students and eliminate many of the differences that students have upon entry to kindergarten. The federal government held local municipalities and schools accountable for providing basic skills to all students despite the disadvantages associated with race, income, or disability.

There were concerns about how federal funds were allocated at the local level and whether they were having the intended consequence.[12] Schools were formerly evaluated based on their inputs, such as the number of books, the number of teachers, and the quality of facilities. For the federal government to monitor its investment, schools were held accountable using their outputs, such as graduation rates and test scores. Tests were considered the best measure of learning.[13]

A Nation at Risk and Education Reform in the 1980s

Between 1965 and the 1980s, urban schools received great attention for their low test scores and deplorable conditions.[14] Cultural arguments blamed minority pathologies for these inequalities.[15] *The Coleman Report* explained that improving schools would not necessarily improve the achievement of students, and this report was taken as evidence that families rather than schools were the cause of inequality.[16] The conservative Reagan administration villainized the poor, and cut spending on education. Public dissatisfaction with the low quality of public schools increased during this time.[17]

The election of Ronald Reagan in 1981 solidified the conservative argument as a foundation for public policy. Part of Reagan's 1980 presidential campaign platform was that he would abolish the Department of Education because it was ineffective at improving outcomes. During his presidency, civil rights–era reforms and legislation focused on alleviating inequalities between racial and socioeconomic groups were abandoned. By the mid-1980s, urban schools were portrayed as dysfunctional and unworthy of any increased public spending. The public discourse at this time was that urban schools were vastly unequal because of social background inequalities and the inefficient use of funding. The public perception was that these schools were not rigorous enough to create a work force that was internationally competitive.

The National Commission on Excellence in Education was created on August 26, 1981, under President Reagan, to investigate "the widespread public perception that something is seriously remiss in our educational system."[18] This report promoted increased high school standards, rigor, and school accountability. This commission produced the report *A Nation at Risk. A Nation at Risk (ANAR)*, like the cries that led to the National Defense of Education Act in the 1950s, argued that the United States would lose its standing as an economic and technological world leader if our students continued to underperform.

ANAR led to increased criticism of the public education curriculum. The report stated that "the public has no patience with undemanding and superfluous high school offerings."[19] The report argued that most students were enrolled in general track courses that did not prepare them for postsecondary success, particularly because they did not improve tested ability in core content areas like math, science, and English. *ANAR* affirmed the sentiment that schools were currently failing American children, and that schools should create rigorous standards, increase data collection from schools, and increase school accountability. *ANAR* recommended an increase in accountability through the reporting of test scores and other data throughout the education system.[20] As a result of this report, the National Assessment of Educational Progress (NAEP), which was initially created in 1964 as an objective test in reading and math to be compared across states, became the benchmark against which to compare schools across the nation.[21]

ANAR decried the practical education of the progressive era, characterized by classes like home economics and cooking. The report recommended that state and local high school graduation requirements be increased. The report recommended that all students seeking a diploma should focus on five areas termed the "new basics" (three to four years of English, math, science, and social studies, plus some work in computer science).[22] It also recommended that test scores be used to evaluate teaching and learning. As a result of this report, public attention focused on increasing the standards of education for American students and on the lack of rigor in public high schools.

The Standards Movement and No Child Left Behind

During the 1990s, former President George H.W. Bush and the National Governor's Association collaborated to create a National Education Goals Panel, to develop America 2000, a federal plan to mandate standardized tests and curricula by the year 2000. The plan contained a choice provision, allowing students to transfer to private or parochial schools and take federal money with them.

The Improving America's Schools Act of 1994 was a reauthorization of the Elementary and Secondary Education Act of 1965 and it focused on increased standards and accountability.[23] Initiated by President George H.W. Bush and passed under President Clinton, it mandated that all schools must administer assessments in grades three through five and 10 through 12. These assessments had to be aligned with content standards that improve student learning. Failing schools were required to develop improvement plans and engage in corrective action.[24] The development of a national test was met with great aversion, and by 2001 many states were still not in compliance with the policy.

The No Child Left Behind (NCLB) Act was the first successful attempt to combine standards, accountability, and choice into a federal policy.

NCLB was a reauthorization of the Elementary and Secondary Education Act of 1965, and it was signed into law on January 8, 2002, under President George W. Bush. The mission of NCLB was "to close the achievement gap with high standards, accountability, flexibility, and choice, so that no child is left behind."[25] NCLB emphasized the need for high standards for all students and mentioned minority students in particular.

NCLB was established on the neoliberal principle of increased accountability. The federal government decentralized its power by allowing each state to set its own standards and curriculum. In exchange for this increased power at the state level, states are held accountable to the government for meeting these standards or else they are penalized. The law mandates that all standardized test scores and outcomes be disaggregated by race, socioeconomic status, English-language proficiency, and disability status in order to track the progress of schools and states in reducing achievement gaps. Under NCLB, schools that fail to meet standards for each subgroup are subject to formal sanctions. If schools fail to meet content or achievement standards, the schools can be closed and the secretary of education can choose to withhold federal funding. The law mandates that any student in a failing school has the option to attend a nonfailing school. This provision encouraged the expansion of school choice for students in failing schools.

NCLB aimed to reduce racial and socioeconomic gaps within and across schools through increased choice and accountability. The policy did not include any mechanism for integrating schools. Although NCLB required every state to make changes, many states were already on the path to test-based accountability and standards-based reforms. In states like New York, Florida, and Texas, there were already accountability systems and statewide standards.

Race to the Top

Race to the Top was initiated in 2009 under President Barack Obama and Secretary of Education Arnie Duncan. This initiative used $4.35 billion in funding from the American Recovery and Reinvestment Act (ARRA). This initiative was a collaboration between the federal government and state governors. It included state governors because it was assumed that they would be above partisan politics or influence from teachers' unions or other interest groups. States were required to submit applications that were graded on a 500-point scale, which were judged according to the following criteria: developing common standards and assessment, improving teacher preparation and evaluation, creating better data systems, and adopting school-turnaround strategies.[26]

President Obama argued that this initiative came from frequent discussions between the secretary and education experts.[27] Tennessee and Delaware were two of the 40 states that were awarded the grant in 2010. Ten states out of 35 were chosen in the second round of applications. The Race to the Top application required at least 23 states to change their laws.[28] The application required that states remove caps on the number of charter schools in operation, and it mandated that student-achievement data be linked to teacher information.

The federal government had never before implemented this type of reform. This reform took lessons from the failures of NCLB by focusing less on sanctions and more on incentives. This shifted the Department of Education's role from one of monitoring and evaluation to one of capacity building and innovation.[29] Race to the Top reinvigorated the role of governors in education reform and invited private organizations like the Bill and Melinda Gates Foundation and Mark Zuckerberg to assist in helping reform schools.

Common Core

The planning for a new series of state standards called the Common Core was started in 2009 to ensure more conformity across schools in what students learn. Governors and school officers worked together to come up with expectations for what students should know by the time they graduated from high school and what they should learn throughout their K–8 years. Beginning in 2011, states could choose to adopt these standards and curricula. Currently, 42 states have adopted the Common Core literacy and math standards, and local schools have been figuring out how to implement them. Textbook, testing, and curriculum development companies have sought to capitalize on these new standards, and some schools with strained budgets find it hard to purchase these new products.

The Common Core has had advocates and critics. Some argue the new standards are well thought-out and based on the expertise of teachers and comments of the public. Advocates say the new standards advance math education in the United States substantially. Critics worry that there is too much conformity across schools, that the Common Core is a way for higher levels of government to mandate what should be taught in local schools. Others worry about the added expenses for struggling schools, and the increased testing for already test-burdened students. Finally, some say the efforts will do little to correct differential outcomes by race and socioeconomic background that the standards were initially designed to ameliorate.

The End of No Child Left Behind?

In December 2015, headlines of major newspapers read "The End of NCLB." President Obama signed a law called the Every Student Succeeds Act, which replaced the No Child Left Behind Act. States are still required to test students in grades three through eight annually on math and reading performance and report to the public scores by race, income, ethnicity, disability, and English-language learner status, but states are given the power to decide how to use those scores in assessing overall school quality and teacher performance. States develop their own goals and plans for improvement, and these need to be approved by the Department of Education. Under this law, the power of the secretary of education is limited, as the secretary cannot influence state decisions about assessment, teacher evaluation, or the adoption of the Common Core standards and curricula. Though the new law shifts power back to states, it is unclear what its effects may be on school inequality, as states vary in the degree to which they have made reducing inequalities by race and ethnicity, socioeconomic background, disability status, and other characteristics of students a priority.

Standards Reforms: Consequences for Inequality

Educational reforms are intended to improve one or more aspects of education. Reforms may be intended to improve overall student learning, to reduce inequality, or both. Often, focusing on one goal can have unintended consequences for others. Sociologists have noted that when schooling expands or experiences reform, often inequality between socioeconomic groups remains the same.[30] Sometimes diminished inequality across some dimensions (like socioeconomic background) can lead to increased inequality in others (like political party membership).[31] When looking at calls for higher standards and greater accountability, researchers need to explore whether the reforms are meeting their stated goals and whether or not reforms are affecting inequality in unintended ways.

Empirical studies find that increased accountability may improve academic achievement. For example, researchers find improvements in reading achievement due to the threat of school failure.[32] Using data from North Carolina public schools, Douglas Lee Lauen and S. Michael Gaddis find that the implementation of accountability metrics for each racial subgroup reduced the black-white test gap in reading and math.[33] They find that black students' test scores improved more than whites if their school failed to make adequate yearly progress, or AYP, the previous year. The impact of accountability on the black-white achievement gap is smallest in the schools serving the most poor students.

Although accountability systems may temporarily improve student achievement, these findings may also reflect gaming and other practices used to dishonestly boost accountability grades. To ensure that schools perform well and meet accountability requirements, research finds, resources are channeled primarily toward the grades during which students take standardized exams.[34] These grades receive more money for books and other learning materials to pass exams. Schools may also target "bubble kids." These are the students who score right beneath the passing score. Schools focus on these students more than students who are further beneath the cutoff, with the hopes that the school will meet accountability measures if they can get these students over the passing threshold.[35]

Other research examines the progress of students whose schools have failed once under federal accountability systems. It finds that performance suffers for students in grade levels not being tested, and for students in traditionally struggling subgroups. There are no gains in nontest subjects.[36] Other research finds that most attention is paid to students who are near the proficiency cut point.[37] This maintains current educational inequalities because the achievement of the lowest-performing students is ignored, and the top-performing students are not impacted by accountability pressures. Despite efforts to improve all students' quality of education, the lowest-performing students do not seem to benefit.

Finally, still other research argues that testing shows what we already know about our society: that it is highly stratified by socioeconomic background and race. Testing alone cannot reduce inequality in students' scores if students' opportunities to learn the material on which they are being tested aren't also distributed more equitably both across and within schools. These researchers argue that testing should be used as one of many pieces of information when making decisions about individual students and schools, but should not form the basis of high-stakes decisions, like school restructuring or take-overs.[38]

THE RISE OF CHOICE AND PRIVATIZATION

Though school choice has become more common over the past several decades, for most of the population, the schools that students attend have been determined by their place of residence. Students attend the school associated with their "feeder area" or "catchment zone." Boundaries drawn on a map show which elementary, middle, and high schools within school districts serve which homes. While throughout most of the history of public schooling in the United States the school attached to one's residence was the only public school option, that is no longer the case. Magnet schools, charter schools, intradistrict transfer programs, and other schools of choice have increased the number of options for families who want their children to attend public schools. Schools are perceived as "choices" rather than public goods, and families are said to behave like "consumers."

A variety of policy efforts and initiatives have expanded the choices that families have for schooling their children. Families, particularly wealthier families, have long had the option to choose private schools for their children. These schools may be affiliated with Episcopal, other Protestant, Quaker, or other religious traditions, or they may be secular, and they may be associated with particular educational philosophies like Montessori or Waldorf. Catholic Schools, originally an educational option for Catholics who were suspicious of the Anglo-Protestant public schools, now often serve disadvantaged, non-Catholic students in urban areas. They offer lower tuitions and more subsidies than other private schools. As a result, Catholic school students make up the largest proportion of private school students.[39]

Though rural students in Maine and Vermont had been using them for a while, school vouchers saw more use nationally in the 1990s as a way to increase school choices for families who did not want to send children to their neighborhood public schools. Milwaukee was one of the first districts to use vouchers on a larger scale. Students who were eligible for the program (who came from low-performing schools, were low-income, had disabilities, or were from military families, for example) were eligible for vouchers to pay for some portion of private school tuition. Schools that accepted vouchers were required to comply with some state standards.

Other school choice options include magnet schools. Magnet schools are public schools that admit students based on academic talent, usually determined by test scores or other criteria like talent in art or music. Magnet schools like Boston Latin were founded as academies in the seventeenth century; however, magnet schools grew most dramatically during the 1970s and 1980s as school integration was attempted. Magnet schools were considered a way to retain academically talented white students who would otherwise leave integrating urban schools for schools in the suburbs.[40]

Efforts to integrate schools also encouraged other types of policies that expanded choice for parents. For example, to achieve racial balance, some school districts decided to allow students to choose any of the schools (or designated schools) within that district. This is called intradistrict transfer. Parents could send their children to schools other than their assigned public school, though usually the goal was to decrease school segregation, so students could not choose any school within the district, only those at which their presence would help achieve racial balance. In some places, urban and suburban districts allowed transfers of students between them (better-known examples of this are Raleigh and Wake County, Charlotte and Mecklenberg County, and St. Louis City and St. Louis County). Students from predominantly minority city schools were allowed to transfer to whiter, suburban schools through these interdistrict transfer programs. While there were few of these programs to begin with, many such as those in North Carolina and Missouri have been dismantled; consequently, schools have become resegregated in these areas. Urban school districts (like Philadelphia) may offer the choice of transfer to particular neighborhood public schools, if there are slots available, and other districts like Cambridge, Massachusetts, require families to choose particular public schools that specialize in areas (like science or art) before entering the public school system; however, the districts do not include suburban neighborhoods typically.

Charter schools have perhaps been the fastest growing sector of expanded school choice. Charter school founders often propose to run a school that is different from local public schools in some ways, perhaps in its teaching style or method, organization, or theme. School district authorities then grant these schools "charters" to operate, providing funding usually based on the number of students they serve. Charter schools do not admit students based on academic talent; rather, students are typically admitted by lottery (though there may be preferences for students based on their neighborhoods or whether or not they have siblings who attend). Starting with two charter schools in Minnesota in 1991, the number of charter schools had grown to 3000 in 2004 and could be found in more than 37 states.[41]

The No Child Left Behind Act of 2001 promoted the use of alternatives to neighborhood schools. After two years of not achieving adequate yearly progress (AYP), schools are labeled "in need of improvement" and a plan must be made to correct this. Students are offered the option to transfer from this school. After another year of missing AYP, students must be offered tutoring or other educational services to improve student performance. Beyond the third year, more drastic actions must be taken, including school and personnel reorganization or school takeover by the state, charter schools, or other private school management companies. Although the implementation of these provisions has not always been straightforward, and it is often not easy for parents to navigate their new choices, NCLB increased the perception that families should have the right to choose alternative schools if their school is not judged "adequate."

So, how might expanded school choice influence school socioeconomic or racial inequality? The stated intentions of NCLB and of the expansion of charter, voucher, and transfer programs are to equalize outcomes between race groups (shrinking racial test score gaps) by expanding opportunities among those who face the lowest-quality schools—those who have fewer resources and members of some racial and ethnic minority groups. The argument made by many advocates of expanded choice is that once options increase, those schools that are not serving the needs of their target populations will cease to exist, as students leave these schools (and take their funding with them).[42] So, ideally, expanded school choice should reduce inequality in outcomes as students leave poorly performing schools for better-quality ones.

Improvement in outcomes across races and socioeconomic groups is based on several assumptions, though, that researchers have questioned. First, is information about the quality of alternative schools available to all families equally? Researchers like Jack Buckley and Mark Schneider suggest that some parents act as "marginal consumers," considering several options.[43] They gather information about potential schools in order to make informed decisions, but these researchers find differences in information-gathering by race and social background. For example, high-income parents are less likely than those families with lower incomes to use relatives to find out about schools.[44] Middle-class parents rely more heavily on their social networks for information about schools so they consult fewer other sources of information than working-class parents.[45] They also find that blacks and other minorities have smaller networks than whites.[46] Middle- and upper-middle class parents, particularly those without strong network connections, rely on reports of school performance in their decision-making far more than working-class parents.[47]

Families' decision-making about schools may differ according to their views on public education and these may also vary by social background. For example, some working-class families may believe that their local schools provide an education that is good enough and students are responsible for their own failures.[48] On the other hand, middle- and upper-class families may explicitly decide to match the values and attributes of their family (perhaps race, status, or cultural background) and those of the child (artistically talented, scientifically inclined, and the like) to the best-fitting school.[49]

Apart from different decision-making processes, families of different races and ethnicities and with different amounts of resources may face different sets of constraints when making choices. Lower-income and minority parents in Cincinnati and St. Louis are more concerned about transportation when choosing schools for their children than middle-class, white parents, for example.[50] Claire Smrekar and Ellen Goldring also find that in St. Louis 74% of parents with incomes over $50,000 reported academic reputation as their main reason for choosing a magnet school, compared to 26% of the lower-income parents.[51] Anna Rhodes and Stephanie DeLuca suggest that school choice is not realistic for many parents who move frequently and are constrained by transportation and after-school care for children. Students may move among schools that are of equally low quality.[52]

Others question whether there are enough quality schools to meet demand for them. There are numerous media accounts of families who wait overnight in long lines to get children a place in desirable-choice schools, and the film *Waiting for Superman* showed how heartbreaking it can be when there are so few slots open to families who believe they are the only option for their children. And still others wonder whether the bulk of charter schools are better than the neighborhood schools from which children came.[53] While there are charter schools that produce high test scores among their students, most charter schools perform similarly to their local, neighborhood counterparts.[54] What is true is that parents seem more satisfied with their choice of charter schools than parents of children in public schools.[55]

A final issue for those who worry about the expansion of charter schools is what happens to those students who do not, for whatever reasons, leave their neighborhood schools. As other students leave these schools for charters and resources go with them, who is left? Until these schools close and students are forced out of them, will those students left behind get an even poorer-quality education than if charter schools did not exist? Is this justified because these students did not leave these schools, as others did?

Researchers have worried that the existence of charter schools maintains racial and socioeconomic inequality or even exacerbates it. Upper-income families typically do not take advantage of charter schools.[56] These families prefer to send children to the largely segregated local, neighborhood schools that are supported by local taxes, sometimes having double the per capita spending of surrounding schools. They may seek to maximize the academic and social advantages schools are able to provide.

Even though the school they "chose" was a neighborhood, public school, these parents gathered information about a variety of public schools before locating to their neighborhood, and chose that neighborhood because of its public school.[57] Those who take advantage of charter schools are largely urban, lower-income students who may not necessarily be gaining increased school quality (at least not measured by test scores).

Other researchers wonder how the presence of charter schools affects neighborhood schools. Some find that the proportion of nonwhite students in public schools affects the likelihood of white enrollment in private, charter, and magnet schools, even when controlling for measures of school quality, including graduation rates, test scores, safety, and student-teacher ratios.[58] Rather than moving from integrating neighborhoods, families may use public school choice programs to avoid neighborhood-based schools. For example, Salvatore Saporito and Salvatore Saporito and Deenesh Sohoni find that white children are more likely to leave public neighborhood schools for magnet schools as the proportion of non-white children in their assigned neighborhood school increases, even after accounting for school characteristics such as average test scores and poverty rates.[59] Further evidence based on interviews suggests that white parents are averse to sending their children to schools where there are many black and Latino children.[60] Similarly, Linda Renzulli and Lorraine Evans find that whites are more likely to attend charter schools in districts with greater degrees of racial integration.[61] Latino students are also more likely to leave public schools for private schools when there is a greater the percentage of blacks in their neighborhood public schools.[62] Studies such as these cause concern for educators and policy-makers who had hoped that having options such as magnet and charter schools and vouchers would serve to integrate schools.

Another school choice that families may make is to opt out of formal, institutional schooling altogether by homeschooling. Only about 2.2% of school-aged children were home-schooled in 2003,[63] but this option is often chosen by those who dislike or do not trust educational institutions for religious or other reasons, and by those who feel that these institutions cannot well serve the needs of their child or children.[64] It is unclear whether or how homeschooling might affect school inequality since such a small proportion of families choose it.

School choice innovations largely occur in urban areas, so the majority of the research on school choice has been conducted in and around large cities like Milwaukee, Detroit, Montgomery County (in Maryland), New York, San Antonio, St. Louis, and Cincinnati.[65] However, charter schools and other school choice programs are expanding into suburban and even rural areas.[66] Increasing school choices lead to the increasing perception that school is less of a public good and more of a private choice, but how that influences school inequality is unclear. As people more and more perceive school to be a family's choice, they may choose homes in particular neighborhoods, and residential segregation could increase as middle- and upper-middle-class white families cluster together around schools that they believe are of high quality. Or, as options for nonneighborhood public schools proliferate, families may feel freer to enact their ideal residential preferences without concern for schooling quality. This may decrease racial residential segregation and, though perhaps to a lesser extent, school segregation. Families who want to live in cities but are concerned about the quality of public schools may move to cities if they have their choice of neighborhood or charter schools across a city. Finally, it is possible that both could be occurring: Families with resources may be better able to take advantage of nonneighborhood public schools, particularly in gentrifying urban areas, and may also be more likely to use homes as a means of securing their ideal schools.

Alongside the growth of school choice programs has been an increase in alternatives to certify and supply teachers to schools in need. Many of these teachers are placed in charter schools and other public schools with few resources. Teach for America started in 1990 with the mission to place teachers straight from undergraduate programs (with or without education training) into challenging schools. Many have questioned whether those recruited by Teach for America produce the same learning gains as those more traditionally trained and certified teachers and whether they have higher turnover than traditionally trained teachers, with mixed results.[67] Other programs to provide alternatively certified teachers, like New York City's Teaching Fellows Program, designed to attract professionals in noneducation fields to teaching, show few differences between alternatively certified and traditionally certified teachers in student outcomes and teacher turnover.[68]

Currently, public school systems are heavily influenced by the privatization movement. Schools are increasingly shaped by private or philanthropic agencies through partnerships, some that provide alternatively certified teachers, and some that support charter schools.[69] Schools are also being held accountable to parents, states, and even the federal government in unprecedented ways through testing. Schools, students, and teachers are increasingly evaluated using test scores as a metric, a metric that determines whether or not they continue to operate. While test scores are steadily increasing in many schools, so is racial and socioeconomic segregation between and within schools.[70] These reforms may have been intended to improve educational outcomes for all students, and particularly for racial and ethnic minority students and those who are socioeconomically disadvantaged, but inequality between groups is pervasive and may be even starker today than before these reforms were attempted.

9 If We Don't Like Educational Inequality, Why Is It So Hard to Make It Go Away?

Structured, systematized education—education that occurs in schools— intimately involves how we believe our society does look and should look. Education is one means that a society uses to prepare children for their futures. Education prepares children for their roles as adults—as Americans, workers, professionals, men, women, blacks, whites, Hispanics, Asians, straight people, gays, or lesbians.

Early in this book, I introduced two concepts that involve different aspects of children's preparation for their future roles: socialization and stratification. Socialization involves how children learn acceptable behaviors, values, beliefs, and social rules called norms. Socialization prepares us, for better or worse, for our roles as members of different races, classes, genders, sexual orientations. Through socialization, we learn how to be a member of a group, of a society.

Education also stratifies; it sorts us. There are two views about how education does this. One is the functionalist view that sees education as a place where children learn skills that help them compete. Through the education process children ideally get sorted into adult roles efficiently—everyone enters positions where their talents are best used. According to the conflict position, education maintains the status quo stratification system. Children are sorted into roles in which their parents are already situated—workers become workers, professionals become professionals. Positions are maintained, in part, through the education system.

In order to socialize and sort, schools provide children with human, social, and cultural capital. Schools provide children with human capital—knowledge and skills. Schools also provide their students with social capital in the form of information, supervision, and support, and finally schools give students cultural capital, which acts as a membership into certain social groups—and eases entrance into certain types of occupations and adult roles. Schools may also treat students differently based on the types of capital they bring to schools from their families and neighborhoods, or schools may not be able to compensate for the capital that students lack to achieve social mobility that may not be present in their families, peer groups, and neighborhoods.

The acquisition of these types of capitals in schools may vary according to the characteristics of the schools and the characteristics of students. Public schools with different racial, ethnic, and socioeconomic compositions and different amounts of resources may vary in terms of the amounts and types of human, social, and cultural capital they can provide. There is also variation within schools in how these capitals are distributed, and often variation within schools is related to children's ascribed characteristics like socioeconomic background, race, or gender. Course-taking is an example of this. Research has shown that children with lower socioeconomic status and black and Hispanic children are less likely to take advanced math and Advanced Placement courses. In this sense, they get less human capital.

Starting with chapter 4, this book explored contemporary inequality in schools by several characteristics: socioeconomic background, race and ethnicity, and gender, while also touching on differences by disability status, sexual orientation, and immigration. These categories are not distinct, though, and evidence suggests that they "intersect," such that experiences may differ based on a students' combination of statuses. A black female student may have very different experiences with school punishment compared to a black male student. A poor Asian student experiences different pressures from a poor Hispanic student. And so on.

In general, I divided chapters 4 and 5 into two parts: differences in educational experiences (which may result in different "learning opportunities") and differences in educational outcomes. Differences in educational experiences included whether schools received different amounts of funding per student, the extent to which they were racially segregated, whether student bodies comprised many or few poor students, and teacher qualifications and class sizes. I then described students' outcomes: expectations, grades, retention rates, proficiency test scores, SAT scores, course-taking, graduation, and enrollment in postsecondary education.

There is considerable debate over how much schools influence these outcomes independent of the family backgrounds of children, with some scholars arguing that schools play a small role in creating or exacerbating these inequalities. Some argue that, at least in some cases, schools ameliorate them (at least while children are attending schools, that is, during the school year). There is evidence that schools decrease differences in students' learning outcomes by socioeconomic background. However, there is also evidence to show that differences by race and ethnicity increase over the school year and over years spent in school.

One reason to explore both educational experiences *and* outcomes is to emphasize that there are different perspectives on what educational inequality means. If educational opportunity is what is meant by educational equality, then we might consider that children's school environments look somewhat similar in important ways. Others who want to tackle educational inequality suggest that it is outcomes that need to be addressed: that rich and poor, black, white, Asian, and Hispanic, and girls and boys should have similar grades and test scores or enrollment in college. These two ideas become conflated: equal educational opportunities should result in equal outcomes according to many, but I think it is important to separate these two concepts. Hypothetically, even if Asian, Hispanic, black, and white students do not score equally on NAEP tests (and, on average, maybe won't in the near future for a host of other reasons), should they be provided with similar educational facilities? This is one of many questions that separating experiences and outcomes is meant to evoke.

In chapter 7, I tried to provide a picture of inequality in other countries to put the United States in context. Is inequality in educational outcomes by wealth, gender, or urban/rural residence inevitable around the globe?

What are some differences between the United States and places where inequality is lower or higher? The last chapter provided a short history of educational reforms in the United States. These reforms are informed by what the public perceives and what politicians may say are the big problems in education. Though educational inequality has often been identified as one of these big problems, addressing it may compete with other priorities of education and may be in tension with the goals of families with more resources who want to maximize their own children's advantages. If educational inequality were a universal goal with a simple solution, it seems the problem may have been solved by now.

The reforms described in the previous chapter suggest that schools could better address two large problems. The first is low achievement—especially in math and science—among US students, compared to students in other countries. As Linda Darling-Hammond points out, this low average achievement is largely driven by those students who do the worst on exams: those in low-performing, often predominantly poor or minority schools.[1] A second large problem is that inequality by race, gender, socioeconomic background, and other characteristics is in some instances not ameliorated and may even be perpetuated by schools. Some scholars see these issues as inseparable. Schools cannot improve overall achievement if they do not address the underlying inequality that leads students in particular schools to score far worse than students in other schools.

There are perhaps three issues that make it difficult for reforms to be effectively implemented. First, there are trade-offs that make change difficult. Second, schools may be ineffective at battling inequality if they are the only institution charged with doing so and they operate in isolation. Third, political battles about larger issues play out in schools in ways that make change difficult.

TRADE-OFFS

First, let's look at trade-offs both within and across schools and districts that may have to be made in order to implement reforms that might create more equitable school environments and outcomes. Within schools, for example, schools can teach a more culturally inclusive curriculum, adding materials about minorities, gays and lesbians, and women. This takes time from other subjects.

To increase educational equity, groups working together, especially at young ages, could be of mixed ability, not segregated by ability (which also tends to segregate children along race and socioeconomic background). However, parents who believe their children are academically talented or even "gifted" want the best resources for their children. They may believe that their children get bored in classrooms with students who are not ahead academically. At higher levels of education, parents may agitate for more Advanced Placement (AP) or International Baccalaureate (IB) classes and programs, so their children can distinguish themselves on college applications.[2] Teachers may like ability grouping as well, because children who are grouped by ability may be able to be taught more efficiently.

Others suggest that teachers can be better trained about how they may subconsciously expect different levels of achievement from students based on their race or socioeconomic background. Teachers could become aware of cultural differences between themselves and the groups they teach, and try to bridge those differences. Those reforms require professional development for teachers and the time to process these issues.

Others argue that changes that occur within schools are not enough. There need to be widespread, perhaps federal policies that address inequality that occurs across schools, and, again there are trade-offs to such reforms. Choice programs, for example, have trade-offs. They do provide mostly disadvantaged urban children with more choices of where to go to school, and some of these schools are large improvements over their assigned, neighborhood schools. There is great demand for some charter schools, particularly ones with track records for improving student achievement. However, public schools that lose students to charter schools or other schools of choice lose the funding associated with these students and often become worse off than before, further disadvantaging the students who remain.

One potentially effective way to reduce gaps in educational outcomes is to reach students before school even starts. Large gaps by socioeconomic background and race exist before students begin kindergarten,[3] and schools face challenges in erasing such large initial gaps. Disadvantages may build cumulatively as students do poorly in schools over time, and early efforts to reduce these disadvantages may reduce the power of this accumulation. Federal efforts like increasing the reach of Head Start programs, providing subsidies for preschool education, or mandating universal preschool may also diminish inequalities by socioeconomic background and possibly race, but there is a cost to the public (through increased taxes perhaps or less government spending on other things) that some are unwilling to pay.

Another potentially effective policy to reduce gaps in learning, particularly by socioeconomic background, is to increase students' time in schools. That could mean a longer school day or a longer school year. This would result in more pay for teachers and in other expenses that taxpayers may not support. Others have suggested attending school for a similar number of days, but replacing the long summer break by interspersing shorter vacations throughout the year as they do in most other countries. Families, many of whom are privileged, (and teachers) resist giving up an uninterrupted summer break, as that is the time when children may participate in different types of activities like study abroad experiences, camps, or extended family vacations, or gain job or internship experiences.

One reform that is rarely considered is to change the ways schools are funded that lead to different amounts of money being spent on students per capita across states and across schools within states. Efforts have been directed through the courts, both state and federal, to sue state and federal governments on behalf of students who are not getting an "equal" education. Some states like Oregon, Kansas, Louisiana, and Texas (through a system called recapture) redistribute resources across districts in a variety of ways, though all of these plans have met with opposition. This reform, which spreads more money across schools in a county or in a state, appears to "take" resources from advantaged schools, a cost that many voters and taxpayers are unwilling to bear. And, in those places where low- and high-resource schools must share funding, parents have taken children out of schools or have raised additional funds for their neighborhood schools. Wealthier parents are better able to raise these funds, while poorer parents cannot.

Chapter 4 shows that the funds available to educate children vary widely by state and by district. School funding continues to be largely funded by local property taxes, a process that perpetuates itself.

High-quality schools drive up home prices, which results in a higher tax base. Wealthy neighborhoods that know their schools are a draw for movers may devote even more of their tax base to schools. Richer schools get richer, and, as researchers are beginning to find, there is a growing divide between the wealthiest families and those with less wealth, and a shrinking divide between poor, working-class, and middle-class families.[4]

It is in these debates about funding that the opposition to diminishing inequality is starkest. Parents who are able to do so move to the neighborhoods where they perceive their children will receive the best education.[5] Once established in these schools, they do not support plans to redistribute funding more equitably across districts, as it is perceived as a "zero-sum game"—any shared funding is a reduction in the amount of resources available to their students (no matter how many resources these students already have). State and local politicians dare not suggest policies that equalize funding across districts, so governments have limited funds to supplement poorer schools—only those that come from current state taxes or proposed state tax increases, which are already allocated to many other functions of state governments.

There are also trade-offs to promoting desegregation (let alone mandating it). It is important to remember that desegregation itself—simply allowing black students to attend all-white schools—was met with great protest. In some places, white parents would not send their children to school, and the US National Guard had to be called to protect those few, brave black students who attended previously all-white schools. Busing, a policy tried in the 1970s, sparked violent protest among parents and students. Some of the protest sprung from racism, though other stated reasons for white protest included being sent away from neighborhood schools and spending long durations on a bus. One consequence of busing, according to some researchers, is that white families fled schools in the city—either by moving to the suburbs or by using private schools.[6] A few magnet schools were not enough to stem the tide of whites leaving urban schools.

So, these are some, just some, ideas about how to address the large problems facing schools today. This chapter and the previous one show a smattering of the kinds of educational reforms that have been proposed to combat these large problems, but they also give you a sense of why reforms are so hard to implement. The trade-offs are generally consequential for one or more groups in society and people have opposing ideas about the best ways to combat problems that we all may agree we face.

CAN SCHOOLS DO EVERYTHING?

Although reformers, and perhaps we ourselves, have the goal for education that it should reduce inequality in outcomes or experiences, or at least minimize the influence that ascribed characteristics like socioeconomic background, race and ethnicity, gender, disability status, and sexual orientation (among others) have on a person's chances to have her or his abilities and talents recognized, it is unclear whether this goal is realistic. Students come to schools differently prepared and with different resources. Students live in different neighborhoods and socialize with different peers. Politicians and reformers are often shocked and dismayed by the inequalities in test scores and graduation rates across socioeconomic and racial groups and blame schools for these differences (or at least charge schools with fixing them). Can schools make up for other inequalities in resources and experiences that occur outside of schools? Can schools make up for differences in preparation before school? Can schools provide students with trips, extracurricular activities, cultural experiences, and educational tutoring and resources that more advantaged families are able to provide on their own? Can schools make sure students are well fed and healthy enough to be able to focus on schoolwork? Can schools provide counseling and other psychological services to students from families that experience disruptions due to anything from divorce or remarriage to unemployment, relocation, imprisonment, or death of peers or family members? Can schools keep children safe in their neighborhoods and make up for those services that neighborhoods provide?

It seems that this may be a tall order for schools alone, yet most policymakers and the public seek solutions to educational inequality only in schools. The most successful programs at improving educational outcomes for children, like Harlem Children's Village, realize that children are nurtured in families and live in neighborhoods. Families need to be supported in their efforts to feed, house, and provide learning opportunities for their children. Neighborhoods need to be safe places with opportunities for children to be active and engaged. If we charge only schools with the task of remedying educational inequality, then we may doom them to failure.

Scholars like Richard Rothstein have argued that while schools can make some inroads into closing achievement gaps between groups, they cannot be the sole source of change.[7] Students need stable housing, good health care and nutrition, safe neighborhoods, and activities that keep them engaged after school and during the summers. To some extent, school-based initiatives can address these issues: through policies that promote racial integration, through school-based health clinics and nutrition programs, through expanded early childhood education, and through expanded after-school and summer programs. However, schools alone are unlikely to be able to create policies that decrease the widening income gap, promote residential stability, and decrease the crime and concentrated disadvantages in highly segregated neighborhoods.

POLITICS AND SCHOOL INEQUALITY

For better or worse, how we as a society educate our children is a political issue. It involves different visions of how we want our social world and our governing institutions to work. Some believe that schools should receive federal support and that funds should be distributed more equitably among schools. Others think that schools should be accountable to their local constituencies and that educational issues are better decided by states and districts. These clashes are mirrored in larger political battles over the role of the federal government in our daily lives. Schools become sites where these issues play out, and it becomes hard to mandate change.

Schools are also places where other political battles take place. Those who believe in less government control may be in favor of more privatization of schools. This argument has resulted in the tremendous growth of charter schools and some growth in voucher programs. Others argue that schools are very different from private institutions that are consumer-oriented and provide consumable "products." Schools, they argue, are best conceived as public services that are for the good of the society and not entirely oriented toward the individual. They provide a public good, above and beyond the ways that they serve individual students and families.[8]

Schools are also places where liberal and conservative ideas get contested. Schools may promote acceptance of LGBTQ families and students, and they may be places where racial diversity is celebrated. They may also be places where sex education is abstinence-only, and until very recently, they were places where black and white students held separate proms. They may be places where creationism is taught and where climate change is challenged. They may be places that teach alternative histories of the United States that place the voices of women and minorities in the center or they may be places where teachers and students believe that too much emphasis is placed on historical wrongdoing in the US past, as recently occurred in Arizona.

Schools are also places where the values of unions get challenged. Teachers' unions have been and continue to be politically powerful groups. Politicians who do not support unions generally may agitate to erode some of the conditions guaranteed to teachers in their contracts. And, on the part of teachers, they may be unwilling to compromise for fear that their unions will be weakened.

All of these political battles are centered in the institution of education. Politicians who seek to realize their political visions may either knowingly or inadvertently also maintain or worsen school inequality, and this is yet another challenge for those seeking to minimize educational inequality.

One of my goals for this book, apart from providing a portrait of educational inequality in the United States, is to get you, the reader, to think of education as something that is accomplished by a society, and, as a member of that society, you have a role in shaping it. As students, and later as parents, people often think of schools in terms of the ways that they serve themselves—what their own experiences were and how they could be improved, or they think about the quality of education their own children get. They think of schools according to their private functions, as Labaree would say.[9] That is one vantage point from which to view education, but I hope throughout this book to have also given some ways to view the other vantage point that Labaree identifies, the public function. As a member of society, you have a say in how you want your society to look. Education is one means by which we accomplish that vision—and it is a powerful means. Education then is intimately tied to how you want the world to look. So, when we think about educational inequality, I pose these two important questions for you to hopefully think about:

What is your ideal vision of society?

Can schools be changed to better accomplish this vision? If so, how? What else needs to change?

Notes

CHAPTER 1. THE PROMISE(S) OF EDUCATION

1. www.brainyquote.com/quotes/quotes/h/horacemann137201.html.
2. Benavot and Riddle 1988.
3. Gerth and Mills 1946.
4. Shavit and Blossfeld 1993.
5. Meyer 1977.
6. Thompson 1985.
7. Bowles and Gintis 1976.
8. See Sadker and Sadker 1994.
9. See Davis and Moore 1945; Parsons 1959.
10. See Heath 1983; Rist 1970.
11. Labaree 1997.
12. E.g., McCall 2005.

CHAPTER 2. COMPETING VISIONS OF PUBLIC
EDUCATION: WHO AND WHAT SHOULD IT BE FOR?

1. For a good review of the history of American public education, see Tyack (1974) and Urban and Wagoner (2009). Much of the following review is drawn from those two sources.

2. Reese 2001.

3. Benavot and Riddle 1988.

CHAPTER 3. WHAT DOES EDUCATION DO?
PARADIGMS AND THEORIES ABOUT HOW
EDUCATION WORKS

1. Parsons 1959.

2. E.g., Davis and Moore 1945.

3. Turner 1960.

4. Buchmann, Diprete, and McDaniel 2008.

5. Orfield and Yun 1999; Rickles et al. 2001; Stroub and Richards 2013.

6. E.g., Hout, Raftery, and Bell 1993; Mare 1981.

7. Collins 1971.

8. Lemann 2000.

9. For more on testing, see Grodsky, Warren, and Felts 2008.

10. Rist 1970.

11. Gerth and Mill 1946.

12. Wyatt and Hecker 2006.

13. National Center for Education Statistics 2015.

14. Sewell, Haller, and Ohlendorf 1970; Sewell, Haller, and Portes 1969.

15. Bourdieu and Passeron 1977.

16. Blau and Duncan 1967.

17. E.g., Hauser, Tsai, and Sewell 1983; Looker and Pineo 1983; Sewell, Haller, and Ohlendorf 1970; Sewell, Haller, and Portes 1969.

18. Wilson and Portes 1975.

19. Conklin and Dailey 1981; Looker and Pineo 1983; Picou and Carter 1976; Reitzes and Mutran 1980.

20. Reitzes and Mutran 1980.

21. Cheng and Starks 2002.

22. E.g., Farkas et al. 1990; Kao 1995.

23. Bourdieu and Passeron 1977.

24. Lamont and Lareau 1988.

25. DiMaggio 1982.

26. Kohn 1977.

27. Lareau 1989.

28. Lareau 2001.

29. Bourdieu and Passeron 1977; Dumais 2002; Horvat, Weininger, and Lareau 2003; Lamont and Lareau 1988; Lareau and Horvat 1999; Lee and Bowen 2006.

30. Goffman 1959.

31. E.g., Parsons 1975.

32. Thorne 1993.
33. Conchas 2006; Ferguson 2000; Lee 2005.
34. Conchas 2006.
35. Dewey 1916; Freire 1970.
36. Apple 2013.
37. Kozol 1991.

CHAPTER 4. INEQUALITY BY SOCIOECONOMIC BACKGROUND AND CLASS

1. E.g., Kozol 1991.
2. Sorensen 1996.
3. Bowles and Gintis 1976.
4. Lareau 1989.
5. Lareau 2001.
6. Anyon 1997; Kozol 1991.
7. Reardon and Owens 2014.
8. Logan, Stowell, and Oakley 2002.
9. E.g., Hanushek 1997.
10. Baker, Sciarra, and Farrie 2010.
11. Baker and Corcoran 2012.
12. Darling-Hammond 2000; Goe 2007; Kane, Rockoff, and Staiger 2008.
13. Boyd et al. 2008.
14. Neild and Spiridakis 2003.
15. Glass and Smith 1979; for an opposing view, see Hoxby 2000.
16. Alon and Tienda 2007; Soares 2015.
17. Klugman 2013.
18. Klugman 2013.
19. Coleman et al. 1966 [1999]; Reardon 2011.
20. Condron 2009; Downey, Von Hippel, and Broh 2004.
21. Jensen 1998.
22. Bouchard and McGue 1981.
23. Evans and Martin 2000.
24. Kamin 1974.
25. Grodsky, Warren, and Felts 2008.
26. Miele 1979; Neisser et al. 1996.
27. Orfield, Basa, and Yun 2001.
28. Rothstein 2004.
29. Wightman and Danziger 2014.
30. Lareau 2001.
31. Manski and Wise 1983.

32. Bourdieu and Passeron 1977.

33. Kohn 1977.

34. E.g., Heath 1983.

35. Magnuson, Meyers, Ruhm, Waldfogel 2004.

36. Lareau 1989.

37. Fan and Chen 2001; Lee and Bowen 2006.

38. Robinson and Harris 2014.

39. Lin, Ensel, and Vaughn 1981.

40. Coleman 1988; Coleman and Hoffer 1987.

41. Coleman 1988.

42. Lareau 1989.

43. Wilson 1987.

44. Walker, Keane, and Burke 2010.

45. Sharkey and Elwert 2011.

46. E.g., Ainsworth 2002; Bowen and Bowen 1999; Leventhal and Brooks-Gunn 2000.

47. Rothstein 2004.

48. Sanbonmatsu, Kling, Duncan, and Brooks-Gunn 2006.

49. Swanson and Schneider 1999.

50. Pribesh and Downey 1999.

51. MacLeod 1987.

52. Willis 1977.

53. Tyson 2011.

54. Lee and Burkham 2002.

55. Alexander, Entwisle, and Olson 2014.

56. Diprete and Eirich 2006.

57. Coleman at al. 1966 [1999].

58. E.g., Jencks 1972; Jencks and Brown 1975.

59. Betts, Reuben, and Danenberg 2000.

60. Reardon 2011.

61. McDonough 1997.

62. Wayne and Youngs 2003.

63. Hanushek 1997.

64. Eder 1981; Oakes 1985; Rist 1970.

65. Gamoran 1992.

66. Lucas 1999.

67. Lucas 1999.

68. Klugman 2013; Lucas 1999.

69. E.g., Alexander, Entwisle, and Olson 2007; Condron 2009; Downey, Von Hippel, and Broh 2004.

70. Downey, Von Hippel, and Hughes 2008.

71. Alexander, Entwisle, and Olson 2007.

72. Condron 2009.

CHAPTER 5. INEQUALITY BY RACE AND ETHNICITY, IMMIGRANT STATUS, AND LANGUAGE ABILITY

1. Xie and Goyette 1997.

2. Williams 2009.

3. Wollenberg 1978.

4. Loewen 1988.

5. Patterson 2001.

6. Ramos 2004.

7. Stout 2012.

8. Goldring and Smrekar 2002.

9. Clark 1987; Clotfelter 1976; Farley, Richards, and Wurdock 1980; Giles 1978; Smock and Wilson 1991.

10. Patterson 2001.

11. Mikelson 2005.

12. Kruse 2005; Lassiter 2006; Sugrue 2008.

13. Stroub and Richards 2013.

14. Kozol 1991.

15. *New York Times* 1990.

16. Rist 1970.

17. Ferguson 2000.

18. Conchas 2006; Tatum 2003.

19. Gurin, Dey, Hurtado, and Gurin 2002.

20. Khan 2011.

21. Ferguson 2003.

22. Hoelter 1982.

23. Kozol 1991.

24. McCarty 2002.

25. Stroub and Richards 2013.

26. Hoxby 2000.

27. Kao and Tienda 1998; Ogbu 1991.

28. Mikelson 1990.

29. MacLeod 1987.

30. Perry, Steele, and Hilliard 2003.

31. Kao, Tienda, and Schneider 1996.

32. Warren, Hoffman, and Andrew 2014.

33. E.g., Harry and Klingner 2014; Hosp and Reschly 2004.

34. Tyson 2011.

35. Lucas 1999.

36. E.g., Ferguson 2000.

37. Herrnstein and Murray 1994.

38. E.g., Fischer et al. 1996; Jencks and Phillips 1998.

39. Xie and Goyette 2003.

40. Bennett and Xie 2003.

41. Steele and Aronson 1995.

42. DeNavas-Walt and Proctor 2014.

43. http://factfinder.census.gov/faces/tableservices/jsf/pages/productview .xhtml?pid = ACS_13_3YR_S0201&prodType = table.

44. Kao and Tienda 1998; Kao, Tienda, and Schneider 1996; Jencks and Philipps 1998.

45. Kochar and Fry 2014.

46. Orr 2003.

47. www.census.gov/hhes/socdemo/education/data/cps/2014/tables.html, table 3.

48. Phillips et al. 1998.

49. Fryer and Levitt 2006; Lee and Burkham 2002; Phillips, Crouse, and Ralph 1998.

50. Steinberg, Dornbusch, and Brown 1992.

51. Chen and Stevenson 1995; Kitano 1976; Schneider and Lee 1990.

52. Steinberg 1989.

53. Lewis 1959.

54. Wilson 1987.

55. Ladson-Billings 2009; Perry, Steele, and Hilliard 2003.

56. Wilson 1987.

57. Card and Rothstein 2007.

58. Goldsmith 2009.

59. Ogbu 1991.

60. Fordham and Ogbu 1986.

61. Carter 2005.

62. E.g., Ainsworth-Darnell and Downey 1998; Downey 2008; Harris 2008; Horvat and Lewis 2003; Tyson, Darrity, and Castellino 2005.

63. Tyson 2011.

64. Harris 2011.

65. Goldsmith 2009; Mikelson 2001.

66. Valenzuela 1999.

67. Lareau and Horvat 1999; Roscigno and Ainsworth-Darnell 1999.

68. Lareau 2001.

69. Conchas 2006; Ferguson 2003.

70. Lee 2005.

71. Ferguson 2000.
72. Downey, Von Hippel, and Broh 2004.
73. Condron 2009; Phillips, Crouse, and Ralph 1998.
74. Caplan, Choy, and Whitmore 1992.
75. Steinberg 1989; Takaki 1993.
76. Caplan, Choy, and Whitmore 1992; Steinberg 1989.
77. Kao and Tienda 1998; Rong and Brown 2001.
78. Portes and Zhou 1993.
79. Feliciano 2005.
80. Chen and Stevenson 1995; Schneider and Lee 1990.
81. Coleman 1988.
82. Zhou and Bankston 1998.
83. Kao and Tienda 1998.
84. Schneider and Lee 1990.
85. The National Center for Education Statistics: http://nces.ed.gov/programs/coe/indicator_cgf.asp.
86. The National Center for Education Statistics: https://nces.ed.gov/programs/coe/pdf/coe_cnc.pdf.
87. www.ed.gov/news/press-releases/achievement-gap-narrows-high-school-graduation-rates-minority-students-improve-faster-rest-nation.
88. Kao, Vaquera, and Goyette 2013.
89. Kanno and Cromley 2013.
90. Mouw and Xie 1999.
91. Smith-Hefner 1993.
92. Desmond and Turley 2009.
93. Ericksen 1987.
94. Kao, Vaquera, and Goyette 2013.
95. Cheng 2003; Cheng and Lively 2009; Cheng and Klugman 2010.

CHAPTER 6. INEQUALITY BY GENDER AND DISABILITY

1. Barnett and Rivers 2006; Orr 2011; Sax 2007. For those who argue the "boy crisis" is a myth, see, e.g., Husain-Millimet 2009; Perkins-Gough 2006.
2. Webb 2006.
3. Reese 1999.
4. Current Population Survey 2013, table 1, www.census.gov/hhes/school/data/cps/2013/tables.html.
5. DiPrete and Buchmann 2013.
6. DiPrete and Buchmann 2013; Steinmayr and Spinath 2008.
7. Hamre and Pianta 2001.

8. National Center for Education Statistics 2011.

9. Skiba et al. 2002.

10. Ferguson 2000.

11. Fagot, Rodgers, and Leinbach 2000.

12. Cunningham 2001.

13. Moen, Erickson, and Dempster-McClain 1997.

14. Jacobs, Chhin, and Bleeker 2006.

15. Lee 2001; Valenzuela 1999.

16. Zhou and Bankston 2001.

17. López 2002.

18. Martin 1998.

19. DiPrete and Buchmann 2013.

20. Pascoe 2007.

21. Willis 1977.

22. www.menteach.org/resources/data_about_men_teachers.

23. National Center for Education Statistics 2013.

24. Paradise and Wall 1986.

25. Thorne 1993.

26. Messner 1995.

27. Eder and Parker 1987.

28. For a good review, see Linn and Petersen 1985.

29. Spencer, Steele, and Quinn 1999.

30. Looker and Magee 2000.

31. Lockwood 2006.

32. Jones and Wheatley 1990.

33. See figure 2.26 in Jeff Allum, *Graduate Enrollment and Degrees: 2003 to 2013*, Council of Graduate Schools and Graduate Record Examinations Program, published in 2014: http://cgsnet.org/ckfinder/userfiles/files/GED_report_2013.pdf.

34. E.g., Fikar 1992; O'Conor 1993.

35. Pascoe 2007.

36. www.npr.org/sections/codeswitch/2015/03/05/388464316/transgender-students-learn-to-navigate-school-halls.

37. US Department of Education 2010.

CHAPTER 7. EDUCATIONAL INEQUALITY IN OTHER NATIONS

1. Baker and LeTendre 2005; Boli, Ramirez, and Meyer 1985; Meyer 1977.

2. Altbach 2004.

3. Darling-Hammond 2010.

4. Darling-Hammond 2010.

5. To further explore inequality in these other dimensions across non-US nations, see www.education-inequalities.org/.

6. Carnoy and Rhoten 2002.

7. E.g., Benavot and Riddle 1988.

8. Hanushek, Woessmann, and Zhang 2011.

9. www.oecd.org/edu/eag2013%20(eng)—FINAL%2020%20June%202013 .pdf.

10. Condron 2009; Downey, Von Hippel, and Broh 2004.

11. OECD 2013.

12. Baker et al. 2001; Bray and Lykins 2012; Park, Byun, and Kim 2011.

13. Stevenson and Stigler 1994.

14. Chen and Stevenson 1995.

15. Sahlberg 2010.

16. Fullan 2010.

CHAPTER 8. EDUCATION REFORMS AND INEQUALITY

1. Labaree 2010; Rury 2005; Snyder 1993.

2. Goldin 1998; Stambler 1968.

3. Kessinger 2011.

4. Reese 2011.

5. Graves 2010.

6. Tyack and Cuban 1995.

7. Rury 2005.

8. Kessinger 2011.

9. Patterson 2001.

10. Rury 2013.

11. Good and McCaslin 2008.

12. Reese 2011.

13. Bracey 1995.

14. Kozol 1991.

15. Lewis 1966; Office of Policy Planning and Research 1955.

16. Coleman et al. 1966 [1999].

17. Tyack and Cuban 1995.

18. National Commission on Excellence in Education 1983.

19. National Commission on Excellence in Education 1983.

20. Bracey 1995.

21. Tyack and Cuban 1995.

22. Labaree 2010: 33.

23. Lee and Wong 2004.

24. McGuinn 2006.

25. No Child Left Behind Act 2001: Statute 1425.

26. McGuinn 2012.

27. Shear 2009.

28. McGuinn 2012.

29. Nee 2010.

30. Pfeffer 2008; Raftery and Hout 1993.

31. Korinek 2006.

32. Figlio and Rouse 2006.

33. Lauen and Gaddis 2012.

34. Booher-Jennings 2005; Diamond and Spillane 2004.

35. Ho 2008.

36. Chakrabarti 2014.

37. Neal and Schazenbach 2010.

38. Grodsky, Warren, and Felts 2008.

39. US Department of Education 2012.

40. Goldring and Smrekar 2002.

41. US Department of Education 2004.

42. E.g., Chubb and Moe 1990.

43. Buckley and Schneider 2003.

44. Schneider et al. 1997.

45. Schneider 2001.

46. Schneider et al. 1997.

47. Weininger 2014.

48. Fuller, Elmore, and Orfield 1996; Reay and Ball 1998; Wells and Crain 1997.

49. Ball 2003; Bowe, Ball, and Gewirtz 1994; Holme 2002.

50. Smrekar and Goldring 1999.

51. Smrekar and Goldring 1999: 33.

52. Rhodes and DeLuca 2014.

53. Patillo, Delale-O'Connor, and Butts 2014.

54. Logan and Burdick-Will 2015.

55. Manno et al. 1998.

56. Logan and Burdick-Will 2015.

57. Holme 2002.

58. Bankston and Caldas 2000; Fairlie and Resch 2002; Hess and Leal 2001; Renzulli and Evans 2005; Saporito 2003; Saporito and Sohoni 2006; Wrinkle, Stewart, and Polinard 1999.

59. Saporito 2003; Saporito and Sohoni 2006.

60. Saporito and Lareau 1999.

61. Renzulli and Evans 2005.

62. Fairlie 2002.

63. Princiotta and Bielick 2006.

64. Stevens 2001.

65. E.g., Henig 1995; Lee, Croninger, and Smith 1996; Martinez, Godwin, and Kemerer 1996; Smrekar and Goldring 1999; Wells and Crain 1997; Witt and Thorn 1996.

66. Kane and Luricella 2001.

67. Darling-Hammond et al. 2005; Raymond and Fletcher 2002; Xu, Hannaway, and Taylor 2011.

68. Kane, Rockoff, and Staiger 2008.

69. For an excellent account of how philanthropy was promoted in Newark, New Jersey, schools, see Russakoff 2015.

70. Orfield, Kucsera, and Siegel-Hawley 2012.

CHAPTER 9. IF WE DON'T LIKE EDUCATIONAL INEQUALITY, WHY IS IT SO HARD TO MAKE IT GO AWAY?

1. Darling-Hammond 2010.

2. Klugman 2013.

3. Lee and Burkham 2002.

4. E.g., Reardon 2011; Reardon and Owens 2014.

5. Holme 2002.

6. E.g., Wilson 1985.

7. Rothstein 2004.

8. Labaree 1997.

9. Labaree 1997.

References

Advisory Committee on Head Start Research and Evaluation. 2012. *Final Report*. U.S. Department of Health and Human Services.

Ainsworth, James W. 2002. "Why Does It Take a Village? The Mediation of Neighborhood Effects on Educational Achievement." *Social Forces* 81 (1): 117–152.

Ainsworth-Darnell, James W., and Douglas B. Downey. 1998. "Assessing the Oppositional Culture Explanation for Racial/Ethnic Differences in School Performance." *American Sociological Review* 63 (4): 536–553.

Alexander, Karl L., Doris R. Entwisle, and Linda Steffel Olson. 2007. "Lasting Consequences of the Summer Learning Gap." *American Sociological Review* 72 (2): 167–180.

———. 2014. *The Long Shadow: Family Background, Disadvantaged Urban Youth, and the Transition to Adulthood*. New York: Russell Sage Foundation.

Alon, Sigal, and Marta Tienda. 2007. "Diversity, Opportunity, and the Shifting Meritocracy in Higher Education." *American Sociological Review* 72 (4): 487–511.

Altbach, Philip G. 2004. "Globalisation and the University: Myths and Realities in an Unequal World." *Tertiary Education & Management* 10 (1): 3–25.

Alwin, Duane, and Luther B. Otto. 1977. "High School Context Effects on Aspirations." *Sociology of Education* 50 (4): 259–273.

Anyon, Jean. 1997. *Ghetto Schooling: A Political Economy of Urban Educational Reform*. New York: Teachers College Press.

Apple, Michael W. 2013. *Education and Power.* New York: Routledge.

Baker, Bruce D., and Sean P. Corcoran. 2012. *The Stealth Inequities of School Funding: How State and Local School Finance Systems Perpetuate Inequitable Student Spending.* Center for American Progress.

Baker, Bruce D., David G. Sciarra, and Danielle Farrie. 2010. *Is School Funding Fair? A National Report Card.* Newark, NJ: Education Law Center.

Baker, David P., Motoko Akiba, Gerald K. Le Tendre, and Alexander Wiseman. 2001. "Worldwide Shadow Education: Outside-School Learning, Institutional Quality of Schooling, and Cross-National Mathematics Achievement." *Educational Evaluation and Policy Analysis* 23 (1): 1–17.

Baker, David, and Gerald K. LeTendre. 2005. *National Differences, Global Similarities: World Culture and the Future of Schooling.* Stanford: Stanford University Press.

Ball, Stephen J. 2003. *Class Strategies and the Education Market: The Middle Classes and Social Advantage.* London: Routledge Farmer.

Bankston, Carl L., III, and Stephen J. Caldas. 2000. "White Enrollment in Nonpublic Schools, Public School Racial Composition, and Student Performance." *Sociological Quarterly* 41 (4): 539–550.

Barnett, Rosalind, and Caryl Rivers. 2006. "The Boy Crisis-Fact or Myth?" *Teachers College Record* 2.

Benavot, Aaron, and Phyllis Riddle. 1988. "The Expansion of Primary Education, 1870–1940: Trends and Issues." *Sociology of Education* 61:191–210.

Bennett, Pamela R., and Yu Xie. 2003. "Revisiting Racial Differences in College Attendance: The Role of Historically Black Colleges and Universities." *American Sociological Review* 68 (4): 567–580.

Betts, Julian R., Kim S. Reuben, and Anne Danenberg. 2000. *Equal Resources, Equal Outcomes? The Distribution of School Resources and Student Achievement in California.* San Francisco: Public Policy Institute of California.

Blau, Peter M., and Otis Dudley Duncan. 1967. *The American Occupational Structure.* New York: John Wiley & Sons.

Boli, John, Francisco O. Ramirez, and John W. Meyer. 1985. "Explaining the Origins and Expansion of Mass Education." *Comparative Education Review* 29 (2): 145–170.

Booher-Jennings, Jennifer. 2005. "Below the Bubble: 'Educational Triage' and the Texas Accountability System." *American Educational Research Journal* 42 (2): 231–268.

Bouchard, Thomas J., and Matthew McGue. 1981. "Familial Studies of Intelligence: A Review." *Science* 212 (4498): 1055–1059.

Bourdieu, Pierre, and Jean-Claude Passeron. 1977. *Reproduction in Education, Society and Culture.* London: Sage.

Bowe, Richard, Stephen Ball, and Sharon Gewirtz. 1994. "'Parental Choice,' Consumption, and Social Theory: The Operation of Micromarkets in Education." *British Journal of Educational Studies* 42 (1): 38–52.

Bowen, Natasha K., and Gary L. Bowen. 1999. "Effects of Crime and Violence in Neighborhoods and Schools on the School Behavior and Performance of Adolescents." *Journal of Adolescent Research* 14 (3): 319–342.

Bowles, Samuel, and Herbert Gintis. 1976. *Schooling in Capitalist America*. Vol. 57. New York: Basic Books.

Boyd, Donald, Pam Grossman, Hamilton Lankford, Susanna Loeb, and James Wyckof. 2008. *Who Leaves? Teacher Attrition and Student Achievement*. No. w14022. National Bureau of Economic Research.

Bracey, Gerald. 1995. *Final Exam*. Bloomington, IN: TECHNOS Press.

Bray, Mark, and Chad Lykins. 2012. *Shadow Education: Private Supplementary Tutoring and Its Implications for Policy Makers in Asia*. Mandaluyong City, Philippines: Asian Development Bank.

Brookover, Wilbur. 1957. *The Sociology of Education*. New York: American Book Company.

Buchmann, Claudia, Thomas A. DiPrete, and Anne McDaniel. 2008. "Gender Inequalities in Education." *Annual Review of Sociology* 34:319–337.

Buckley, Jack, and Mark Schneider. 2003. "Shopping for Schools: How Do Marginal Consumers Gather Information about Schools?" *Policy Studies Journal* 3 (2): 121–145.

Burke, Ronald J., and Mary C. Mattis, eds. 2007. *Women and Minorities in Science, Technology, Engineering, and Mathematics: Upping the Numbers*. Cheltenham, UK: Edward Elgar.

Caplan, Nathan, Marcella H. Choy, and John K. Whitmore. 1992. "Indochinese Refugee Families and Academic Achievement." *Scientific American* 266 (2): 36–42.

Card, David, and Jesse Rothstein. 2007. "Racial Segregation and the Black–White Test Score Gap." *Journal of Public Economics* 91 (11): 2158–2184.

Carnoy, Martin, and Diana Rhoten. 2002. "What Does Globalization Mean for Educational Change? A Comparative Approach." *Comparative Education Review* 46 (1): 1–9.

Carter, Prudence L. 2005. *Keepin' It Real: School Success beyond Black and White*. Oxford: Oxford University Press.

Chakrabarti, Rajashri. 2014. "Incentives and Responses under No Child Left Behind: Credible Threats and the Role of Competition." *Journal of Public Economics* 110: 124–146.

Chen, Chuansheng, and Harold W. Stevenson. 1995. "Motivation and Mathematics Achievement: A Comparative Study of Asian-American, Caucasian-American, and East Asian High School Students." *Child Development* 66 (4): 1215–1234.

Cheng, Hsu-chih. 2003. *Standing in the Middle of Interracial Relations: The Educational Experiences of Children from Multiracial Backgrounds.* Bloomington: Indiana University Press.

Cheng, Simon, and Joshua Klugman. 2010. "School Racial Composition and Biracial Adolescents' School Attachment." *Sociological Quarterly* 51 (1): 150–178.

Cheng, Simon, and Kathryn J. Lively. 2009. "Multiracial Self-Identification and Adolescent Outcomes: A Social Psychological Approach to the Marginal Man Theory." *Social Forces* 88 (1): 61–98.

Cheng, Simon, and Brian Starks. 2002. "Racial Differences in the Effects of Significant Others on Students' Educational Expectations." *Sociology of Education* 75 (4): 306–327.

Chubb, John E., and Terry M. Moe. 1990. *Politics, Markets, and America's Schools.* Washington, DC: Brookings Institution Press.

Clark, William A.V. 1987. "School Desegregation and White Flight: A Reexamination and Case Study." *Social Science Research* 16 (3): 211–228.

Clotfelter, Charles T. 1976. "The Detroit Decision and 'White Flight.'" *Journal of Legal Studies* 5 (1): 99–112.

———. 2001. "Are Whites Still Fleeing? Racial Patterns and Enrollment Shifts in Urban Public Schools, 1987–1996." *Journal of Policy Analysis and Management* 20 (2): 199–221.

Coleman, James S. 1988. "Social Capital in the Creation of Human Capital." *American Journal of Sociology* 94 (Supplement): S95–S120.

Coleman, James, Ernest Campbell, Carol Hobson, James McPartland, Alexander Mood, Frederic Weinfeld, and Robert York. 1966 [1999]. "The Coleman Report [Excerpts from Equality of Educational Opportunity]." In *The Structure of Schooling: Readings in the Sociology of Education,* edited by R. Arum and I.R. Beattie, 154–167. Boston: McGraw-Hill.

Coleman, James, and Thomas Hoffer. 1987. *Public and Private Schools: The Impact of Communities.* New York: Basic Books.

Collins, Randall. 1971. "Functional and Conflict Theories of Educational Stratification." *American Sociological Review* 36 (6): 1002–1019.

———. 1979. *The Credential Society: An Historical Sociology of Education and Stratification.* New York: John Wiley.

Conchas, Gilberto Q. 2006. *The Color of Success: Race and High-Achieving Urban Youth.* New York: Teachers College Press.

Condron, Dennis J. 2009. "Social Class, School and Non-School Environments, and Black/White Inequalities in Children's Learning." *American Sociological Review* 74 (5): 685–708.

Conklin, Mary E., and Ann Ricks Dailey. 1981. "Does Consistency of Parental Encouragement Matter for Secondary School Students?" *Sociology of Education* 54 (4): 254–262.

Cookson, Peter W., Jr., and Caroline Hodges Persell. 1985. *Preparing for Power: America's Elite Boarding Schools*. New York: Basic Books.

Cunningham, Mick. 2001. "The Influence of Parental Attitudes and Behaviors on Children's Attitudes toward Gender and Household Labor in Early Adulthood." *Journal of Marriage and Family* 63 (1): 111–122.

Darling-Hammond, Linda. 2000. "Teacher Quality and Student Achievement." *Education Policy Analysis Archives* 8 (1): 1–44.

———. 2010. *The Flat World and Education: How America's Commitment to Equity Will Determine Our Future*. New York: Teachers College Press.

Darling-Hammond, Linda, Deborah J. Holtzman, Su Jin Gatlin, and Julian Vasquez Heilig. 2005. "Does Teacher Preparation Matter? Evidence about Teacher Certification, Teach for America, and Teacher Effectiveness." *Education Policy Analysis Archives* 13(42): 1–51.

Davis, Kingsley, and Wilbert E. Moore. 1945. "Some Principles of Stratification." *American Sociological Review* 10 (2): 242–249.

Demos, John Putnam. 1986. *Past, Present, Personal: The Family and the Life Course in American History*. New York: Oxford University Press.

DeNavas-Walt, Carmen, and Bernadette D. Proctor. 2014. *Current Population Reports, P60–249, Income and Poverty in the United States: 2013*. Washington, DC: US Census Bureau, US Government Printing Office.

Desmond, Matthew, and Ruth N. López Turley. 2009. "The Role of Familism in Explaining the Hispanic-White College Application Gap." *Social Problems* 56 (2): 311–334.

Dewey, John. 1916. *Democracy and Education*. Edited by Jo Ann Boydston, and Patricia Baysinger. Carbondale: Southern Illinois University Press, 1985.

Diamond, John B., and James P. Spillane. 2004. "High-Stakes Accountability in Urban Elementary Schools: Challenging or Reproducing Inequality?" *Teachers College Record* 106 (6): 1145–1176.

DiMaggio, Paul. 1982. "Cultural Capital and School Success: The Impact of Status Culture Participation on the Grades of U.S. High School Students." *American Sociological Review* 47 (2): 189–201.

DiPrete, Thomas A., and Claudia Buchmann. 2013. *The Rise of Women: The Growing Gender Gap in Education and What It Means for American Schools*. New York: Russell Sage Foundation.

DiPrete, Thomas A., and Gregory M. Eirich. 2006. "Cumulative Advantage as a Mechanism for Inequality: A Review of Theoretical and Empirical Developments." *Annual Review of Sociology* 32:271–297.

Downey, Douglas B. 2008. "Black/White Differences in School Performance: The Oppositional Culture Explanation." *Annual Review of Sociology* 34:107–126.

Downey, Douglas B., Paul T. Von Hippel, and Beckett A. Broh. 2004. "Are Schools the Great Equalizer? Cognitive Inequality during the Summer Months and the School Year." *American Sociological Review* 69 (5): 613–635.

Downey, Douglas B., Paul T. Von Hippel, and Melanie Hughes. 2008. "Are 'Failing' Schools Really Failing? Using Seasonal Comparison to Evaluate School Effectiveness." *Sociology of Education* 81 (3): 242–270.

Dumais, Susan A. 2002. "Cultural Capital, Gender, and School Success: The Role of Habitus." *Sociology of Education* 75 (1): 44–68.

Eder, Donna. 1981. "Ability Grouping as a Self-Fulfilling Prophecy: A Micro-Analysis of Teacher-Student Interaction." *Sociology of Education* 54 (3): 151–161.

Eder, Donna, and Stephen Parker. 1987. "The Cultural Production and Reproduction of Gender: The Effect of Extracurricular Activities on Peer-Group Culture." *Sociology of Education* 60 (3): 200–213.

Erickson, Frederick. 1987. "Transformation and School Success: The Politics and Culture of Educational Achievement." *Anthropology & Education Quarterly* 18 (4): 335–356.

Evans, David M., and Nicholas G. Martin. 2000. "The Validity of Twin Studies." *GeneScreen* 1 (2): 77–79.

Fagot, Beverly I., Carie S. Rodgers, and Mary D. Leinbach. 2000. "Theories of Gender Socialization." In *The Developmental Social Psychology of Gender*, edited by Thomas Eckes and Hanns Martin Trautner, 65–89. Oxon, UK: Psychology Press.

Fairlie, Robert W. 2002. "Private Schools and 'Latino Flight' from Black School Children." *Demography* 39 (4): 655–674.

Fairlie, Robert, and Alexander Resch. 2002. "Is There 'White Flight' into Private Schools? Evidence from the National Educational Longitudinal Study." *Review of Economics and Statistics* 84 (1): 21–33.

Fan, Xitao, and Michael Chen. 2001. "Parental Involvement and Students' Academic Achievement: A Meta-Analysis." *Educational Psychology Review* 13 (1): 1–22.

Farkas, George, Robert P. Grobe, Daniel Sheehan, and Yuan Shuan. 1990. "Cultural Resources and School Success: Gender, Ethnicity, and Poverty Groups within an Urban School District." *American Sociological Review* 55 (1): 127–142.

Farley, Reynolds, Toni Richards, and Clarence Wurdock. 1980. "School Desegregation and White Flight: An Investigation of Competing Models and Their Discrepant Findings." *Sociology of Education* 53 (3): 123–139.

Feliciano, Cynthia. 2005. "Educational Selectivity in US Immigration: How Do Immigrants Compare to Those Left Behind?" *Demography* 42 (1): 131–152.

Ferguson, Ann Arnett. 2000. *Bad Boys: Public Schools in the Making of Black Masculinity*. Ann Arbor: University of Michigan Press.

Ferguson, Ronald F. 2003. "Teachers' Perceptions and Expectations and the Black-White Test Score Gap." *Urban Education* 38 (4): 460–507.

Figlio, David N., and Cecilia Elena Rouse. 2006. "Do Accountability and Voucher Threats Improve Low-Performing Schools?" *Journal of Public Economics* 90:239–255.

Fikar, Charles R. 1992. "Gay Teens and Suicide." *Pediatrics* 89 (3): 519–520.

Fischer, Claude S., Michael Hout, Martin Sanchez Jankowski, Samuel R. Lucas, Ann Swidler, and Kim Voss. 1996. *Inequality by Design: Cracking the Bell Curve Myth.* Princeton: Princeton University Press.

Fordham, Signithia, and John Ogbu. 1986. "Black Students' School Success: Coping with the Burden of 'Acting White.'" *Urban Review* 18 (3): 176–206.

Fox, Sherwood D., trans. 1956. *Émile Durkheim: Education and Sociology.* Glencoe, IL: Free Press.

Freire, Paulo. 1970. *Pedagogy of the Oppressed.* New York: Continuum.

Frey, William. 1979. "Central City White Flight: Racial and Nonracial Causes." *American Sociological Review* 44 (3): 425–448.

Fryer, Roland G., and Steven D. Levitt. 2006. "The Black-White Test Score Gap through Third Grade." *American Law and Economics Review* 8 (2): 249–281.

Fullan, Michael. 2010. *All Systems Go: The Change Imperative for Whole System Reform.* Thousand Oaks, CA: Corwin.

Fuller, Bruce, Richard F. Elmore, and Gary Orfield. 1996. "Policy-Making in the Dark: Illuminating the School Choice Debate." In *Who Chooses? Who Loses? Culture, Institutions, and the Unequal Effects of School Choice,* edited by Bruce Fuller and Richard F. Elmore, 1–24. New York: Teachers College Press.

Gamoran, Adam. 1992. "The Variable Effects of High School Tracking." *American Sociological Review* 57 (6): 812–828.

Gerber, Theodore P., and Sin Yi Cheung. 2008. "Horizontal Stratification in Postsecondary Education: Forms, Explanations, and Implications." *Annual Review of Sociology* 34:299- 318.

Gerth, H. H., and C. Wright Mills. 1946. *From Max Weber: Essays in Sociology.* New York: Oxford University Press.

Giles, Micheal W. 1978. "White Enrollment Stability and School Desegregation: A Two-Level Analysis." *American Sociological Review* 43 (6): 848–864.

Glass, Gene V., and Mary Lee Smith. 1979. "Meta-Analysis of Research on Class Size and Achievement." *Educational Evaluation and Policy Analysis* 1 (1): 2–16.

Goe, Laura. 2007. "The Link between Teacher Quality and Student Outcomes: A Research Synthesis." *National Comprehensive Center for Teacher Quality.*

Goffman, Erving. 1959. *The Presentation of Self in Everyday Life.* Garden City, NY: Anchor.

———. 1961. *Asylums: Essays on the Social Situation of Mental Patients and Other Inmates.* Garden City, NY: Anchor.

Goldin, Claudia. 1998. *Labor Markets in the 20th Century*. Cambridge, MA: National Bureau of Economic Research.

Goldring, Ellen, and Claire Smrekar. 2002. "Magnet Schools: Reform and Race in Urban Education." *Clearing House* 76 (1): 13–15.

Goldsmith, Pat Rubio. 2009. "Schools or Neighborhoods or Both? Race and Ethnic Segregation and Educational Attainment." *Social Forces* 87 (4): 1913–1941.

Good, Thomas L., and Mary McCaslin. 2008. "What We Learned about Research on School Reform: Considerations for Practice and Policy." *Teachers College Record* 110 (11): 2475- 2495.

Goyette, Kimberly. 2008. "Race, Social Background, and School Choice Options." *Equity & Excellence in Education* 41 (1): 114–129.

Graves, Karen. 2010. "The Cardinal Principles: Mapping Liberal Education and the American High School." *American Educational History Journal* 37 (1): 95–107.

Grodsky, Eric, John Robert Warren, and Erika Felts. 2008. "Testing and Social Stratification in American Education. " *Annual Review of Sociology* 34:385–404.

Gurin, Patricia, Eric L. Dey, Sylvia Hurtado, and Gerald Gurin. 2002. "Diversity and Higher Education: Theory and Impact on Educational Outcomes." *Harvard Educational Review* 72 (3): 330–367.

Hallinan, Maureen T. 1994. "Tracking: From Theory to Practice." *Sociology of Education* 67 (2): 79–84.

Hamre, Bridget K., and Robert C. Pianta. 2001. "Early Teacher–Child Relationships and the Trajectory of Children's School Outcomes through Eighth Grade." *Child Development* 72 (2): 625–638.

Hanson, Sandra L. 1994. "Lost Talent: Unrealized Educational Aspirations and Expectations among U.S. Youths." *Sociology of Education* 67 (3): 159–183.

Hanushek, Eric A. 1997. "Assessing the Effects of School Resources on Student Performance: An Update." *Educational Evaluation and Policy Analysis* 19 (2): 141–164.

Hanushek, Eric A., Ludger Woessmann, and Lei Zhang. 2011. *General Education, Vocational Education, and Labor-Market Outcomes over the Life-Cycle*. No. w17504. Washington, DC: National Bureau of Economic Research.

Harris, Angel L. 2008. "Optimism in the Face of Despair: Black-White Differences in Beliefs about School as a Means for Upward Social Mobility." *Social Science Quarterly* 89 (3): 608–630.

———. 2011. *Kids Don't Want to Fail: Oppositional Culture and the Black-White Achievement Gap*. Cambridge, MA: Harvard University Press.

Harry, Beth, and Janette K. Klingner. 2014. *Why Are So Many Minority Students in Special Education? Understanding Race & Disability in Schools*. New York: Teachers College Press.

Hauser, Robert M., Shu-Ling Tsai, and William H. Sewell. 1983. "A Model of Stratification with Response Error in Social and Psychological Variables." *Sociology of Education* 56 (1): 20–46.

Heath, Shirley Brice. 1983. *Ways with Words: Language, Life and Work in Communities and Classrooms.* Cambridge: Cambridge University Press.

Henig, Jeffrey R. 1995. "Race and Choice in Montgomery County, Maryland, Magnet Schools." *Teachers College Record* 96 (4): 729–735.

Herrnstein, Richard J., and Charles Murray. 1994. The *Bell Curve: Intelligence and Class Structure in American Life.* New York: Free Press.

Hess, Frederick, and David Leal. 2001. "Quality, Race, and the Urban Education Marketplace." *Urban Affairs Review* 37 (2): 249–266.

Ho, Andrew Dean. 2008. "The Problem with 'Proficiency': Limitations of Statistics and Policy under No Child Left Behind." *Educational Researcher* 37:351–360.

Hoelter, Jon W. 1982. "Segregation and Rationality in Black Status Aspiration Processes." *Sociology of Education* 55 (1): 31–39.

Holme, Jennifer Jellison. 2002. "Buying Homes, Buying Schools: School Choice and the Social Construction of School Quality." *Harvard Educational Review* 72 (2): 177–206.

Horvat, Erin McNamara, and Kristine S. Lewis. 2003. "Reassessing the Burden of 'Acting White'": The Importance of Peer Groups in Managing Academic Success." *Sociology of Education* 76 (4): 265–280.

Horvat, Erin McNamara, Elliot B. Weininger, and Annette Lareau. 2003. "From Social Ties to Social Capital: Class Differences in the Relations between Schools and Parent Networks." *American Educational Research Journal* 40 (2): 319–351.

Hosp, John L., and Daniel J. Reschly. 2004. "Disproportionate Representation of Minority Students in Special Education: Academic, Demographic, and Economic Predictors." *Exceptional Children* 70 (2): 185–199.

Hout, Michael, Adrian E. Raftery, and Eleanor O. Bell. 1993. "Making the Grade: Educational Stratification in the United States, 1925–1989." In *Persistent Inequality: Changing Educational Attainment in Thirteen Countries,* edited by Yossi Shavit and Hans-Peter Blossfeld, 25–20. Boulder: Westview.

Hoxby, Caroline M. 2000. "The Effects of Class Size on Student Achievement: New Evidence from Population Variation." *Quarterly Journal of Economics* 115 (4): 1239–1285.

Husain, Muna, and Daniel L. Millimet. 2009. "The Mythical 'Boy Crisis'?" *Economics of Education Review* 28 (1): 38–48.

Jacobs, Janis E., Christina S. Chhin, and Martha M. Bleeker. 2006. "Enduring Links: Parents' Expectations and Their Young Adult Children's Gender-

Typed Occupational Choices." *Educational Research and Evaluation* 12 (4): 395–407.

Jencks, Christopher. 1972. *Inequality: A Reassessment of the Effect of Family and Schooling in America*. New York: Basic Books.

Jencks, Christopher, and Marsha Brown. 1975. "Effects of High Schools on Their Students." *Harvard Educational Review* 45 (3): 273–324.

Jencks, Christopher, and Meredith Phillips, eds. 1998. *The Black-White Test Score Gap*. Washington, DC: Brookings Institute.

Jensen, Arthur. 1998. *The G Factor: The Science of Mental Ability*. Santa Barbara: Praeger Press.

Jones, M. Gail, and Jack Wheatley. 1990. "Gender Differences in Teacher-Student Interactions in Science Classrooms." *Journal of Research in Science Teaching* 27 (9): 861–874.

Kamin, Leon J. 1974. *The Science and Politics of IQ*. East Sussex, UK: Psychology Press.

Kane, Pearl Rock, and Christopher J. Luricella. 2001. "Assessing the Growth and Potential of Charter Schools." In *Privatizing Education: Can the Marketplace Deliver Social Choice, Efficiency, Equity, and Social Cohesion?*, edited by Henry M. Levin, 203–233. Boulder: Westview.

Kane, Thomas J., Jonah E. Rockoff, and Douglas O. Staiger. 2008. "What Does Certification Tell Us about Teacher Effectiveness? Evidence from New York City." *Economics of Education Review* 27 (6): 615–631.

Kanno, Yasuko, and Jennifer G. Cromley. 2013. "English Language Learners' Access to and Attainment in Postsecondary Education." *Tesol Quarterly* 47 (1): 89–121.

Kao, Grace. 1995. "Asian-Americans as Model Minorities? A Look at Their Academic Performance." *American Journal of Education* 103 (2): 121–159.

Kao, Grace, and Marta Tienda. 1998. "Educational Aspirations of Minority Youth." *American Journal of Education* 106:349–384.

Kao, Grace, Marta Tienda, and Barbara Schneider. 1996. "Racial and Ethnic Variation in Academic Performance." In *Research in Sociology of Education and Socialization*, vol. 11, edited by Aaron M. Pallas, 263–297. Greenwich, CT: JAI Press.

Kao, Grace, Elizabeth Vaquera, and Kimberly Goyette. 2013. *Education and Immigration*. Cambridge: Polity.

Kerr, Clark. 1979. "Five Strategies for Education and Their Major Variants." *Comparative Education Review* 23 (2): 171–182.

Kessinger, Thomas A. 2011. "Efforts toward Educational Reform in the United States since 1958." *American Educational History Journal* 38 (2): 263–276.

Khan, Shamus Rahman. 2011. *Privilege: The Making of an Adolescent Elite at St. Paul's School*. Princeton: Princeton University Press.

Kitano, Harry H. L. 1976. *Japanese Americans: The Evolution of a Subculture.* Upper Saddle River, NJ: Prentice Hall.

Klugman, Joshua. 2013. "The Advanced Placement Arms Race and the Reproduction of Educational Inequality." *Teachers College Record* 115 (5): 1–34.

Kochar, Rakesh, and Richard Fry. 2014. "Wealth Inequality Has Widened along Racial, Ethnic Lines since End of Great Recession." Pew Research Center. www.pewresearch.org/fact-tank/2014/12/12/racial-wealth-gaps-great-recession/.

Kohn, Melvin. 1977. "Social Class and Parental Values." In *Class and Conformity: A Study in Values,* 17–37. 2nd ed. Chicago: University of Chicago Press.

Korinek, Kim M. 2006. "The Status Attainment of Young Adults during Market Transition: The Case of Vietnam." *Research in Social Stratification and Mobility* 24 (1): 55–72.

Kozol, Jonathon. 1991. *Savage Inequalities: Children in America's Schools.* New York: Crown.

Kruse, Kevin Michael. 2005. *White Flight: Atlanta and the Making of Modern Conservatism.* Princeton: Princeton University Press.

Labaree, David F. 1997. "Public Goods, Private Goods: The American Struggle over Educational Goals." *American Educational Research Journal* 34 (1): 39–81.

———. 2010. *Someone Has to Fail: The Zero-Sum Game of Public Schooling.* Boston: Harvard University Press.

Ladson-Billings, Gloria. 2009. *The Dreamkeepers: Successful Teachers of African American Children.* New York: John Wiley & Sons.

Lamont, Michele, and Annette Lareau. 1988. "Cultural Capital: Allusions, Gaps, and Glissandos in Recent Theoretical Developments." *Sociological Theory* 6 (2): 153–168.

Lareau, Annette. 1989. *Home Advantage: Social Class and Parental Intervention in Elementary Education.* London: Falmer Press.

———. 2001. *Unequal Childhoods: Class, Race, and Family Life.* Berkeley: University of California Press.

Lareau, Annette, and Erin McNamara Horvat. 1999. "Moments of Social Inclusion and Exclusion: Race, Class, and Cultural Capital in Family-School Relationships." *Sociology of Education* 72 (1): 37–53.

Lassiter, Matthew D. 2006. *The Silent Majority: Suburban Politics in the Sunbelt South.* Princeton: Princeton University Press.

Lauen, Douglas Lee, and S. Michael Gaddis. 2012. "Shining a Light or Fumbling in the Dark? The Effects of NCLB's Subgroup-Specific Accountability on Student Achievement." *Educational Evaluation and Policy Analysis* 34:185–209.

Lee, Jaekyung, and Kenneth K. Wong. 2004. "The Impact of Accountability on Racial and Socioeconomic Equity: Considering Both School Resources and Achievement Outcomes." *American Educational Research Journal* 41 (4): 797–832.

Lee, Jung-Sook, and Natasha K. Bowen. 2006. "Parent Involvement, Cultural Capital, and the Achievement Gap among Elementary School Children." *American Educational Research Journal* 43 (2): 193–218.

Lee, Marlene, and Mark Mather. 2008. *US Labor Force Trends*. Vol. 63. No. 2. Population Reference Bureau.

Lee, Stacey J. 2001. "More Than 'Model Minorities' or 'Delinquents': A Look at Hmong American High School Students." *Harvard Educational Review* 71 (3): 505–529.

———. 2005. *Up against Whiteness: Race, School, and Immigrant Youth*. New York: Teachers College Press.

Lee, Valerie E., and Anthony S. Bryk. 1986. "Effects of Single-Sex Secondary Schools on Student Achievement and Attitudes." *Journal of Educational Psychology* 78 (5): 381–395.

Lee, Valerie E., and David T. Burkham. 2002. *Inequality at the Starting Gate: Social Background Differences in Achievement as Children Begin School*. Washington, DC: Economic Policy Institute.

Lee, Valerie, Robert Croninger, and Julia Smith. 1996. "Equity and Choice in Detroit." In *Who Chooses, Who Loses: Culture, Institutions, and the Unequal Effects of School Choice*, edited by Bruce Fuller and Richard Elmore, 70–91. New York: Teachers College Press.

Lemann, Nicholas. 2000. *The Big Test: The Secret History of the American Meritocracy*. New York: Macmillan.

Leventhal, Tama, and Jeanne Brooks-Gunn. 2000. "The Neighborhoods They Live In: The Effects of Neighborhood Residence on Child and Adolescent Outcomes." *Psychological Bulletin* 126 (2): 309–337.

Lewis, Oscar. 1959. *Five Families: Mexican Case Studies in the Culture Of Poverty*. New York: Basic Books.

———. 1966. *La Vida: A Puerto Rican Family in the Culture of Poverty—San Juan and New York*. New York: Random House.

Lin, Nan, Walter M. Ensel, and John C. Vaughn. 1981. "Social Resources and Strength of Ties: Structural Factors in Occupational Status Attainment." *American Sociological Review* 46 (4): 393–405.

Linn, Marcia C., and Anne C. Petersen. 1985. "Emergence and Characterization of Sex Differences in Spatial Ability: A Meta-Analysis." *Child Development* 56 (6): 1479–1498.

Lockwood, Penelope. 2006. "'Someone Like Me Can Be Successful': Do College Students Need Same-Gender Role Models?" *Psychology of Women Quarterly* 30 (1): 36–46.

Loewen, James W. 1988. *The Mississippi Chinese: Between Black and White*. Long Grove, IL: Waveland Press.

Logan, John R., and Julia Burdick-Will. 2015. "School Segregation, Charter Schools, and Access to Quality Education." *Journal of Urban Affairs* (September).

Logan, John R., Jacob Stowell, and Deirdre Oakley. 2002. *Choosing Segregation: Racial Imbalance in American Public Schools, 1990–2000*. Report from the Lewis Mumford Center for Comparative Urban and Regional Research, University at Albany.

Looker, E. Dianne, and Pamela A. Magee. 2000. "Gender and Work: The Occupational Expectations of Young Women and Men in the 1990s." *Gender Issues* 18 (2): 74–88.

Looker, E. Dianne, and Peter C. Pineo. 1983. "Social Psychological Variables and Their Relevance to the Status Attainment of Teenagers." *American Journal of Sociology* 88 (6): 1195–219.

López, Nancy. 2002. "Race-Gender Experiences and Schooling: Second-Generation Dominican, West Indian, and Haitian Youth in New York City." *Race, Ethnicity and Education* 5 (1): 67–89.

Lucas, Samuel Roundfield. 1999. *Tracking Inequality: Stratification and Mobility in American Schools*. New York: Teachers College Press.

———. 2001. "Effectively Maintained Inequality: Education Transitions, Track Mobility, and Social Background Effects." *American Journal of Sociology* 106 (6): 1642–1690.

MacLeod, Jay. 1987. *Ain't No Makin' It: Leveled Aspirations in a Low-Income Neighborhood*. Boulder: Westview.

Magnuson, Katherine A., Marcia K. Meyers, Christopher J. Ruhm, and Jane Waldfogel. 2004. "Inequality in Preschool Education and School Readiness." *American Educational Research Journal* 41 (1): 115–157.

Manno, Bruno, Chester Finn Jr., Louann Bierlein, and Gregg Vanourek. 1998. "Charter Schools: Accomplishments and Dilemmas." *Teachers College Record* 99 (3): 537–558.

Manski, Charles F., and David A. Wise. 1983. *College Choice in America*. Cambridge, MA: Harvard University Press.

Mare, Robert D. 1981. "Change and Stability in Educational Stratification." *American Sociological Review* 46 (1): 72–87.

Marini, Margaret Mooney, and Ellen Greenberger. 1978. "Sex Differences in Occupational Aspirations and Expectations." *Sociology of Work and Occupations* 5 (2): 147–178.

Martin, Karen A. 1998. "Becoming a Gendered Body: Practices of Preschools." *American Sociological Review* 63 (4): 494–511.

Martinez, Valerie R., Kenneth R. Godwin, and Frank R. Kemerer. 1996. "Public School Choice in San Antonio: Who Chooses and with What Effects?" In

Who Chooses, Who Loses? Culture, Institutions, and the Unequal Effects of School Choice, edited by Bruce Fuller, Richard F. Elmore, and Gary Orfield, 50–69. New York: Teachers College Press.

McCall, Leslie. 2005. "The Complexity of Intersectionality." *Signs* 30 (3): 1771–1800.

McCarty, Teresa L. 2002. *A Place to Be Navajo: Rough Rock and the Struggle for Self-Determination in Indigenous Schooling.* New York: Routledge.

McDonough, Patricia M. 1997. *Choosing Colleges: How Social Class and Schools Structure Opportunity.* Albany: State University of New York Press.

McGuinn, Patrick. 2006. *No Child Left Behind and the Transformation of Federal Education Policy, 1965–2005.* Lawrence: University Press of Kansas.

———. 2012. "Stimulating Reform: Race to the Top, Competitive Grants and the Obama Education Agenda." *Educational Policy* 26 (1): 136–159.

Messner, Michael A. 1995. *Power at Play: Sports and the Problem of Masculinity.* Boston: Beacon.

Meyer, John W. 1977. "The Effects of Education as an Institution." *American Journal of Sociology* 83 (1): 55–77.

Miele, Frank. 1979. "Cultural Bias in the WISC." *Intelligence* 3 (2): 149–163.

Mikelson, Roslyn Arlin. 1990. "The Attitude-Achievement Paradox among Black Adolescents." *Sociology of Education* 63 (1): 44–61.

———. 2001. "Subverting Swann: First-and Second-Generation Segregation in the Charlotte- Mecklenburg Schools." *American Educational Research Journal* 38 (2): 215–252.

———. 2005. "The Incomplete Desegregation of the Charlotte-Mecklenburg County Schools and Its Consequences." In *School Resegregation: Must the South Turn Back?,* edited by John Charles Boger and Gary Orfield, 87–110. Chapel Hill: University of North Carolina Press.

Moen, Phyllis, Mary Ann Erickson, and Donna Dempster-McClain. 1997. "Their Mother's Daughters? The Intergenerational Transmission of Gender Attitudes in a World of Changing Roles." *Journal of Marriage and the Family* 59 (2): 281–293.

Mouw, Ted, and Yu Xie. 1999. "Bilingualism and the Academic Achievement of First- and Second-Generation Asian Americans: Accommodation with or without Assimilation?" *American Sociological Review* 64 (2): 232–252.

National Center for Education Statistics. 2011. *Digest of Education Statistics: 2010.* NCES 2011–015. US Department of Education: Institute of Education Sciences.

———. 2013. *Characteristics of Public and Private Elementary and Secondary School Principals in the United States: Results from the 2011-12 Schools and Staffing Survey: First Look.* NCES 2013–313. US Department of Education: Institute of Education Sciences.

————. 2015. *Demographic and Enrollment Characteristics of Nontraditional Undergraduates: 2011-12*. Web Tables. NCES 2015-025. US Department of Education: Institute of Education Sciences.

National Commission on Excellence in Education. 1983. *A Nation at Risk: The Imperative for Educational Reform*. Washington, DC: US Department of Education.

Neal, Derek, and Diane Whitmore Schazenbach. 2010. "Left Behind by Design: Proficiency Counts and Test-Based Accountability." *Review of Economics and Statistics* 92 (2): 263–283.

Nee, E. 2010. "Q&A: Joanne Weiss." *Stanford Social Innovation Review* 15. www.ssireview.org/aritcles/entry/qa_joann_weiss.com.

Neild, Ruth Curran, and Kurt Spiridakis. 2003. "Teachers in the School District of Philadelphia: Tables on Teacher Retention and the Distribution of Teachers' Certification Levels and Experience in the District by School Type, Poverty Level, and School Racial Composition." Philadelphia: Research for Action.

Neisser, Ulric, Gwyneth Boodoo, Thomas J. Bouchard Jr., A. Wade Boykin, Nathan Brody, Stephen J. Ceci, Diane F. Halpern, John C. Loehlin, Robert Perloff, Robert J. Sternberg, and Susana Urbina 1996. "Intelligence: Knowns and Unknowns." *American Psychologist* 51 (2): 77.

New York Times. 1990. "The Nation: In Pupil 'Tracks' Many See a Means of Resegregation." February 18.

No Child Left Behind (NCLB) Act of 2001. 2002. Pub. L. No. 107–110, § 115, Stat. 1425.

Oakes, Jeannie. 1985. *Keeping Track: How Schools Structure Inequality*. New Haven: Yale University Press.

O'Conor, Andi. 1993. "Who Gets Called Queer in School? Lesbian, Gay and Bisexual Teenagers, Homophobia and High School." *High School Journal* 77 (1/2): 7–12.

OECD. 2013. *Education at a Glance 2013: OECD Indicators*. OECD Publishing. www.oecd.org/edu/eag2013%20(eng)—FINAL%2020%20June%202013.pdf.

Office of Policy Planning and Research. 1965. "The Moynihan Report."

Ogbu, John U. 1991. "Minority Coping Responses and School Experience." *Journal of Psychohistory* 18 (4): 433–456.

Orfield, Antonia, Frank Basa, and John Yun 2001. "Vision Problems of Children in Poverty in an Urban School Clinic: Their Epidemic Numbers, Impact on Learning, and Approaches to Remediation." *Journal of Optometric Vision Development* 32 (3): 114–141.

Orfield, Gary, and Erica Frankenberg. 2012. *Educational Delusions? Why Choice Can Deepen Inequality and How to Make Schools Fair*. Berkeley: University of California Press.

Orfield, Gary, John Kucsera, and Genevieve Siegel-Hawley. 2012. *E Pluribus . . . Separation: Deepening Double Segregation for More Students*. University of California, Los Angeles: Civil Rights Project.

Orfield, Gary, and John T. Yun. 1999. "Resegregation in American Schools." Harvard University, Civil Rights Project.

Orr, Amy J. 2003. "Black-White Differences in Achievement: The Importance of Wealth." *Sociology of Education* 76 (4): 281–304.

———. 2011. "Gendered Capital: Childhood Socialization and the 'Boy Crisis' in Education." *Sex Roles* 65 (3/4): 271–284.

Paradise, Louis V., and Shavaun M. Wall. 1986. "Children's Perceptions of Male and Female Principals and Teachers." *Sex Roles* 14 (1/2): 1–7.

Park, Hyunjoon, Soo-yong Byun, and Kyung-keun Kim. 2011. "Parental Involvement and Students' Cognitive Outcomes in Korea Focusing on Private Tutoring." *Sociology of Education* 84 (1): 3–22.

Parsons, Talcott. 1959. "The School Class as a Social System: Some of Its Functions in American Society." *Harvard Educational Review* 29 (4): 297–318.

———. 1975. "The Sick Role and the Role of the Physician Reconsidered." *Milbank Memorial Fund Quarterly: Health and Society* 53 (3): 257–278.

Pascoe, C. J. 2007. *Dude, You're a Fag: Masculinity and Sexuality in High School.* Berkeley: University of California Press.

Patillo, Mary, Lori Delale-O'Connor, and Felicia Butts. 2014. "High-Stakes Choosing." In *Choosing Homes, Choosing Schools,* edited by Annette Lareau and Kimberly Goyette, 237–267. New York: Russell Sage.

Patterson, James T. 2001. *Brown v. Board of Education: A Civil Rights Milestone and Its Troubled Legacy.* New York: Oxford University Press.

Perkins-Gough, Deborah. 2006. "Do We Really Have a 'Boy Crisis'?" *Educational Leadership* 64 (1): 93–94.

Perry, Theresa, Claude Steele, and Asa Hilliard III. 2003. *Young, Gifted, and Black: Promoting High Achievement among African-American Students.* Boston: Beacon.

Pfeffer, Fabian. 2008. "Persistent Inequality in Educational Attainment and Its Institutional Context." *European Sociological Review* 24 (5): 543–565.

Phillips, Meredith, Jeanne Brooks-Gunn, Greg Duncan, Pamela Klebanov, and Jonathan Crane. 1998. "Family Background, Parenting Practices, and the Black-White Test Score Gap." In *The Black-White Test Score Gap,* edited by Christopher Jencks and Meredith Phillips, 103–148. Washington, DC: Brookings Institute.

Phillips, Meredith, James Crouse, and John Ralph. 1998. "Does the Black-White Test Score Gap Widen after Children Enter School?" In *The Black-White Test Score Gap,* edited by Christopher Jencks and Meredith Phillips, 229–272. Washington, DC: Brookings Institute.

Picou, J. Steven, and T. Michael Carter. 1976. "Significant Other Influence and Aspirations." *Sociology of Education* 49 (1): 12–22.

Portes, Alejandro, and Min Zhou. 1993. "The New Second Generation: Segmented Assimilation and Its Variants." *Annals of the American Academy of Political and Social Science* 530 (1): 74–96.

Pribesh, Shana, and Douglas B. Downey. 1999. "Why Are Residential and School Moves Associated with Poor School Performance?" *Demography* 36 (4): 521–534.

Princiotta, Daniel, and Stacey Bielick. 2006. *Homeschooling in the United States, 2003*. NCES 2006–042. Washington, DC: US Department of Education, National Center for Education Statistics.

Raftery, Adrian E., and Michael Hout. 1993. "Maximally Maintained Inequality: Expansion, Reform, and Opportunity in Irish Education, 1921–75." *Sociology of Education* 66 (1): 41–62.

Ramirez, Francisco O., and John Boli. 1987. "The Political Construction of Mass Schooling: European Origins and Worldwide Institutionalization." *Sociology of Education* 60:2–17.

Ramos, Lisa Y. 2004. "Dismantling Segregation Together: Interconnections between the Mendez v. Westminster (1946) and Brown v. Board of Education (1954) School Segregation Cases." *Equity & Excellence in Education* 37 (3): 247–254.

Raymond, Margaret, and Stephen Fletcher. 2002. "Teach for America." *Education Next* 2 (1).

Reardon, Sean F. 2011. "The Widening Academic Achievement Gap between the Rich and the Poor: New Evidence and Possible Explanations." In *Whither Opportunity: Rising Inequality, Schools, and Children's Life Chances*, edited by Greg J. Duncan and Richard J. Murnane, 91–116. New York: Russell Sage.

Reardon, Sean F., and Ann Owens. 2014. "60 Years after Brown: Trends and Consequences of School Segregation." *Annual Review of Sociology* 40:199–218.

Reardon, Sean F., and John T. Yun. 2001. "Suburban Racial Change and Suburban School Segregation: 1987–1995." *Sociology of Education* 74 (2): 79–101.

Reay, Diane, and Stephen J. Ball. 1998. "'Making Their Minds Up': Family Dynamics of School Choice." *British Educational Research Journal* 24 (4): 431–448.

Reese, William J. 1999. *The Origins of the American High School*. New Haven: Yale University Press.

———. 2001. "The Origins of Progressive Education." *History of Education Quarterly* 41 (1): 1–24.

———. 2011. *America's Public Schools: From the Common Schools to No Child Left Behind*. 2nd ed. Baltimore: Johns Hopkins University Press.

Reitzes, Donald C., and Elizabeth Mutran. 1980. "Significant Others and Self-Conceptions: Factors Influencing Educational Expectations and Academic Performance." *Sociology of Education* 53 (1): 21–32.

Renzulli, Linda, and Lorraine Evans. 2005. "School Choice, Charter Schools, and White Flight." *Social Problems* 52 (3): 398–418.

Renzulli, Linda A., and Vincent J. Roscigno. 2005. "Charter School Policy, Implementation, and Diffusion across the United States." *Sociology of Education* 78 (4): 344–366.

Rhodes, Anna, and Stefanie DeLuca. 2014. "Residential Mobility and School Choice among Poor Families." In *Choosing Homes, Choosing Schools*, edited by Annette Lareau and Kimberly Goyette, 137–166. New York: Russell Sage Press.

Rickles, Jordan, Paul M. Ong, Shannon McConville, and Doug Houston. 2001. "The Relationship between School and Residential Segregation at the Turn of the Century." Los Angeles: Ralph and Goldy Lewis Center for Regional Policy Issues, UCLA.

Rist, Ray C. 1970. "Student Social Class and Teachers' Expectations: The Self-Fulfilling Prophecy in Ghetto Education." *Harvard Educational Review* 40 (3): 411–450.

Robinson, Keith, Angel L. Harris. 2014. *The Broken Compass: Parental Involvement with Children's Education*. Cambridge, MA: Harvard University Press.

Rong, Xue Lan, and Frank Brown. 2001. "The Effects of Immigrant Generation and Ethnicity on Educational Attainment among Young African and Caribbean Blacks in the United States." *Harvard Educational Review* 71 (3): 536–566.

Roscigno, Vincent J., and James W. Ainsworth-Darnell. 1999. "Race, Cultural Capital, and Educational Resources: Persistent Inequalities and Achievement Returns." *Sociology of Education* 72 (3): 158–178.

Rosenthal, Robert, and Lenore Jacobson. 1968. *Pygmalion in the Classroom: Teacher Expectation and Pupils' Intellectual Development*. New York: Holt, Rinehart & Winston.

Rothstein, Richard. 2004. *Class and Schools: Using Social, Economic, and Educational Reform to Close the Black-White Achievement Gap*. New York: Teachers College.

Rury, John L. 2005. "Introduction: The Changing Social Contours of Urban Education." In *Urban Education in the United States: A Historical Reader*, edited by J. L. Rury, 1–12. New York: Palgrave Macmillan.

———. 2013. "The Historical Development of Urban Education." In *Urban Education: A Model for Leadership and Policy*, edited by K. S. Gallagher, R. Goodyear, D. J. Brewer, and R. Rueda. London: Routledge.

Russakoff, Dale. 2015. *The Prize: Who's in Charge of America's Schools?* Boston: Houghton Mifflin Harcourt.

Sadker, Myra, and David Sadker. 1994. *Failing at Fairness: How America's Schools Cheat Girls*. New York: Charles Scribner's Sons.

Sahlberg, Pasi. 2010. *Finnish Lessons: What Can the World Learn from Educational Change in Finland?* New York: Teachers College Press.

Sanbonmatsu, Lisa, Jeffery R. Kling, Greg J. Duncan, and Jeanne Brooks-Gunn. 2006. "Neighborhoods and Academic Achievement Results from the Moving to Opportunity Experiment." *Journal of Human Resources* 41 (4): 649–691.

Saporito, Salvatore. 2003. "Private Choices, Public Consequences: Magnet School Choice and Segregation by Race and Poverty." *Social Problems* 50 (2): 181–203.

Saporito, Salvatore, and Annette Lareau. 1999. "School Selection as a Process: The Multiple Dimensions of Race in Framing Educational Choice." *Social Problems* 46 (3): 418–439.

Saporito, Salvatore, and Deenesh Sohoni. 2006. "Mapping Educational Inequality: Concentrations of Poverty among Poor and Minority Students in Public Schools." *Sociology of Education* 79 (2): 81–105.

Sax, Leonard. 2007. "The Boy Problem: Many Boys Think School Is Stupid and Reading Stinks—Is There a Remedy?" *School Library Journal* 53 (9): 40–43.

Schneider, Barbara, and Yongsook Lee. 1990. "A Model for Academic Success: The School and Home Environment of East Asian Students." *Anthropology & Education Quarterly* 21 (4): 358–377.

Schneider, Mark. 2001. "Information and Choice in Educational Privatization." In *Privatizing Education: Can the Marketplace Deliver Choice, Efficiency, Equity, and Social Cohesion?*, edited by Henry M. Levin, 72–102. Cambridge, MA: Westview.

Schneider, Mark, Paul Teske, Christine Roch, and Melissa Marschall, 1997. "Networks to Nowhere: Segregation and Stratification in Networks of Information about Schools." *American Journal of Political Science* 41 (4): 1201–1223.

Sewell, William H., Archibald O. Haller, and George W. Ohlendorf. 1970. "The Educational and Early Occupational Status Attainment Process: Replication and Revision." *American Sociological Review* 35 (6): 1014–1027.

Sewell, William H., Archibald O. Haller, and Alejandro Portes. 1969. "The Educational and Early Occupational Attainment Process." *American Sociological Review* 34 (1): 82–92.

Sharkey, Patrick, and Felix Elwert. 2011. "The Legacy of Disadvantage: Multigenerational Neighborhood Effects on Cognitive Ability." *American Journal of Sociology* 116 (6): 1934–1981.

Shavit, Yossi, and Hans-Peter Blossfeld. 1993. *Persistent Inequality: Changing Educational Attainment in Thirteen Countries.* Social Inequality Series. Boulder: Westview.

Shear, Michael D. 2009. "President Obama Discusses New 'Race to the Top' Program." *Washington Post,* July 23.

Skiba, Russell J., Robert S. Michael, Abra Carroll Nardo, and Reece L. Peterson. 2002. "The Color of Discipline: Sources of Racial and Gender Disproportionality in School Punishment." *Urban Review* 34 (4): 317–342.

Smith-Hefner, Nancy J. 1993. "Education, Gender, and Generational Conflict among Khmer Refugees." *Anthropology & Education Quarterly* 24 (2): 135–158.

Smock, Pamela J., and Franklin D. Wilson. 1991. "Desegregation and the Stability of White Enrollments: A School-Level Analysis, 1968–84." *Sociology of Education* 64 (4): 278–292.

Smrekar, Claire, and Ellen Goldring. 1999. *School Choice in Urban America: Magnet Schools and the Pursuit of Equity.* New York: Teachers College Press.

Snyder, Thomas D. 1993. "Education Characteristics of the Population." In *120 Years of American Schooling: A Statistical Portrait,* edited by T. D. Snyder and the Center for Education Statistics, 5–24. Washington, DC: Office of Education Research and Improvement.

Soares, Joseph A. 2015. *SAT Wars: The Case for Test-Optional College Admissions.* New York: Teachers College Press.

Sorensen, Aage B. 1996. "Educational Opportunities and School Effects." In *James S. Coleman,* edited by Jon Clark, 207–222. London: Routledge.

Spencer, Steven J., Claude M. Steele, and Diane M. Quinn. 1999. "Stereotype Threat and Women's Math Performance." *Journal of Experimental Social Psychology* 35 (1): 4–28.

Stambler, Moses. 1968. "The Effect of Compulsory Education and Child Labor Laws on High School Attendance in New York City, 1898–1917." *History of Education Quarterly* 8 (2): 89–214.

Steele, Claude M., and Joshua Aronson. 1995. "Stereotype Threat and the Intellectual Test Performance of African Americans." *Journal of Personality and Social Psychology* 69 (5): 797.

Steinberg, Laurence, Sanford M. Dornbusch, and B. Bradford Brown. 1992. "Ethnic Differences in Adolescent Achievement: An Ecological Perspective." *American Psychologist* 47 (6): 723–729.

Steinberg, Stephen. 1989. *The Ethnic Myth: Race, Ethnicity, and Class in America.* Boston: Beacon.

Steinmayr, Ricarda, and Birgit Spinath. 2008. "Sex Differences in School Achievement: What Are the Roles of Personality and Achievement Motivation?" *European Journal of Personality* 22 (3): 185–209.

Stevens, Mitchell L. 2001. *Kingdom of Children: Culture and Controversy in the Homeschooling Movement.* Princeton: Princeton University Press.

Stevenson, Harold, and James W. Stigler. 1994. *Learning Gap: Why Our Schools Are Failing and What We Can Learn from Japanese and Chinese Education.* New York: Simon & Schuster.

Stout, Mary. 2012. *Native American Boarding Schools.* Santa Barbara: Greenwood, ABC-CLIO.

Stroub, Kori J., and Meredith P. Richards. 2013. "From Resegregation to Reintegration: Trends in the Racial/Ethnic Segregation of Metropolitan

Schools, 1993–2009." *American Educational Research Journal*. March 6, 2013.

Sugrue, Thomas J. 2008. *Sweet Land of Liberty: The Forgotten Struggle for Civil Rights in the North*. New York: Random House.

Swanson, Christopher B., and Barbara Schneider. 1999. "Students on the Move: Residential and Educational Mobility in America's Schools." *Sociology of Education* 72 (1): 54–67.

Swift, David W. 1969. "Ideology and Control in Public Institutions: The Public Schools." *Sociological Focus* 3 (1): 78–95.

Takaki, Ronald. 1993. *A Different Mirror: A History of Multicultural America*. Boston: Little, Brown.

Tatum, Beverly Daniel. 2003. *Why Are All the Black Kids Sitting Together in the Cafeteria?: And Other Conversations about Race*. New York: Basic Books.

Thompson, Kenneth, ed. 1985. *Readings from Émile Durkheim*. London: Routledge.

Thorne, Barrie. 1993. *Gender Play: Girls and Boys in School*. New Brunswick, NJ: Rutgers University Press.

Turner, Ralph H. 1960. "Sponsored and Contest Mobility and the School System." *American Sociological Review* 25 (6): 855–867.

Tyack, David B. 1974. *The One Best System: A History of American Urban Education*. Cambridge, MA: Harvard University Press.

Tyack, David, and Larry Cuban. 1995. *Tinkering toward Utopia: A Century of Public School Reform*. Cambridge, MA: Harvard University Press.

Tyson, Karolyn. 2011. *Integration Interrupted: Tracking, Black Students, and Acting White after* Brown. Oxford: Oxford University Press.

Tyson, Karolyn, William Darity, and Domini R. Castellino. 2005. "It's Not 'a Black Thing': Understanding the Burden of Acting White and Other Dilemmas of High Achievement." *American Sociological Review* 70 (4): 582–605.

Urban, Wayne J., and Jennings L. Wagoner. 2009. *American Education: A History*. Routledge, 2009.

US Department of Education. 2004. *Evaluation of the Public Charter Schools Program: Final Report*. Washington, DC: Office of the Under Secretary.

———. 2010. *Thirty-Five Years of Progress in Educating Children with Disabilities through IDEA*. Washington, DC: Office of Special Education and Rehabilitation Services, US Department of Education.

———. 2012. *The Condition of Education 2012*. Washington, DC: National Center for Education Statistics.

Valenzuela, Abel. 1999. "Gender Roles and Settlement Activities among Children and Their Immigrant Families." *American Behavioral Scientist* 42 (4): 720–742.

Valenzuela, Angela. 2010. *Subtractive Schooling: US-Mexican Youth and the Politics of Caring*. Albany: State University of New York Press.

Walker, Renee E., Christopher R. Keane, and Jessica G. Burke. 2010. "Disparities and Access to Healthy Food in the United States: A Review of Food
Deserts Literature." *Health & Place* 16 (5): 876–884.

Warren, John Robert, Emily Hoffman, and Megan Andrew. 2014. "Patterns and
Trends in Grade Retention Rates in the United States, 1995–2010." Table 2.
Educational Researcher. http://edr.sagepub.com/content/early/2014/12/03
/0013189X14563599.full.pdf+html?ijke y = 6zOILNJscZEP2&keytype =
ref&siteid = spedr.

Wayne, Andrew J., and Peter Youngs. 2003."Teacher Characteristics and
Student Achievement Gains: A Review." *Review of Educational Research* 73
(1): 89–122.

Webb, L. Dean. 2006. *The History of American Education.* Upper Saddle River,
NJ: Merrill Prentice Hall.

Weininger, Elliot B. 2014. "School Choice in an Urban Setting." In *Choosing
Homes, Choosing Schools,* edited by Annette Lareau and Kimberly Goyette,
268–294. New York: Russell Sage Press.

Wells, Amy Stuart, ed. 2002. *Where Charter School Policy Fails: The
Problems of Accountability and Equity.* Vol. 12. New York: Teachers
College Press.

Wells, Amy Stuart, and Robert L. Crain. 1997. *Stepping over the Color Line:
African-American Students in White Suburban Schools.* New Haven: Yale
University Press.

Wightman, Patrick, and Sheldon Danziger. 2014. "Multi-Generational Income
Disadvantage and the Educational Attainment of Young Adults." *Research in
Social Stratification and Mobility* 35: 53–69.

Williams, Heather Andrea. 2009. *Self-Taught: African American Education in
Slavery and Freedom.* Durham: University of North Carolina Press.

Willis, Paul E. 1977. *Learning to Labor: How Working Class Kids Get Working
Class Jobs.* New York: Columbia University Press.

Wilson, Franklin D. 1985. "The Impact of School Desegregation Programs on
White Public-School Enrollment, 1968–1976." *Sociology of Education* 58 (3):
137–153.

Wilson, Kenneth L., and Alejandro Portes. 1975. "The Educational Attainment
Process: Results from a National Sample." *American Journal of Sociology* 81
(2): 343–363.

Wilson, William Julius. 1987. *The Truly Disadvantaged: The Inner City, the
Underclass, and Public Policy.* Chicago: University of Chicago Press.

Witte, John F., and Christopher A. Thorn. 1996. "Who Chooses? Voucher and
Interdistrict Choice Programs in Milwaukee." *American Journal of Education* 104 (3): 186–217.

Wollenberg, Charles. 1978. *All Deliberate Speed: Segregation and Exclusion in
California Schools, 1855–1975.* Berkeley: University of California Press.

Wrinkle, Robert D., Joseph Stewart Jr., and J. L. Polinard. 1999. "Public School Quality, Private Schools, and Race." *American Journal of Political Science* 43 (4): 1248–1253.

Wyatt, Ian D., and Daniel E. Hecker. 2006. "Occupational Changes during the 20th Century." *Monthly Labor Review* (March): 35–57.

Xie, Yu, and Kimberly Goyette. 1997. "The Racial Identification of Biracial Children with One Asian Parent: Evidence from the 1990 Census." *Social Forces* 76 (2): 547–570.

———. 2003. "Social Mobility and the Educational Choices of Asian Americans." *Social Science Research* 32 (3): 467–498.

Xu, Zeyu, Jane Hannaway, and Colin Taylor. 2011. "Making a Difference? The Effects of Teach for America in High School." *Journal of Policy Analysis and Management* 30 (3): 447–469.

Zhou, Min, and Carl Bankston III. 1998. *Growing Up American: How Vietnamese Children Adapt to Life in the United States.* New York: Russell Sage Foundation.

———. 2001. "Family Pressure and the Educational Experience of the Daughters of Vietnamese Refugees." *International Migration* 39 (4): 133–151.

Index

ability-grouping, 83, 84–85, 94–95, 200. *See also* differential course-taking; educational expectations; tracking
academic self-concept, 69
accountability systems, 172; achievement and, 187; drawbacks of, 187–88; NCLB and, 183–84; Obama administration reforms and, 184–86; reforms in the 1980s and, 181–83
ACT test, 67
adequate yearly progress (AYP), 187, 190
advanced math courses: gender differences and, 143–44, 143*table;* racial and ethnic differences and, 110, 111*fig.*
advanced placement (AP) courses: gender and, 143–44, 143*table;* parent involvement in schools and, 200; racial and ethnic inequality and, 109–10, 110*table,* 197; socioeconomic background and, 69, 70*table,* 85–86, 197. *See also* differential course-taking
affirmative action programs, 95
America 2000 plan, 183
American cultural values: compared with Asian values, 174–75; educational achievement and, 126–27, 129; employer concern with, 35, 39, 40; immigrants and, 123–24,

126–27, 129; socialization goal of schools and, 6–7, 8, 11–12, 22
American Recovery and Reinvestment Act (ARRA), 184
American Spelling Book (Webster), 22
ANAR *(A Nation at Risk)* report, 182–83
AP courses. *See* advanced placement courses
ascribed characteristics vs. achievement, 51, 73, 150, 203; educational inequality and, 10–11, 13–14, 83; intersectionality and, 13–14; social reproduction tradition and, 44–46; social stratification and, 10–11, 41–44. *See also* conflict paradigm; functionalist paradigm; gender inequality; race and ethnicity; socioeconomic background
Asian Americans: advanced courses and, 109, 110*table;* assimilation and, 124–25; as category, 90; college attainment and, 113, 114*fig.;* educational expectations and, 102, 103*fig.;* median incomes and, 116; as "model minority," 118; school discipline and, 111–12, 112*table;* special education programs and, 108–9, 108*table*
Asian educational systems, 173–75
assessment of students: civil rights era and, 180–81; national examinations and, 172–73; progressive era reforms and, 180; rise

243